WHO YOU WERE
MEANT TO BE

WHO YOU WERE MEANT TO BE

A Guide to Finding or Recovering Your Life's Purpose

LINDSAY C. GIBSON, PSY.D.

Second Edition – 2020

Blue Bird Press
1 Columbus Center – Suite 615
Virginia Beach, VA 23462

Gibson, Lindsay C.

Who You Were Meant To Be: A Guide to Finding or Recovering Your Life's Purpose (first edition, 2000) Library of Congress Catalog Card Number: 99-70158

ISBN: 0-88282-187-3

Originally published by New Horizons Press, Far Hills, NJ
Manufactured in the USA.

2004 2003 2002 2001 2000 / s 4 3 2 1

To Skip and Carter, with all my love

TABLE OF CONTENTS

AUTHOR'S NOTE

This book is based on my psychotherapy work with patients, a study of the relevant literature, and my clients' life experiences. Fictitious names and identities have been given to all characters in this book in order to protect individual privacy. Personal characteristics and family circumstances of the individuals in the book have been altered to prevent recognition.

PREFACE TO THE SECOND EDITION

I hope this book will prove a useful guide to your self-discovery. It was written out of my lifelong desire as a psychotherapist to help people extricate themselves from childhood fears and unrealistic loyalties that hold them back in their lives. *Who You Were Meant to Be* came to me as a message from the heart, the ideas arising from my deep feelings about this subject. I was seeking not just to educate but also to cheer and encourage my reader, whose difficulties I knew so well. I hope its wholeheartedness shines through.

This second edition – self-published when the publishing rights reverted to me after nearly twenty years of publication – came about because I wanted to make sure that the book didn't go out of print. To judge from enthusiastic readers, it has found a home in the hearts of many people. I am hoping that new readers will discover it too as it reemerges on the coattails of my later books. A few changes such as roomier formatting, clearer divisions, and larger font size, hopefully make this edition an even more comfortable read. In this new edition, I tried to preserve the book's clear and rhythmic voice while updating a few of the terms and topics in ways that better explain its concepts to new readers. Relevant new psychological and neurological research also has been added in places, to support the spirit of the book's mission: to find or recover who you were meant to be.

INTRODUCTION

How did we get to be so uncomfortable with who we really are? Why do creative and capable people turn their energies away from their truest longing for self-expression? As a psychotherapist and concerned human being, these are questions that interest me deeply. I have been troubled all my life by watching bright and talented people not do what they were happiest doing – and often for the noblest reasons.

In my early days as a therapist, I was a real cheerleader. It was second nature for me to jump in and start offering my clients ideas for how they could make themselves feel better. Like a smiling waiter offering a dessert tray, I would ask them to consider this solution or that idea. I was eager to whet their appetites for growth by showing them possibilities. My clients listened with interest, but they rarely followed up on these great suggestions. Worse, they seemed to feel badly about not being able to go along with me when I so obviously wanted to help them. I also recommended excellent self-help books, thinking some good ideas from outside sources would help. No dice.

There were forces operating in my consulting room that went beyond the scope of enthusiasm or positive thinking. There was something unseen standing in the way between my client and me, unperceived by us both, but which bounced back my ideas and encouragements as if I had hurled them against a wall. Finally I learned to sit back and fix my gaze in the middle distance. What was that wall? What was standing between my client and me? What was keeping this person from receiving help and growing? Soon I began to figure out what these forces were that joined us in every session, working as hard against my clients' growth as I was to help them. Their power over my clients was formidable, yanking them back into depression or walloping them with an anxiety attack just when things started to get better.

When I began to relax and stopped trying so hard to fight through these psychological protectors, they became easier to see. As though materializing before my eyes, I began to discern patterns in my clients' struggles that had a very consistent form. I began to understand how and why those unseen defenders got there. *They were commissioned out of the deepest levels of love, fear, and protectiveness.* These psychological defenses were charged with protecting sacred family loyalties, arising from deep empathy for parents or loved ones. Their purpose was ultimately so self-sacrificing, I stood in awe before what these people had given up in order not to hurt someone they loved.

What I was seeing was the retarding effect of inner forces that existed solely to keep my clients stuck in a certain role in their family or a certain self-image in their own minds. Growth itself did not have to be so slow or hard. In fact, I often marveled at how quickly and totally clients could bloom with psychological health on a good day, making it seem that they had suddenly gotten it all together. And so they had. *Their growth was real.* However, on other days, because of these invisible negative forces, these bodyguards of the status quo, my clients often gave up the ground they had gained and the struggle started all over again.

As time went on, I also became aware of the depth of my clients' fears about growth, how frightened they were at times about getting in touch with their true selves. It was as though a vast space of complicated loyalties and terrors opened up before my eyes, and I saw like never before what these people were really up against. It was then I realized that there was a need for a special approach to living one's life effectively without being sabotaged by past demons. An approach designed to deal not only with the hurts from the past, but also to address *people's profound anxieties about how their growth might affect their loved ones.*

Around the time of this realization, I woke up from a sound sleep one night with the words "Who You Were Meant To Be" in the forefront of my mind. Immediately I knew that *this* was what my clients were really trying to figure out when they came to me for help. They suffered because they were sick of living an unfulfilling life, but had no idea how to live any differently. Not knowing who they were meant to be, *they had no way of knowing what would make them truly happy.*

Later that spring I started a Growth Group, subtitled "Who You Were Meant To Be." Some of the most earnest people I have ever met came to that group, and continued to come over the next two years. My clients and group members had one thing in common: they realized that they did not know what to do with their lives, but were terribly ready to find out.

Through a new understanding of their fears and family loyalties, my clients and group members began to recover their lost motivation. They began to express renewed creativity and an itch for accomplishment, as though some intrinsic energy had been released. However, this was often a challenging period in their lives, as these courageous people see-sawed between their new selves and their old self-doubts. Surprising ups and downs frequently followed in their lives, and often my role was simply to educate them about the growth process and to reassure them that they were on the right track. As my clients calmed down and grew steadily more sure of their new way of being in the world, the rest of their lives fell into place too, obedient now to a soul that knew where it was going.

Like the people I have helped in the past, this book is for people who want to discover their true purpose in life but have had trouble figuring it out, or who feel intimidated and overwhelmed when they get close to taking steps toward changing their lives, leading to feelings of disappointment or hopelessness. What you are about to read in this book honors the bravery that goes into real growth. It explains why so many people have had to unhitch from their dreams and from who they were meant to be.

The approach I take gently and methodically takes apart the reasons why so many of us do not end up doing what brings us energy and joy. It will help you understand your conflicts, and feel compassion for what you have been struggling with all these years. You will see how your finest qualities of empathy, love, loyalty, and conscience have been turned against your best interests in favor of other people. The ideas in this book have worked for my clients and they will work for you.

⎯ᴄ⎯

The first half of the book deals with why you have not been able to follow the dream of who you were meant to be. Until these psychological forces are uncovered and understood, they tend to keep exerting their influences unseen, remaining all the more powerful for their invisibility. When you read about the forces of family loyalties and the conflicts about becoming your own person, you will begin to understand why it has seemed so hard to get what you really want, and how you can stop standing in your own way.

The second half of the book provides you with a roadmap for how to go about answering the question of who you were meant to be, and thereby recover your life's true purpose. It describes the process of growth and reassures you through the inevitable rough spots. It shows you how growth and success *really* occur, information that was not given to many of us when we were growing up. Instead, in far too many families, children are taught how to continue being their parents' children, which is no preparation at all for a fulfilling adult life.

That is what this book is for: preparation for your new life. It will help you move aside the tangled debris of old loyalties and mistaken self-identities in order to find the part of you that is still green and growing. Because the process of becoming our true selves has a universal pattern, the steps toward growth can be clearly defined and predicted. I will help you recognize these steps for what they are. You will relax instantly from self-criticism and guilty fears when you understand the hidden agenda behind these awful feelings. I will help you gain compassion for yourself and your family, and when necessary I will encourage you to draw your line in the sand. When you need to escape or go backwards, we can deal with that too, because it is often hard. I promise you that you will not be left feeling that I don't understand, or that no one knows how hard it is. Having practiced psychotherapy for over thirty years, I have a good idea what kind of work it takes.

No one on this earth is a 100 percent success story. It is easy to bring yourself down by holding unrealistic expectations about your ability to sustain feelings of success. Discouragement happens to everyone, but you may become unnecessarily demoralized by it if you do not realize it is a natural part of the growth process. That is the purpose of this book, not only to help you find or recover your life's purpose, but to give you confidence for dealing with the dragons you may encounter along the way.

My belief is that we gain our strength and joy from the success *moments* in our lives, not whether or not our lives are turning out to be overall "success stories." Just because we slip backwards at times does not mean we're not making progress. Often it actually means just the opposite. For most people who are trying to grow and do things differently, these disruptions of progress are the norm. As we will see later in the book, we are usually tempted to give up right at the moment of greatest potential change. That is because imminent change stirs up the frantic urge to return to some kind of familiar stability, something we know about – even when it is frustration or unhappiness!

If you are a serious self-builder you will find answers here. While there is an important place for self-help books that stress positive thinking and behavioral solutions, this book goes a little deeper. Relax and let's be honest together about the things that hold you back. When you want to move forward, read on. Use this book for inspiration and practical suggestions. When you feel discouraged and have been knocked back, go right to the chapters that catch your eye. You will know which ones to read.

There is no need to read the book in order. The chapters stand on their own. But if you find yourself resisting some of the suggestions and ideas in the second half of the book, go back and check out the earlier chapters. The book is planned to deal with resistance first, then growth. Just as in a therapy session, we might have to explore what is holding you back before you can move forward.

In the pages to follow, you will be reading the stories of real people who've been actively engaged in discovering who they were meant to be. While I have changed all identifying data in order to preserve confidentiality, the underlying process and pattern of growth is faithfully reported. This invariable pattern of growth holds across many different stories, because it is an ancient human struggle, a challenge faced by all people who have ever outgrown their families and tribes and felt compelled to follow their own personal visions.

It is important to note here that the very personal stories in this book are from lives in progress, with no final endings. Life never rides off into the sunset. I do not want to imply that the people whose lives I tell about have achieved total success and everything from then on out was a perfect dream. No, their lives continued after the publication of this book, just like yours and mine. They're still out there, wrestling with their egos and listening to the little voice inside. Every one of these people continues to have challenges, setbacks, and incredible growth. They are living their lives, and each day they come home from the wars, a little more victorious than the day before. *Their biggest success is that they have become the main characters in their own lives.* These lives may not be perfect dreams, but getting as much of the dream as possible into our lives is the goal.

SECTION I

HOW OUR LEGACIES HOLD US BACK

CHAPTER ONE

WHO WERE YOU MEANT TO BE?

There is nothing you can do about what interests you or energizes you. It is simply who you are. Trying to change this - not accepting this - will always result in a tiring, frustrating struggle.

Nora was back. She perched on my tufted office chair in poised anticipation. Her large designer scarf graced her neckline with élan and confidence, richly complementing the long dress that draped across her knees. Nora's black paperboard portfolio of artwork rested against her chair, as she updated me on her vocational dilemma. I had not seen her in over a year; our last contact had been a vocational assessment interview. She had appreciated my help back then, but now needed more. Nora's winsome blue eyes and softly waving blonde hair defined her femininity at a glance, and when she spoke her whispery, melodious voice was full of intelligence and insistence. "I have two diametrically opposed selves," she complained. "Whichever one I try to satisfy, I'm damned if I do and damned if I don't. I'm sitting on a fence, paralyzed. It's depressing to be this indecisive!" Nora had come to me for answers. I asked myself, *Can she stand to hear the truth?*

The truth was that Nora was scared to death to fulfill her talent's purpose. I knew what to expect from the portfolio, because I had seen samples of her work the year before. Nora had attained national recognition in her areas of

3

expertise, turning out exquisite art that had been acclaimed in print, yet she could not bring herself to insist upon a career in art. Nora occasionally made money with commissioned art projects, but when these dried up, she began to think long and hard about other careers.

This interview marked the latest in a series of crises in Nora's life over who she would become. The first had occurred when she was seventeen. Having shown promising talent in high school, Nora was offered a small scholarship to art school by a benefactor. Nora chose nursing school instead. Later, a divorce and the demands of a handicapped child made it a struggle for her to keep her head above water over the years.

But as things calmed down and her child got older, Nora had come to see me for occupational direction. At that point, the year before, she had decided she could not make enough money at art, and chose instead to pursue a degree in social work. This had proved to be a huge bore, and she did more doodling than note-taking in her classes. Now Nora was back in my office. She handed me a sheaf of her latest art work, which was stunningly imaginative and of professional quality. As I looked through her drawings, transfixed by their strange and moving beauty, Nora implored me anxiously, "So what do you think? I've been considering getting a degree in biology or genetics."

Here was Nora's split. As her striking artwork wordlessly declared its unmistakable message about her life's purpose, Nora spoke about an advanced degree in science. She was agonizing over the original conflict she had never resolved. *Should she help others, or express herself?*

This is the dilemma that this book addresses. You are probably familiar with Nora's predicament for it is one many of us encounter: to choose one direction would mean giving up our deepest desires for self-fulfillment, but to choose the other would mean feeling irresponsible. The good news is that this dilemma is an illusion. *No one is really stuck like this.* We have been taught to think in absurd extremes, as if we had to choose one or the other: our happiness or the good of others.

Is This You?

Take a moment to see if you recognize yourself in the following description:

> **You are unfulfilled in a key area of your life. You would like a change, but cannot see a way to make it. Often you feel frustrated and blocked. You are very attuned to the needs of your loved ones, whether you show this outwardly or not. Duty is taken seriously. You have a humanitarian streak and want to improve the lives of other people. You daydream about a different kind of life and have a strong desire to be free of the burdens you carry. Perhaps you have bought some of the tools needed to fulfill your dream or plan, and even allowed yourself limited time for its pursuit. You may have come close to making a major change in your life, but it never quite happened. Responsibilities sidetracked you, and you turned back to the familiar life you already knew how to do. This was a relief, because you did not want to appear selfish or egocentric. You hate the thought of not pulling your own weight. For instance, depending on someone else's financial support while you train in a new field, or borrowing money for a new venture, seems irresponsible to you. Often you have thought to yourself, "How can I pursue my plans and dreams when others still need me so much?"**

Now circle below how closely you feel this description fits you:

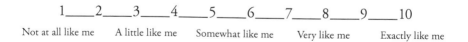

1___2___3___4___5___6___7___8___9___10

Not at all like me   A little like me   Somewhat like me   Very like me   Exactly like me

This description may not be a perfect fit, because these things rarely are. But if you scored yourself five or above, you match up well. If so, there are a few things we can tell about you from the preceding description:

- **You notice your own feelings and the feelings of others.**

- **You want to improve your life.**

- **You tolerate unhappiness to fulfill your responsibilities to others.**

- **You know how to act and what is expected of you.**

- **You have a strong conscience and sense of duty.**

- **You are a humanitarian and want to help improve others' lives.**

- **You feel alive when you are creative.**

- **You do not want to be selfish or egocentric.**

- **You like to be helpful, but try not to trouble others for help.**

Don't you think this reads like a resume for the kind of person this world needs more of? These are exceptional qualities that show concern for others, creative potential, and a well-developed sense of responsibility. The trouble is, we can be such good citizens that we stop leading our own lives.

Let me add here that there are phenomenally successful people who have very creative careers, and yet they too experience the same inner clash between what they *want* to do and what others *need* them to do. It is not the nature of the job that defines whether or not you have this conflict; it is the *reasons* you are doing the job at that moment. If you are pursuing a job in order to fulfill the needs of someone else, your true self will find a way to object.

Are We Afraid to Know Ourselves?

It amazes me how ready we are to jump through hoops, fulfill all kinds of numbing job requirements, and top it off with acts at home that could cinch Oscars. However, when it comes to pursuing our dreams, or even just expressing our true longing for a different life, we suddenly collapse into a mass of anxiety and embarrassment. The ease and skill we show in our daily life evaporates when we consider changing our lives to reflect more of who we really feel ourselves to be. High on our list of anxieties is the fear of selfishness, followed closely by the fear of looking foolish. People who would not turn a hair in making expensive decisions in other areas of their lives suddenly can become indecisive and guiltridden over spending small amounts of time or money on their dreams.

Every one of us has a sense of who he or she really is. This instinct has been with us from the beginning, observing all that we do with the perplexed and frustrated air of an impotent advisor. You know deep down whether something is right for you. There is no one who cannot tell when an activity stirs up life-giving energy or, conversely, exhausts and frustrates. We come equipped as infants to know this in our viscera, where the tide of hormones tells us what feels good and what does not. You too came fully equipped to tell the difference within yourself between what is genuine and what is imposed.

Our Amazing Adaptability

The sad and marvelous thing about human beings is that we can be taught how to choose *against* ourselves. We are so adaptable, so smart, and so attached to our early caretakers that we can learn how to turn ourselves inside out, just to be who somebody else needs us to be. Human beings have the remarkable capacity to become something other than what they really are, and *make it their reality.* We are all prodigies when it comes to this talent, and we get started on it early in life.

Perhaps this is why we are so fascinated by royal families and celebrities. We know what they are up against! There is something riveting about watching a famous person caught in their role like a fox in a trap, and struggling to be a real person in spite of it. We cannot get enough of a princess with an eating disorder or a celebrity who risks everything for a momentary high. We all know very well what it is like to want to escape from our "success," when success has meant turning ourselves into something that we are not. But why have we become such masterful actors? Why do we spend our whole adult lives continuing to chase accomplishments that no longer satisfy our souls?

My job in this book is to help you figure out how you can build a life based on who you were meant to be, rather than who everybody else needs you to be. At a deep level you already know the answer to the question of who you are meant to be, but for many reasons you have forgotten. Now you will reawaken the knowledge of what makes you feel alive and full of energy.

Two Cases of Misplaced Lives

Let's look now at a couple of my clients who lost track of who they really were.

Shelley's Story

Shelley did not really want to die, but every time she looked out the balcony of her hotel room toward the turquoise Caribbean, all she could think about was swimming so far out she would never be able to get back. Why did she keep thinking this? And why now of all times? She and her husband, Matthew, had planned an anniversary trip for three years. When Matthew heard about a business conference in St. Thomas, it seemed like a sensible way to save money. Shelley had plenty of time on her hands while Matthew attended sales meetings, and she liked to sit on the balcony and look out over the water as she sipped her coffee. But after a day or two, every time her mind relaxed, she would catch herself on that mental swim to nowhere. Each evening she shook off the morbid image, and got ready to join Matthew and his sales associates for dinner.

A year later in therapy, Shelley marveled at how unaware she had been of the reasons for her unhappiness on that trip. A depressive crisis six weeks after the trip had finally brought her face to face with how empty her life felt, and how terrified she was to do anything about it. She realized, looking back, that the anniversary trip was the perfect metaphor for her whole life. Pretty, intelligent, and an accomplished hostess, Shelley had become the ultimate accessory, the peripheral support for her husband's center-stage life as super-salesman. Even the anniversary trip had served his career needs. With her two children grown and married, Shelley's family role had evaporated away into superfluity. Her husband would be inconvenienced by her absence, but who would really notice if she were to disappear? She knew her parents would be upset, for they loved her dearly as their only child. However, their love was like the love of her husband. They loved what she could do for them, but they had no idea who she really was, or what she wanted to do with her life. It had not occurred to them to look for signs of Shelley's unique interests. Instead Shelley's parents selectively rewarded the traits in her they liked best, especially her warmth and concern for others.

Shelley was a perfect little caretaker from early childhood on. Her mother had been sure Shelley would become a nurse. However, Shelley's impulsive early marriage and rapid-fire pregnancies had ended that hope. Her parents were bitter about Shelley's life decisions for years, even refusing to help her financially when Matthew was out of work for several months. Shelley was left feeling like she was always letting someone down every time she sought happiness for herself.

Tim's Story

The dynamics of Tim's story were different than Shelley's. He was a handsome, boyish looking physician in his early thirties, with two small children and a wife to support. Becoming a family doctor had been his plan for so long, he no longer remembered when he decided to do it. His goal to be a physician seemed to have always been there, like the color of his eyes or the unruly cowlick on the back of his hair. Each stage of growing up, like going to first grade or getting his driver's license, merely seemed to be another step on the way to medical school.

The strange thing was that Tim never really enjoyed his science classes or medical courses. He was smart enough to get good grades, but it was torture for him to work such long hours and deal constantly with complaining patients. Yet every hard-won step in his career seemed worth it just to see the pride in his mother's face when she introduced her son, the doctor. He knew how much it meant to his hard-working mother that her eldest son had made her dream come true. Tim was convinced that his secret wish to become a writer was the height of ingratitude and irresponsibility. Besides, how would he ever make his physician's income as a writer? Tim began to feel depressed and his irritability at work sapped his strength.

⸺

Both Tim and Shelley had misplaced the responsibility for their lives. Each had mistaken sacrifice for loyalty and felt guilty for not feeling more satisfied. They may have shown some differences in the *way* they sacrificed their lives to meet the needs of others, but deep down they were facing the same question. The question that needed answering was not, "Do you have a successful job?" nor "Do you have a stable marriage?" but rather, "Is this job *about you?*" and "Is this marriage *for you?*" Many people might have felt envious of Shelley, the successful man's pretty wife, or Tim, the doctor who rose out of the working class to fulfill every mother's dream. They certainly looked good from the outside. But that was the problem. They had been looking at *themselves* from the outside. In fact, Shelley and Tim had built whole lives around how they would look to family, friends, and society at large. Yet at a certain point for both, the hollowness of their efforts became too painful to ignore any longer.

The Peculiar Satisfaction of Sacrifice
Tim and Shelley had practically offered themselves on serving dishes to be made into whatever their loved ones needed most, and for quite awhile that was enough. Not just enough; their sacrifices were actually deeply satisfying for a time. You see, to be able to get it right and become who loved ones think we should be is a psychological accomplishment of the highest order. Think of the patience, empathy, fortitude, and dedication it takes to rearrange one's true self into someone else's pattern. It is staggering to consider the personality resources people must use up to do that. Yet when it comes to using these resources for *themselves,* to further *their* dreams and deeply personal sense of purpose, many people suddenly feel confused, scared, and profoundly unsure

of themselves. This moment is the "panic attack," which will be discussed in greater detail later.

There is a good reason why we trade in our true interests for goals that other people have set for us. The payoff in this deal is that at least you have some one who believes in you. In Shelley's case, her parents were proud of her abilities as a good caretaker, and Tim's mother knew her son could do anything. To know that someone sees a potential in you, *even if it is the wrong one,* has a tremendous impact on your choices, especially when you are a child. The fact that someone believes in us lifts us to heights we could never achieve all by ourselves. To be believed in, even if our parents are missing our truest interests, is a compelling and inspiring experience. It easily eclipses the little voice inside that cautions us against taking that path. If you follow your loved ones' advice, you need never fear the loneliness of separation from your family. Making their dream your future is one way of sidestepping the uncomfortable realization that you might be very different from them.

The Necessity of Knowing Who We Are

We do not want to arrive at the end of our lives feeling like we have not fully lived, that something vital was left undone. Within ourselves, we have parts that can tell the difference between living our true lives – the ones we were meant to have – and lives that have been dictated to us by other people.

This part of us that knows is our Core, the inviolate True Self, the Real Self, the Higher Self. This inner touchstone tells us who we really are, and who we are meant to be. It is the white stone on which our true name is written. Not the "name" our parents pinned on us in this lifetime, but our soul's identity. In his book, *The Soul's Code,* James Hillman uses his "acorn theory"[1] to describe the inevitability of our personal destiny. Just as a tiny acorn holds the code for a spreading oak tree, so each of us is born with an intent that seeks to express itself every chance it gets.

You are the most important person in your life. You may have tried to believe otherwise, but you have paid for this misperception with the discontent you feel or the symptoms you suffer. Perhaps you still clutch onto the illusion that you are harming no one when you give up your dreams. We can twist our potential into strange shapes of conformity without wincing, yet are seized with panic when we are invited to unbend and follow our true desires.

What Kind of Force Are You Going to be in the World?

Discovering the desires of your real self is not an esoteric exercise. You have a moral duty to recover your happiness.

Does that surprise you? What you do with your life affects the way you drive your car, talk to your children, treat your employees, and relate to your spouse or life partner. You are choosing every day what kind of force you are going to be in the world: a force for growth, or a force for resignation. These may sound like abstract ideals, but their practical outcomes are *very* real. There is not a person in this world who has resigned himself to an unhappy and unrewarding existence who has not had demoralizing effects on the most cherished people in his life.

Unhappiness and a lack of fulfillment get passed down from generation to generation like bad genes, and they affect the more vulnerable, sensitive members of the family until someone shows serious symptoms of emotional problems.

What you decide to do with your life, in your generation, is not just about you. It is about what you are going to be giving to the world and passing down the line. Taking responsibility for your own life being satisfying and fulfilling is not a selfish act in the old sense of that word. Think of it as psychological pollution control: we are obliged to clean up our own dissatisfactions before they contaminate our relationships with others. Put to rest your fears that your desire for fulfillment is "selfish."

Your Right Purpose

Our obligation or duty is to play our parts in life so that our particular strengths and weaknesses, our very individuality, can interweave with the fabric of the world in ways that enrich and strengthen both the world and ourselves. Our individuality is our one perfect gift to our parents and the world. And it must be *given,* put out into the world in exchange and sharing; otherwise it withers and curls into unrecognizable shapes that bear little resemblance to the pattern of intent that crystallized at our birth.

However, many of us are anxious to not harm anyone with the pursuit of our purpose. Our wish to do no harm can become so primary we try to kill off our real selves. *Few people want to know their life-purpose if they think that following this purpose would lead to suffering for themselves or their loved ones.* Yet the right purpose for your life is never dangerous or harmful. There is always a path to take that fulfills you without harming others. Of course, if you have not found this way yet, you rightly hesitate to act. However, together in this book we are going to seek your solution. A true life's purpose always has some benefits for other people as well as yourself. This is the principle of *overflow*, and will be dealt with in chapter eight, which takes up the subject of putting the self first.

When people initially get the urge to follow their dreams, it is often in the form of fantasies about total breaks from their everyday lives. We daydream about leaving our spouses, quitting our jobs, moving to the tropics. After being stifled for so long, can you blame the true self for going a little overboard? The subconscious mind is histrionic; like a bad stage actor it goes to extremes to show us a subtle truth. Learn to listen to its underlying message – "You need change" – instead of the harebrained solutions with which it first peppers the mind.

Your true right purpose is trying to find you, but you may not know yet what it looks like. You must find out how to recognize this stranger if it approaches you. Below is a checklist that may be a good match for some of your thoughts and ideas about your true purpose (for an in-depth quiz on finding your true direction, see Appendix A):

The Right Purpose Checklist

❑ You feel energized and deeply interested in it.

❑ You feel fully engaged, "clicking on all cylinders," as you do it.

❑ You feel like you belong there.

❑ It has a constructive purpose, directly or indirectly.

❑ It does not exploit, humiliate, or harm others.

❑ It has built-in potential for your continuing development.

❑ You have a sense of pride and "rightness" about it.

❑ Signs of it popped up all through your life; even from childhood.

You will notice that the checklist does *not* say that your purpose will never cause your parents any worry, or that your spouse will surely think it is a good idea. Jostling, bumping into others, occasionally stepping on toes, all may be unavoidable when we follow our true purpose, a result of being genuinely focused on getting where we want to go. As long as the harm is not intentional, other people can be amazingly understanding of our need to be single-minded about these things.

When you make good choices about your life's purpose, you will have an influence on other people's lives, but *you cannot know in advance who they will be.* Many people want the assurance that if they follow their dreams, they will end up directly helping *their* loved ones, or improving the lives of *their* families. This cannot be guaranteed, especially if your interests are very different from those of your family. It could well be that the people to whom you will bring satisfaction or happiness are far removed from your family.

Your job as an adult human being is to go out into the world and contribute what you can as you engage in self-fulfilling work and the pursuit of happiness. It is very possible that you could end up helping many other people while being utterly unable to improve your own family. Your family may be unable to receive your contribution, because they're not interested in it. They might not "get" it. Other people better suited to your family's needs may be there for them. Meanwhile, your job is to head out to where you can do the most good.

It seems to be a rare event when family members have enough things in common to make staying inside the family maximally fulfilling and productive. Sometimes people feel that they are at cross-purposes with their families, and this is often quite literally true. Our first and foremost job as grown-ups is not to avoid hurting the feelings of loved ones at all costs or to protect our parents from the emotional distress of an empty nest. Our jobs are to find our destinies and become productive contributors to our chosen adult communities.

What Do You Want?

Before reading any further in this book, take a sheet of paper and start writing down answers to the question, "What do I want?" Jot down everything you can think of, from the big to the small. The only requirement is that you be scrupulously honest and put down only the things you really *want*, not the things you think would be good for you. If more ideas occur to you later, go back and add them on.

When we do this exercise in the Growth Group, we use unlined white paper and have everyone hold up his or her pages afterwards - not to read but just to see how the writing looks on the page. The thing that always stands out is how much white space is usually left on the pages. People write, think, write, and still end up with plenty of paper left blank. It is the equivalent of going speechless in front of a genie who has just granted you unlimited wishes. We are so trained to think about what is good for us or what other people need, that it can be hard at first to get back in touch with what we really want. The point of this exercise is to start somewhere. Later, as you develop your talent for knowing what you want, you may find it much easier to add to your list.

Another reason why the page is not filled is that we have learned how to condense many of our wishes and wants under a few abstract headings, such as "I want a satisfying relationship" or "I want to be successful." But suppose you were the genie: wouldn't you need a lot more information in order to fill those requests? For instance, to fill the first wish above, wouldn't the genie need to know exactly what kind of person would be satisfying to *you* in a relationship? As for the "I want to be successful" wish, what precisely is success in *your* mind? If you see a sweeping generalization on your list that would confuse a genie, circle it. Later on you can come back and add the specifics.

Which Area of Your Life Do You Want to Start With?

Different people have unfulfilled dreams in different areas. Some people know who they were meant to be in the career field, and may even have pursued it successfully. But they may never have defined what they needed for real happiness in their relationships. Other people might feel very good about their marriage and yet be disappointed over their unsatisfying career. In some cases, there is dissatisfaction in many or all areas of life. It is important for you to identify in which areas of your life you have unfulfilled needs. These are called **Life Choice Areas,** because in each of these areas we have made choices that have led to either fulfillment or frustration.

Our dissatisfaction in any life choice area is not accidental. It was probably part of a complex pattern of accommodation designed to please or impress someone else. We may feel okay about success in one area, but we may pull back in other parts of our lives if we fear we are venturing too far beyond what others expect of us.

In the following pie chart, there are sections allotted to important areas of life. Do the following exercise to see where you want to put your focus.

1. Without giving it too much thought, circle the sections in which you feel you need help. What areas are not fulfilling who you were meant to be? What important parts of your life are going unlived?

2. The next question, of course, is whether or not you want to change them. There may be things you know are going unfulfilled in your life, but for many complicated reasons you may decide that now is *not* the time to try to change them. So pick the *one* area that you are most motivated to pursue at this time. Put a big star on it. You can change your choice or add a new one at any time during the reading of this book, but because we have to start somewhere, picking one area now will give you a focus.

Life Choice Areas

Where do you feel the need for more?

How Do I Figure Out What My Purpose Is?

Originally we all came into this life well equipped to sense what we need in order to become our most satisfied selves. Later we are often encouraged to forget or suppress this natural knowledge; therefore, some reminders will come in handy.

There are a handful of psychological tools that help us find our right purpose. They give us crucial information through our *reactions.* These tools work whether we know about them or not, just as gravity holds our feet to the ground. The goal is to make them obvious and available for everyday use. All you have to do is be willing to notice your reactions on a daily basis. You have always had this information, but you may not have realized what it had to offer. Like a magnet being pulled north, we respond predictably whenever we are close to something that reminds us of who we were meant to be.

The Tools of Self-Discovery

Our true purpose in life is as unique as each one of us, but the tools your true self uses to communicate with you are common to everyone. Many people enjoy hearing from their subconscious mind, and allow themselves to be guided accordingly. When we are receptive, the process of communication with our true self is so smooth and natural that it requires no conscious effort on our part. If years of stifling yourself have dulled your ability to read these cues, however, then you can use the following Tools of Self-Discovery:

- **The Tool of Energy Shifts:** what makes your **energy** level change

- **The Tool of Recognition:** who or what you **recognize** as being like you

- **The Tool of Envy:** who or what you **envy**

- **The Tool of Appeal:** what undeniably **appeals** to you

- **The Tool of Physical Response:** what evokes a **physical** reaction

- **The Tool of Mental Response:** what elicits a positive **mental** state

Now let's see how you can use these tools to begin shaping your dream. As you practice with these tools, you will automatically shift your life path away from frustration and toward fulfillment.

1. *The Tool of Energy Shifts*

   Every time you get close to an area of interest that connects with who you were meant to be, you will feel a definite increase in energy. Involvement in – or even thinking about – this topic will stimulate you, making you look forward to it and want to do more of it. Your energy will shift like an infallible weathervane; it has no choice but to point in the right direction.

   If you force yourself to pursue things that are not in line with your deepest interests, you will find yourself losing energy, feeling tired, bored, and stifled. It will feel as if something inside you is not willing to go along.

2. *The Tool of Recognition*

   Things will catch your attention in the area of your true purpose. Robert, a client of mine who was a frustrated actor, was unable to watch television programs without thinking about how he would have played each scene. It was such a normal part of Robert's television viewing that he had never realized what this was indicating. Bettina, a young woman who wanted to become a children's book illustrator, could not read her daughter a bedtime story without analyzing the painting technique in the pictures, or whether or not the illustrator's style fit the tone of the story. *These people were "recognizing" the occupational skills needed to express their underlying life purposes .* This sense of recognition is often accompanied by thoughts like *I could do that* or ideas for how you could have done it better. The critical undertone comes from the natural evaluative instinct of a person who may belong in that field. We cannot help but appraise someone else's skill in "our" area. *We recognize it before we become it.*

3. The Tool of Envy

Look at what makes you envious and critical. It tells you that there is something you feel should have been yours, but you have allowed it to go unclaimed. Envy is one of the most reliable indicators of what we were meant to be, because it is so childishly honest. The proper purpose of envy is to spur us toward getting the object for ourselves. The trick is not to get stuck in envy, nor to content ourselves with resenting people who have what we want, but to understand the meaning of the emotion.

Jennifer's Envy

Jennifer, a very intelligent woman, came to see me about finding some direction in her life, but instead she filled her sessions with complaints about her husband. According to her, he was obsessed with buying the latest four-wheel drive vehicle, and making sure that he had the very best in fly-casting equipment. Her husband owned his own business, provided her with a comfortable living, and was certainly able to afford his pleasures. Her attitude was so critical it began to tell me more about her than him. We explored what bothered her so much about her husband's pursuit of these special interests. It turned out that she was deeply envious; not of his all-terrain vehicle or fishing rods, but of his guilt-free pursuit of his dreams. She did not know what she wanted to do with her own life, and it drove her crazy to see her husband follow his inclinations so easily. Jennifer was close to convincing herself that she had married a shallow, petty man who was obsessed with his possessions, when the real problem was that she had not allowed herself to focus on what *she* wanted.

4. The Tool of Appeal

Appeal is the attracting pull that desirable people and things exert upon us. In a store, some items appeal to us, while others are passed over without a second glance. In a room full of people, we sneak peeks at a certain person because there is something about him or her that we find "appealing." This subtle experience is a reliable guide, nudging you toward something or someone who reminds you of what you need.

5. The Tool of Physical Response

Physical sensations are among the best tools for self-discovery, because they are less likely to be filtered through family expectations or cultural norms. When we get close to our purpose in life, we all have physical reactions. A heightened sense of energy has already been mentioned. Physical pleasure is a giveaway as well. What is exciting to your heart and mind easily extends into pleasant body feelings. Feelings of warmth and well-being are very common, often accompanied by pleasant, full feelings in the chest area. Connecting with our true purpose can give us tingles or a feeling of physical lightness, especially noticed as a feeling of weight being taken off our back and shoulders. It is also characteristic to feel physically *able* in the pursuit of our true purpose, as though our nerves and muscles were preparing to make physical action easy.

There are also unpleasant responses to things that would pull you away from your purpose. Feelings of disgust, fatigue, boredom, depression, headache, nausea, and irritability are just a few of the physical sensations that occur when you're moving *away* from your right direction. (There is one exception in this category of negative reactions: anxiety, an unquestionably noxious sensation. Anxiety and fear are natural knee-jerk reactions many of us have toward any kind of change – good or bad – and therefore are not always indicators you're going the wrong way.)

It is important to "tag" these feelings when they occur so you'll learn to recognize their messages in the future. "Tagging" the feeling means that you notice in detail how it feels, and then name it so you can quickly identify it later on.

6. *The Tool of Mental Response*

Just as our bodies respond to what we like, so do our thoughts. For instance, if you are considering an interesting career that fits you well, you will probably experience hope, optimism, and a sense of possibility. Uplifting fantasies will pop into your mind about how it would be to live that way. These pleasant and stimulating mental responses occur when you are on the right track, moving toward your true purpose in life.

If you review these tools for self-discovery, you will probably recognize every one of them as familiar experiences. Perhaps you will even wonder what the big deal is, since you already were well aware of these feelings. The point is that these naturally occurring human feelings are *tools,* designed to be used for guidance. Too often we dismiss these experiences as simple random reactions, lacking any particular usefulness. The truth is that these feelings and reactions exist for the crucial purpose of *telling* us when we are on track toward finding fulfillment. If you don't know where to start, utilizing these tools will begin to point you in the right direction within a single day.

_6

Accepting What Our Feelings Are Telling Us

Sometimes we know what we want before we are ready to accept it We can be surprised when a simple desire pops up, and the dilemma that results can make us intensely uncomfortable. This is what happened to Michael.

Michael was a thirty-seven-year-old sociology professor who liked to stop in at a local bookshop on his lunch hour. One particular day, he hovered around a certain bookshelf for over a half-hour, picking up a large paperback on spirituality and art, and putting it back again. He made a point of investigating other titles on nearby shelves, pushing his glasses up on his nose and thumbing through books he had no intention of buying. Michael could not walk away from the book with its thrilling, mystical cover art, but he could not bring himself to buy it either. It was getting late; he had to be back for his next class. He told himself his ambivalence was absurd. Putting a stop to his dithering, Michael plucked the spirituality book off the shelf and tried to look casual as he strolled to the checkout counter. Inside, however, Michael felt like an adolescent about to buy a sexy magazine. What had been a safe and private fantasy was now exposed on the checkout counter as a declaration of intent.

When Michael talked about his purchase later in a therapy session, he fidgeted in discomfort. He felt as though he had exposed a shameful, unacceptable side of himself, but he also said he _had_ to have the book. One might call this a small act, an inconsequential event. But if we had monitored Michael's pulse, blood pressure, and adrenaline levels at the sales counter, we would've come to the well-founded conclusion that his body was preparing him to run for his life. We can easily understand the anxiety of a mortified teenage boy trying to buy a forbidden magazine. We recognize such symbolic acts of emerging adulthood, and the bridge every adolescent is trying to cross. But for a grown man, a professor and parent himself, feeling such high levels of anxiety about buying a _book_ does not seem natural.

Of course it is not the book itself that so embarrasses Michael or those with seemingly incongruous desires at these critical points of transformation.

In Michael's case, it was the *intent* behind buying the book that felt so forbidden: he wanted to become his own person in a way that his old life could not accommodate. Michael, the ultra-rational, data-based social scientist was responding to an inner call stronger than any professional peer pressure. After many years he was finally admitting his interest in spirituality. As a child, Michael had thought deeply about God and had many questions about why people suffered. In high school he had daydreamed about becoming a minister and leading his own church. But since his college indoctrination into the social sciences, Michael had developed a contemptuous attitude toward religion. Michael also had learned early not to tell his parents too much about his religious inclinations. He knew his engineer father and accountant mother were steering him firmly down the path of practical realism. Research in the social sciences was a good compromise for Michael: it allowed him to ask all kinds of questions – except the ones that interested him the most.

As Michael stood in that bookstore, wavering between growth and fear, he was seized with the embarrassment and anxiety that can grip all of us when we take a step *in public* toward reclaiming our true self. His profound sense of exposure and self-consciousness revealed the highly meaningful nature of his act. As Michael paid for the book he desired, he was symbolically saying to the clerk (the gatekeeper, the authority figure) that he was intending to change the course of his life. Because this felt so taboo to Michael, he had a fit of indecision before taking that step. At a deep level there was a part of Michael that knew exactly what buying the book meant: he was taking back a piece of himself that had been ransomed to family opinion years before.

Over the next couple of years, Michael began to attend a church that encouraged his searching, intellectual questions about God. He ultimately became a leader in his church, and has felt deeply rewarded by this new direction in his life.

Pivot Points

There may be more dramatic events in people's lives than buying a book, but Michael's example illustrates that the most ordinary act can become a watershed event when we are ready to change. At these moments, we become highly conscious that we hold the power of choice. We no longer assume that who we have always been is who we will continue to be. A *pivot point* is when we have the freedom to turn in any direction, *and we know it.* Choosing rightly at these times is a striking experience, never to be forgotten. Many people can look back and cite just such moments when they first risked their allegiance to their deepest desires.

The amazing thing is that over and over life confronts us with such opportunities, such pivot points. To remain the same, you simply choose what you have always chosen. To discover your true purpose, you must experiment with choosing from your soul. These tiny choice points are easy to overlook, just as the tools of self-discovery seem unremarkable until you deliberately start using them. However, it does not matter how small the act or how inconsequential the decision. If you know what you want and finally do it, you are rearranging your universe.

Success Moments

It is hard to see all at once what we should be doing with our lives. However, on any given day, you can use the self-discovery tools already in your possession to gather up the pieces of your life puzzle. Every time you notice a surge of energy, or follow your interests, you are having a success moment. Tag it and keep going.

The goal is not to burden you with unrealistic expectations of perfect mental health or instant total success. Our goal is for you to collect *success moments.* Success on this life quest is getting as close as possible to the bits and pieces of your dream. These are the moments when you know you are living your life through your real self. A success moment is a goal that is completely possible, and without which nothing bigger is possible. A moment of success may be followed by a disappointment or an emotional regression. But that does not cancel out the reality of your success, however brief it may have been. Success is success. People who have successfully followed their dreams have learned the art of nurturing and tagging their success moments, and they take every bit of credit for them.

The Wrong Questions to Ask Right Now

It usually happens that as soon as people come up with an idea for their future, they immediately begin assessing whether or not they think it would be possible. Worry starts over *how* they would go about making these dreams come true. They quickly run through their sum total of ideas related to the topic and, not surprisingly, come to the conclusion that it cannot be done. This demoralizing attitude quickly drains their initiative. The problem is that they launched prematurely into the planning stage, when they had barely begun to formulate ideas for what they wanted to do.

Self-discovery has a predictable course, and skipping over some of the steps never works. The sequence of growth stages is invariable. If you are in the daydreaming stage and try to push yourself ahead into planning, you could easily become so discouraged that you will stop.

Three Words to Remember

A quick overview of the whole process of recovering your life's purpose may be found in just three words:

RESPECT - PROTECT - CONNECT

These will be your touchstone words, practical reminders of what is needed to set your course on finding your true purpose, and also to recover from temporary setbacks. These three words combine the attitudes and actions that will materialize fulfillment in whatever area you choose. They work together in a synergistic way, so that each sparks off the others to create the optimal conditions for your future.

1. ***Respect:*** Your first responsibility is to **respect** your own unique interests and needs. There is nothing you can do about what interests you or what energizes you. It is simply who you are. Trying to change

26

this identity, or not accepting this identity, will always result in a tiring struggle that can never succeed. You are not required to like your unique interests and needs, especially if they make you very different from other members of your family, but sooner or later you will have to grant them respect. The first step in finding your true self is to honor the primacy of your needs and interests in your life and then look for acceptable ways of expressing them, *because they are not going away.*

2. ***Protect:*** Your true self's unique need is something that you must **protect** from other people's opinions. If you do not protect yourself in this area, you will be molded to fit what makes other people or traditions more comfortable. It could be a family member, an employer, or a cultural norm. These outside forces influence you into becoming who they need you to be in order to maintain their view of the world. Everyone in your life has a part they would love you to play and if you do not shield yourself from this pressure, you will end up dominated by activities and roles that will whittle away at your resolve until your future is lost. No matter how much you love or admire these people, you must protect yourself against accepting everything they have to say and consequently losing your own values.

3. ***Connect:*** To **connect** with like-minded, supportive people is the next necessity. We all need to have contact with people who are interested in our ideas and who are energized by similar pursuits. This does not mean that you have to give up relationships with loved ones, your current job, or anything else in your life that may be less than energizing. It just means you need to add people to your life who will support your efforts at growth and change. Without this connection with a few supporters, it is easy to get frustrated and give up.

Taking a new step can be a fearful venture that stirs up anxieties, but it's even more frightening when you lack supportive people in your life. As we will see in the next chapter, taking new steps is even more difficult when the very people who should be most supportive try to hold you back.

CHAPTER TWO

WHO GIVES YOU PERMISSION?

Family members, with their deep needs and attachments, usually don't give up dependency on each other without a fight.

For weeks Carol had trouble starting her therapy sessions. As soon as she sat down, she would nervously ask me, "What should I talk about today?" No amount of interpretation or encouragement could budge her from this ritual. Week after week she began our sessions the same way, always embarrassed to ask the question, but completely unable to start without voicing it. She was coming to me to talk, and yet wanted me to pick the subject! As time went on and Carol confided more experiences of her past, we began to understand. Carol was showing me how she had related to authority figures her whole life. As a child, Carol had to ask permission for practically everything she did. Her behavior in our sessions was demonstrating the painful contortion of permission-seeking that she'd felt forced to do all her life.

It was no wonder Carol suffered from depression, at times even taking to her bed in fits of despondency. Although she lived a comfortable, financially secure life with her husband, Carol felt chronically overwhelmed and often sought social isolation to the point of not wanting to see anyone or answer her telephone. No matter how comfortable it looked from the outside, Carol's life was an uphill battle every day. It was an ordeal for her to make even minor decisions, because she was so afraid her husband might not like what she did. Her husband was a strong, decisive man, but not a cruel one. His strong personality simply rushed in to fill the void created by Carol's hesitation. He said what he thought, expressed his wishes, and Carol folded.

This was exactly the pattern Carol was unintentionally setting up in our sessions. She was so accustomed to doing what others wanted that it had become her main way of relating to other people. Now it was clear why she went so far as even to avoid answering the telephone: for Carol, any contact with other people meant being dominated into something to which she could not say no.

No overbearing character was taking charge and forcing Carol into a subservient role, but she was responding to our therapeutic relationship along the exact lines she had followed in her childhood and with her husband. This was a priceless moment in Carol's therapy. We began to see the other side of her story, the ways in which she was defeating herself – and then blaming others for beating her down.

When Carol solicited direction from her husband or me, she was secretly hoping for validation and support of her desires – without saying so. She asked what her husband thought about things not really to get his opinion, but to indirectly seek approval for what she wanted to do. Her husband, of course, took her requests at face value and gave his opinion, thinking he was being asked to contribute. Carol listened to his suggestions with resentment, feeling angry and victimized. She felt deeply misunderstood, as though he had steamrolled her. *Why was everybody always running over her?* she asked herself.

It was not unusual that Carol wanted to talk things over before making decisions. Soliciting advice and input promotes a feeling of harmony and closeness with the important people in our lives. Successful people who value others' insights like to keep an open mind and listen to other ideas, but they have no intention of blindly following other people's advice and they definitely are not asking permission. Talking it out and hearing another viewpoint simply serves to clarify their thoughts and feelings on the matter. This kind of sharing is used in the service of what will ultimately be an independent decision.

This was not what Carol was doing. She in no way enjoyed getting the advice she felt compelled to seek. Her compulsive need for permission frustrated both herself and others.

In Carol's childhood, she had been punished for making mistakes and thinking for herself. She was the youngest in a family of tyrannical older siblings and impatient, easily angered and controlling parents. Assertiveness had come to feel dangerous to her, while indecisiveness signified safety. Carol cleverly succeeded in her life by inviting others to run it for her, and fortunately she usually picked the right people to tell her what to do. At a certain point in her late thirties, however, this lifelong trade-off between safety and self-fulfillment became intolerable. Depression hit when she got sick of feeling pushed around, but was too scared to do things differently.

Carol's Next Step

Carol's challenge was to break away from the child-status she had assigned herself in her own mind. Exploring the painful subordination she had suffered as a child, we realized together that permission-seeking had been her best way of coping under the threatening circumstances of her childhood. Unfortunately, she had carried forward her "youngest child" mentality to all her adult relationships, including those with her husband, friends, and employers. She had such a charming way of going along with others that she was well liked and fit in easily. However, once a relationship reached a certain level of closeness, Carol began to tilt back and forth between avoidance and resentment as she struggled to find some way of getting her needs met without openly asserting herself with the other person.

Once she could see how she was unintentionally inviting just the kind of domination she had hated since early childhood, Carol had some new choices. She began to take small steps toward making decisions on her own, and she practiced determination in the face of her husband's initial resistance. The results were amazing. Carol was astounded at how often she was able to have things her way once she stepped up and asked for it. She saw her husband in a new light, no longer impressed by his pronouncements of authority, because she no longer accepted that he knew best *every time*. Carol had decided to give up her childlike status in her relationships. As she did so, her vulnerability to depression faded, and she began to discover new avenues of creativity and enjoyment for herself.

Permission-Seeking Means Never Having to Leave Home

Carol's dilemma had many aspects to it, but at a primal level she was simply seeking the security of childhood. All of us can relate to that wish. Whether our childhood life was happy or miserable, we all had that peculiarly secure feeling that our fate at least was in the hands of grown-ups. We only had choices up to a point, and for most of us nobody was seriously expecting us to know best because we were just children. Under those conditions, a person can only feel minimally responsible.

The enormity of adulthood responsibility can frighten us into giving up the joys of adult freedom. Like Carol, we can settle for self-denying depression rather than feeling the anxiety of adult responsibility and freedom. However, it is only in a grown-up frame of mind that we can pursue who we were meant to be.

Childhood should prepare us to become an adult in our society. Usually this involves the act of leaving home in some form, a circumstance that is honored around the world through many kinds of ceremonies and rituals. Another way of looking at the need for these rituals is that family members, with their deep loves and attachments, usually do not give up dependency on each other without a fight.

Buying the Car

I come by my awareness of permission-seeking honestly. I didn't like to offend people and as a young adult I remember going through the agonies of indecision many of us suffer when we're about to take a major step forward. One such important moment occurred when I bought my first automobile. I was in my early twenties, still in graduate school, and while it would certainly be a convenience, a car was not yet a necessity – except I wanted one badly. While home on summer break, I had an unparalleled opportunity to buy a

WHO YOU WERE MEANT TO BE

great small car. All the conditions were right, and I even had secured my first bank loan, a loan the bank was willing to delay payments on until I was out of school and employed. The whole thing fell right into my lap. Naturally I had to ask my mother what she thought.

In a cautious and objective tone of voice, my mother simply suggested that I consider where I was in my life – still in school, no money and no job – before I made such a decision. Objective or not, I heard her feedback as *you are overstepping your bounds.* To say I felt deflated would be a gross understatement, but at the same time her response didn't dim my desire. Boiling in a pot of conflicting feelings, I broke down in tears. How was I ever going to do this when my mother thought it was a bad idea? It was a big step and I knew it; I was putting myself on the line for a debt I did not yet have the job to support. The other truth was that I was trusting myself to get the job, pay down the loan, and enjoy the car for a whole year before I had to start paying it off.

Perplexed by my tears, my mother reminded me that the decision, of course, was mine, and that she was merely giving me the feedback for which I had asked. This was true, but why did I feel such turmoil? Now I can see that what I was really asking for was her *blessing,* for her to *side* with my strivings for independence and responsibility. I needed her to firmly show she was in favor of my "growing up." Getting her objective advice was a pale and secondary concern. Not being in touch with my real emotions at the time, all I could do was feel completely miserable and totally neurotic as I watched the car deal cool.

Automobiles are often symbolic of our sense of control over our lives and where we want to go. They symbolize our readiness for freedom and express our belief about our place in the world. Most importantly and most basically, they literally take us away from home. How you feel about your vehicle, how it functions, and what it looks like can be fascinating symbols for how psychologically prepared you are to leave home, and how you feel about this separation.

Fortunately, the part of me determined to have what I wanted continued to weasel toward a solution. To my credit, I called the one person I knew on this earth who had no trouble taking a stand. I telephoned my friend, Peggy, who has since used her tough-minded heart to excel in a career of forensic psychology. I dithered and obsessed into Peg's patient ear, until she had finally heard enough. "Screw 'em, Lindsay," she said, "Believe in yourself and buy the car." And that is what I did. I had her blessing.

At the end of this chapter, we'll look more into the importance of blessings and how they can encourage us to create our unique lives.

⁓

The Envious and Bullying Parent

Ask yourself this question: who are *you* waiting for permission from to start your life? This is the person you are afraid will judge or abandon you. If it is hard to see it in those terms, then just ask yourself who has the real power and control in your family. That person may be your particular psychological bully, the person you have given the authority to hold you back.

It may be especially hard to think of our parents as bullies. After all, they only want what is best for us. But the unfortunate fact is that parenthood does not change anybody's personality structure. If a person was angry and controlling before he or she had children, that person will likely continue that behavior when he or she becomes a parent. Biological events do not necessarily create psychological transformations. Envious and bullying parents do not give permission for their children's happy independence – such permission would be contrary to their fundamental attitudes and beliefs.

Bonnie's Story

One of my clients, Bonnie, found her emotional freedom by daring to look at this aspect of her mother. Bonnie was a thirty-year-old woman who had struggled to come to grips with the painful truth about her childhood. Her mother had been a sexually repressed, bitter woman who had been dealt a hard life of oppression by an angry, alcoholic husband. Even though Bonnie was her father's favorite, she had always deemed her father the bad guy, because his rages and lack of responsibility made him such an easy target. Her mother fanned this belief, encouraging Bonnie's disdain and fear of her father. To all appearances, her mother was a selfless victim who stayed with her husband for the sake of the children.

As Bonnie grew up and started to date, a self-defeating pattern began to emerge. Bonnie was a bright and very pretty girl whose good looks and confident flirtatiousness brought her the attentions of Ted, a decent and highly attractive young man. Their mutual attraction was intense, and Ted and Bonnie dated seriously through her last year of high school. Bonnie even found a climate of safety and acceptance within his close, devoted family that she had never felt at home. But when Ted became more serious and seemed about to propose, Bonnie suddenly panicked. She cooled off toward him and soon started making excuses for not returning his calls. No amount of Ted's earnest persuasion could move her, and before long the happy relationship had collapsed.

After graduation, Bonnie continued to work and live at home until she met her husband, Tom, a man who made her feel safe but who held little attraction for her. Accepting *his* marriage proposal was easy. Tom was neither especially handsome nor sexually exciting, and Bonnie settled into married life with relief. But after a few years, Bonnie was no longer placated by the satisfactions of her role as wife and mother of their two children.

Without ever crossing the line into an affair, Bonnie began to form crushes on attractive men with whom she had contact at work. Once again, if the desirable man responded to her, Bonnie became extremely anxious and withdrew. By this time Bonnie had entered therapy to deal with her feelings of inexplicable depression. She was willing to be extremely honest with herself, and soon she was able to identify what she saw in her mind in that split second when a handsome man began to respond to her: "I see my mother," she confessed, "She's furious and is going to attack me. Her face is ugly with hate, as if she wants to kill me."

Bonnie shocked herself when she came out with this image. She had no idea where it came from, but it led her to explore the issue of her mother's envy and anger. Bonnie had always remembered her father's dramatic temper, but now she began to recover memories of her mother's fits of anger, and her bitterness over Bonnie's special place in her father's heart. Bonnie's insight had touched the icy core of her mother's envy.

Rapunzel's Dilemma

Bonnie hit upon the fairy tale of Rapunzel as a vivid metaphor for her childhood relationship with her mother. In this story, the wicked witch isolates the golden-haired Rapunzel in a lonely tower, possessing her youth and beauty as only a jailer can do. When the witch comes with food, Rapunzel must let down her cascade of hair to allow the witch to climb up with her basket. The witch poses as caretaker and protector, but her real purpose is to satisfy her sadistic envy by keeping Rapunzel away from grown-up happiness with a man. The witch uses Rapunzel's hair – her "crowning glory," symbolic of her greatest gifts – in a coarse, unappreciative way, as a ladder for her own ascent.

As long as there is no prince to tempt Rapunzel, she and the witch keep up their uneasy arrangement. But when the prince does come, tricking Rapunzel into letting down her hair for him, he intrudes into the forbidden domain of mother domination and tempts her to freedom. Here was the dilemma of both Rapunzel and Bonnie: pleasure and fulfillment are standing before them – but the witch is on the way. Sure enough, when the witch sees the prince climbing down the priceless hair after a visit, she is enraged. Once inside the tower, the witch confronts Rapunzel and in one horrifying swipe of the shears, cuts off Rapunzel's hair, triumphant in the fury of her revenge.

This is the prototypical metaphor of parental envy. Rather than giving the child permission and encouragement to enter the world, the envious, sadistic parent destroys the child's chance at happiness, even if it requires the psychological mutilation of the child's greatest gifts. The parent may do this unconsciously or deliberately, but the result is the same. The point is that the envious parent will do whatever it takes psychologically to hang on to control of the child; for to see the child go off and experience true fulfillment would be maddeningly painful.

Bonnie's mother prevented Bonnie's healthy mother-daughter separation process by poisoning Bonnie's mind about the motives of men. Perhaps unconsciously, she tried to keep Bonnie's beauty and liveliness for herself, taking pleasure in Bonnie's pretty vivaciousness but making the girl feel guilty for using it with men. Bonnie was deeply confused about her mother's mixed messages to be sexy and pretty, but at all costs not to give in to her sexual feelings or leave her mother by herself. As a result, Bonnie was free to flirt and attract (under her mother's watchful eye), but not to have a real relationship that would psychologically take her away from home for good. Caught in this bind, Bonnie struggled to find some happiness, but not to be so happy that her mother's life would be revealed for what it was: bitter, miserable, and squandered. By marrying a man who did not excite her, Bonnie stayed her mother's little girl and made sure she was not any happier than her mother or anyone else.

Bonnie became conscious of this terrible childhood dilemma only after her husband Tom died, and she was once again free at a relatively early age to explore what she wanted out of life. She met a "prince," one of those men who do not mind pursuing and awakening reluctant ladies. Finally, Bonnie was able to complete the heroic task of braving her mother's anger and dislike of men in order to enjoy life on her own. She cut the negative ties to her childhood, and proceeded to enjoy a love affair that allowed her to complete every unfinished crush she had ever had – without her mother's permission .

Breaking the Rules

Permission-seekers are never good rule-breakers. That's why they need to make a point of breaking rules once in awhile. Bonnie did this by breaking out of a stifling subordination to her mother in order to really live. She broke their secret rule that Bonnie could leave home and marry only if she agreed to never have a more fulfilling life than her mother did.

Most of us have these kinds of old, unexamined "rules" that govern our choices in adulthood. Some of them may be helpful, enabling us to expedite our daily decision. Many other "rules" are just plain harmful, such as when a person unhappily stays in a family-owned business because his parents want him to, or a couple pressures themselves into having a baby because their parents want grandchildren, or a daughter puts off a career change because her parents are proud of her current status. There are many unspoken rules that may need to be broken in order to release us to our own adulthood.

The key is not in the rule-breaking, but in the creativity and productivity that are released when we do things differently than we have always done them.

Joanne's story

Joanne, another client of mine, was an example of a woman who followed all the rules, putting up with her husband's drinking and waiting around for him to come home whenever he pleased. She always prided herself on being a "good wife," but finally her deep frustration resulted in depression, causing her to stay close to home and stop driving her car. She also had a ballooning weight problem. In therapy, Joanne worked on identifying what she really *wanted* to do, instead of waiting around to see what she *had time for* if her errant husband got home in time to help with the children.

One day Joanne decided to try out a new behavior. She informed her husband he had to be home early because she was going out shopping. Laying aside her worries about supper and bedtime, she handed the kids over to him and cruised the store aisles until closing time that night, blissfully savoring her freedom. It was around that time in her life that she began to drive again, something she had given up when her depression started. A tiny broken "rule" about what good mothers should do in the evening opened up a sense of freedom and determination that was just what Joanne needed to begin seeing herself as a separate person with the right to pursue her own goals.

Sara's Story

Another client, Sara, solved an acute depressive crisis by packing up all her favorite books, needlepoint, and writing journal to take a weekend by herself at a local hotel on the beach. She came up with this idea on her own, in response to my question about what she thought would make her feel better. As a young Navy wife with several young children, it was hard to break the rule of frugality and self-sacrifice to take care of herself in this way. In fact, compared to antidepressants and long-term therapy, it turned out to be an inexpensive antidote to her depressive feelings of powerlessness. She returned from her escape with a better self-image which in turn improved her relationships with her husband and children.

Too often the rules we fear to break are the ones that forbid us from taking care of ourselves at the expense of someone else's inconvenience or hurt feelings. We ask too much of ourselves, making up silly rules to follow and then invoking guilt when we fall short. You might be surprised at how much better you feel when you try a little piece of freedom or give yourself a break. Often just the symbolism of a small act of self-caring is enough to open a way out of hopelessness and bring one back into the world of possibility.

The Reassurance Addict

For the overly socialized person – the really good child – asking permission becomes a way of life. The ability to jump in and take advantage of what you need to fulfill yourself gets mixed up with too much concern over doing the right thing. This results in a loss of initiative and a habit of waiting to see what others think every time. There are times when asking for permission goes completely against the flow of life, against the dance of opportunity. It plugs up your inspiration and intuition, preventing you from getting what you need from situations and other people. Permission-seeking is the very opposite of taking charge. There are many moments in our lives when thinking too much about getting permission is the kiss of death to our confidence. We become hesitant and tentative. We lose track of what is okay and we become *reassurance addicts*.

Going ahead with our dreams is all about breaking this habit. In Rapunzel's terms, it means challenging the witch. It necessarily means a degree of separation from loved ones and your old roles in the family. If your parents have brought you up to think for yourself and have respected your ideas, then it is going to be much easier for you to think clearly about where you want to go in your life. However, if your confidence was undermined by a parent who treated you as incompetent – or only gave you love when you were being obedient – then following a freely chosen adult path can feel daunting. Lest you think I am only talking about young adults here, let me reassure you that there are plenty of forty- and fifty-year-olds waiting for permission to do what they want with their lives. Of course, the permission will never come as long as they see themselves as needing to uphold the expectations of their parents or others.

Mature age alone does not mean we have individuated from our parents at a mental and emotional level. That is where the homing pigeon of permission-seeking comes in, bringing with it the urge to seek reassurance for every decision. We crave a source of security to give us permission before we make that next step. And like the addict, we can never get enough.

The Permission of Experts

Asking permission keeps us stuck in a one-sided love affair with another person's power. We get trained early into the habit of looking to experts to tell us what we should do. Often this is helpful, but sometimes expert opinions are the last thing you need These opinions can get in the way of your own knowing, based on your own real experience and intuition.

When you look to other people to tell you something as important as who you were meant to be or what you really want, it takes your eye off the prize. You become like a driver looking backwards over your shoulder, asking the expert in the back seat to tell you where to go, when the road is right in front of you and the wheel is in your hands. Here is where permission-seeking has to end, even when it's in the constructive guise of gathering more and more information. Your ultimate direction has to come from the still, small voice inside you, from synchronicities and serendipities, from moments of enlightenment and moments of hitting bottom. Your job is to make room for your own personal moments of realization. There is no expert on your future but you.

Why Are We So Afraid of Our Own Power?

Many of us give our power away. Why? Because responsibility can be so frightening. It is a bit like a favorite uncle giving us a wonderful toy, which turns out to be a little nuclear bomb. There we sit on the floor, holding the so-called toy in our hands, stunned by the power of it, unable to move for fear we will blow ourselves up. That is often how we handle our own power. We're scared to death of it. Not knowing how to handle the power, we want our uncle to take it back. "You take it!" we say, and feel great relief.

As grown ups, the responsibility of adult power can feel like our very own ticking bomb. We don't want to hold onto it too long for fear of what might happen; so we toss it from our hands into the lap of the next person. Then we ask their permission for what we already had the freedom to do! It's an arrangement many of us accept. It has the familiar appeal of childhood security, as we look to strong adults to take care of us. This is often what we adults secretly wish we could go back to.

But was that really what we wanted, even as children? Look at the behavior of two-year-old children, three-year-olds and four-year-olds. Look at the normal six-year-old boy and twelve-year-old girl. All are in a constant battle for power and self-determination. If they have not been too traumatized by overpowering events, and if they have not been made to lose their natural buoyancy, they are on the lookout for ways in which they can increase their freedom and control. The healthy two-year-old confidently goes around demanding power and declaring his right to have it. Then the adults convince him that his power is dangerous, will hurt him, and he had better trust them to tell him what to do.

The older some of us get, the better childhood dependence looks to us. We even tell our children and grandchildren not to be in a hurry to grow up, to enjoy their childhood. We don't think about it from their point of view. What is there to enjoy about always being told you cannot do something, having your judgment second guessed, and having someone say you can't do such small things as plug in a lamp or work the toaster, when you've seen your mother do those things a thousand times? The child knows better. She is in a hurry to grow up, open her own doors and pick out her own clothes. Nevertheless, in one way or another, she is told that she has to wait for permission. Over and over this inability to make our own decisions is drilled into our heads as children. We gradually learn that it is not a good idea to have too much initiative. After all, we could electrocute ourselves, burn ourselves up, get hit by a car, or whatever the awful outcomes were that our parents scared us with. Out of their desire to protect us, they taught us to be afraid of what we wanted to do.

Here is the tragedy: we don't just learn not to chase balls into the street or put our fingers in light sockets. We also learn to mistrust the go-get-it impulse we had as we saw the ball go into the street. In other words, our *curiosity*, our *urge* to go after what we wanted are tagged as the things to resist, instead of the actual source of danger. *After years of parents filling us with fear*

*and expectations of punishment, we learn that when we feel intense motivation
and burning curiosity, we are about to put ourselves in danger.* This fear of our
own inadequacy becomes an over-generalized belief that extends far beyond
its boundaries of usefulness. From there it is but a short step to fear that we're
going to cause harm to others or ourselves if we eagerly go after what we want.

The rule about not running into the street is not about the *street* being
dangerous; it is about the *cars* on the street being dangerous. However, because we do not trust our children to look for the cars, we teach them that the
street is dangerous. As we grow up, it becomes our responsibility as adults to
figure out which of those old fears are unrealistic. We learn that reasonable
caution allows us to cross all kinds of streets, to try all kinds of things with
safety. We no longer have to stay in our own front yards.

Pleasurable Correctness – Are We Having Fun Yet?

At the beginning of our lives, we get our start using pleasure and pain to define who we are. If it feels good, it is me. If it hurts, it's not me. Pleasure and
pain build our self-concept, and continues to throughout our lives. However,
as children, we can be made ashamed of what we like to do, resulting in desperate inner attempts to change what we cannot change. Part of this is simply
socialization. But when socialization goes overboard, we can reject our true
natures to the point where we can no longer tell what we enjoy. If we don't
know what we enjoy, we don't know who we are.

Pleasure is a funny thing in our culture. Our pleasures are very keenly
observed, defined, and evaluated. If you ask yourself what *really* brings you
pleasure, you may be surprised. Try to be totally honest and open when you
answer this question. If you were given free rein and no one would disapprove
of you, what would you do that brings you the most pleasure?

Whatever they are, your pleasures are about as close to your real self as
you can get. Nothing can convince your true self that something is fun if it's
not. No matter how hard you try, if it's boring, it's boring. As children, our
inborn sense of fun and pleasure can become all tangled up with what other
people approve of. We begin to worry that what we really enjoy may make us
a little too "different." We try to become interested in what we are not, until

by the time we are adults we may be totally confused on the whole subject. Pleasurable correctness has taken us over, dampening our life force with its wet blanket of conformity.

Remember the slogan "Are we having fun yet?" It rang true, this T-shirt plaint. Too often we secretly seek validation to tell us whether or not we are having a pleasurably correct experience. Group reactions tell us what is supposed to be fun, leaving us feeling isolated and baffled if we do not like it. Pleasurable correctness is an important value in our society, and it's often tied to making money: if we can't sell it to you, it can't be the best kind of fun.

If you suspect you've fallen prey to pleasurable correctness, ask yourself, "*Am* I having fun?" If you're not, it means there is something wrong with the situation – not you – and you need to get out of there and do something else. You cannot fake enjoying yourself. It is too personal, too real.

However, most of us have an inner critic who does not care about our real enjoyment. This part of your mind is invested in your remaining a member of the group, the family, the job, the chain gang. It hates uniqueness and personal feeling. It is anti-pleasure, because pleasure is such a heartfelt expression of pure individuality. Our inner critic can make us worry about correctness even when every molecule in us is uncoiling in blissful surrender to a pleasurable experience. Hearing this judgmental voice, we evaluate instead of emancipate; we judge instead of enjoy. The inner critic keeps up a running commentary of what it thinks you ought to be doing or not doing. It stands in your way, and denies permission for certain individual pleasures and interests because it can see exactly where you are headed: away from the group. It springs to its feet in alarm, full defenses bristling, shouting, "You can't do that!" The inner critic gets its start in the family's authority, but it hooks up with the advertisers and media to tell you how to fit in and be more like other people around you. People who honestly follow their pleasures make lousy targets for sales pitches and guilt ploys.

Don't wait for the inner critic's permission to become yourself. By definition, if you depend on others to discover your true self, you never will.

Suicide: The Last Refuge of the Permission-Seeker

When you forbid yourself freedom and happiness, what's left to keep you going? Suicide is just one extreme way of making real the living death that a life of seeking permission brings. It is the one act that is perceived as not under the control of someone else.

Many people who at times have wished they were dead are in fact people who have a very powerful life force, a real drive for growth and enjoyment of pleasure. They are sensitive and strong, and may wish they could expand beyond their family. If this healthy urge is repeatedly criticized and thwarted, and they see no way out, then the idea of death can become the final, tragic way of liberating themselves. Fantasies of death are often only symbolic wishes for freedom. At a subconscious level the person logically but irrationally thinks that if he or she could just stop *this* life, he or she might have a chance to live at last.

Self-destruction is the last self-expressive act of the powerless. It is a peculiar kind of creativity, but that's what it is. A suicidal plan can be the last attempt at taking control over charting your own course. What a tragedy that so right an instinct for freedom could end itself in its own moment of creation. Suicide hopes for the big win in this last dramatic act, but in the end it's a magical wish to become whole and separate without working for it.

Any of us can perform little suicides all day long by not speaking up for our needs or waiting for permissions that never come. But your unmet need will sit indefinitely outside the door and wait for you to call it inside. It is the need to enjoy your life as only you can create it, and to express who you were meant to be. Suicidal feelings tell you how far you have gotten away from your own real life. Suicidal feelings are a cry from the soul, an angry soul that is sick to death of living without air – a soul that no longer agrees to be the perfect victim.

If you have ever felt sick to death of your life, you know this feeling. By the time you get to this stage of frustration and hopelessness, it is extremely difficult to think of another way to solve your problems. Suicidal fantasies satisfy so many neglected urges for power, self-expression, revenge, and escape that they can be hard to give up without help. They become a siren song that lures us toward the thrill of destruction and away from a truly fulfilling life, with no second chances. Don't listen to them. Run, don't walk, to a good therapist who understands such symbolic wishes and can help you figure out how to satisfy all those urges and still be around to enjoy life.

—⟞

Signs and Serendipities

Have you ever had a sense of receiving a "sign" about what you should do at certain key points in your life? I have. At one point in the writing of this book, I was about ready to throw in the towel. I was wondering how I could keep on working on this project when I had so much else going on in my life that was demanding my attention. It seemed that just to turn out the number of pages to which I had committed myself was taking more time and effort than I had to give. The next day as I was driving to work, feeling thoroughly discouraged, the car in front of me slowed down and then stopped to make a turn. Just before he turned left, I looked at the rear of his car. That is when I saw the message on his license plate: DONT KWIT.

My urge to give up collided with the perfect words right in front of me on that license plate, just when I needed to be slowed down and reminded of my real goals. How perfectly in tune with my need. I immediately was reassured.

Is there a way to understand and use these kinds of serendipities? You could give it a mystical explanation, seeing it as a sign from God or a message from a kindly universe devoted to our growth. On the other hand, the scientist in you might say that we program our brains to pick up any cues related to our current need. No matter how you look at the sign, it is an act of recognition. When you see something and feel that charge of meaningful recognition, you are struck by a sensation of knowing this is *your* answer. You feel ownership of it. The sign seems meant for you, and therefore significant and even precious. This sense of recognition often has an intensely comforting feeling to it, telling you that you're on the right track after all.

However, there is another, negative type of sign that is used by people to justify why they cannot have what they want from life. This kind of sign "proves" that their dream was not meant to be and stops them in their tracks.

Often this kind of sign-reading happens when you are just taking the first tentative steps in something new. Maybe you are making the first phone call to check on college courses after being out of school for fifteen years. Maybe you are checking out positions in another company, because you have finally decided you do not want to endure the old job any longer. The "sign" comes when your call does not get through or the conversation does not go as expected. "Oh well, it's a sign," you might say. And you back off. You treat the sign with relief as proof that you were not really meant to go ahead with that plan. This kind of sign serves your fears. It gives you a resigned feeling. It does not energize, inspire, give hope, or lead you onward. It just keeps you stuck.

Disheartening "signs" that your hopes were not meant to be are nothing more than the projection of your own discouragement and fear. When the signs you're noticing are negative like this, your mind is telling you that for whatever reason you are afraid to keep pursuing what you want. *It is not a sign from the heavens about what is not "meant" to be!* As a rule of thumb, always take these negative signs with a grain of salt, as nothing more than simple proof of your reluctance.

On the other hand, you must feel free to take uplifting serendipities at full face value! This is legitimate because you are simply accepting the projection of your own secret confidence that you can and should be following your dream. The right kind of serendipities and synchronicities feel light and encouraging. They lift you into more of life, whereas discouraging signs sink you down with resignation. They are very different states, and are excellent clues as to how ready you are to go after your dreams. Again, evaluate an experience's worth by what it does to your level of energy. If it pumps you up, believe in it. If it brings you down, discount it as quickly as possible. This tool of self-discovery is obvious and simple but it can be easily overlooked

The real benefit of signs and serendipities is that they reflect our inner landscape, our land of dreams and where we stand in relation to them. Learn to read where you really are through the kinds of "signs" you are experiencing. They are very reliable reflections of what you are willing and able to accept at this time. If many negative signs are crossing your path, it merely suggests that you are afraid, lacking in preparation, or are going about it the hard way. That is all it shows. It doesn't mean your dream is wrong.

The signs and serendipities you see and feel will tell you whether you are primarily committed or primarily reluctant. Remember that serendipities confirm a rightful order to the universe and hopefulness about your life. In contrast, negative signs are agents of your own fear, the voice of the old guard telling you that the world does not want you to come play. "See," the voice says, "they didn't return your call. They don't want to play with you. Come home," it whispers, "back where you are safe." Surely *this* is not what you want to listen to for the rest of your life. Such a life, as Thoreau said, would be one "of quiet desperation."

Getting Your Blessing

Who does not crave a parent's blessing when he or she steps out into the world? Giving one's blessing is an old custom often neglected in our culture, but it is still psychologically crucial. In the old days, a young man getting ready to set off on his self-supporting life would go to his parents for a blessing. This ritual put the stamp of approval on his transformation from child to grown man. It required the parent to give up complete ownership of the child, so he could become a man in his own right. It also gave notice to the young man that his childhood was officially done. (While young women in the old days may not have had a similar ritual release into a life of their own, it is certainly something that can be claimed now.)

These days, instead of sitting down with our parents and getting a clear go-ahead to grow up, we leave this very important matter hanging. We inch into adulthood without a ritual that says explicitly, "This is the end of my childhood, it is now up to me." For many people in our culture, this final necessary step is not fully experienced until middle age when elderly parents die. We have ceremonies for school graduation, for marriage and baptisms, but none of these provide the psychological ritual we need: the official recognition that grown children are people with a right to unique lives apart from their parents' expectations.

When parents are not required to give their formal blessing to their child's independence, they can continue subconsciously to influence and even rule their children's lives. No matter how they feel about us, many parents don't want to let go. The role of parent is too important to them. They continue to need their children, way past the point of what is good for parent or child. Emotionally mature parents release their children anyway, but the insecure parent keeps an iron grip on the attachment. In such families, an ambitious child may be able to get out on his own with few problems, while one of his siblings may continue to be stuck in some version of the baby role, awaiting the permission to grow up that never comes.

It is not how often a person has contact with her family that identifies her level of independence. It is whether or not the person has taken hold of directing her own life. It is perfectly possible to grow up, leave home, get a job, and still be caught in the role of lifelong child because you care too much about what your parents think. How can you tell if you care too much? You find yourself thinking twice – once for yourself and once for your parents – before you pursue what you really want.

Think again about the person from whom you feel you need permission. Who it is will be obvious if you give it a moment of honest reflection. It may be a disapproving parent, a depressed or needy spouse, or maybe even a domineering friend. But the people from whom you need permission are the people who are mentally holding you back. You worry about what they would think; you hear their criticisms and warnings inside your head. Wanting permission from someone tells you that you have accepted that person's domination over your life.

Asking for *permission* puts us in an infantile, dependent state, but asking for a *blessing* is a step toward adulthood. With a blessing request, we already know what we want to do and are planning to do it. When we make the bold move of asking for a blessing, it is because we want the most important people in our lives to support us. The most compassionate and empowering parents do not wait for their child to ask for a blessing; instead they give it spontaneously at each new crossroad in their child's life. However, if you are like many of us, your parents overlooked that step, leaving you always feeling a little uneasy about your adult status in their eyes. Therefore, you may need to get your blessing someplace else.

This new kind of permission, this blessing, can come from other sources: a mentor, a supportive friend, or yourself. In many cases, it's up to you to give the permission and blessing to yourself in order to grow up and leave home, no matter how old you are. Think about it this way: you have already done your time in the family. You have put sheer numbers of years into what other people wanted you to do. You must now do something for yourself. Whatever your age, don't wait for a mid-life crisis. Seek self-understanding now, and look for your blessing from the people who will give it ungrudgingly.

Find people who love to see you stretch your wings, who applaud it when you strike out on your own. Let them be the ones from whom you seek your blessing, because they will certainly give it. Look for people who are not threatened by your dreams and who would rejoice in your success.

Mature, loving parents like to give their blessing, even if their own dreams have gone unfulfilled. This kind of parent is happy for his child's future even if there may be some envy of the child's freedom. Even if your parents don't or can't extend this kind of support, you can still give yourself the blessing of a compassionate parent – the parent you have become to yourself.

CHAPTER 3
EGO: THE ENEMY WITHIN

Whatever you call it, the ego's mission boils down to one aim: your unhappiness and lack of personal fulfillment. The ego does not want you to find yourself nor feel your unique purpose and power.

Standing in the shadows, running the show but taking no responsibility, is the ego, your inner saboteur. The ego is the hit man of the psyche, funded by ancient prohibitions against real individuality. In its most seductive form, the ego brings euphoria and the kind of inflated self-image that guarantees busted ambitions. At its worst, it crushes hope and incentive, and will not rest until you agree to give up the dream. The ego, our inner enemy, undermines us in the most insidious and subtle ways by keeping us too frightened – or too grandiose – to live out our dreams. No matter which route it takes – fear or grandiosity – the ego has but one goal: to make sure you never fulfill who you were meant to be. It is anti-happiness and anti-destiny.

The ego has no interest in your happiness; it just wants you to stay safe by maintaining the self-image you adopted in childhood. It tells you to live according to the expectations of others in return for tidbits of love and security. It has no intention of letting you grow up, much less find your true destiny.

Carl's Story

My client Carl was in the grip of his ego for years. Carl was an artist by talent and desire. However, growing up in a working class family, Carl had memories of his mother throwing his drawings in the trash and his father telling him art was for losers. With phenomenal integrity and drive, Carl went ahead, despite his lack of parental support, and got a graduate degree in fine arts, intending a career as a professional artist. *Then his ego got hold of him.* Unfortunately, Carl began to become more and more high-minded, inflated, and entitled about the terms he would accept from the art world. Carl's ego whispered in his ear to be suspicious of commercialized art galleries that might make him compromise his high artistic ideals. The last straw came when he was not accepted for an advanced arts fellowship he'd desperately wanted. Now the ego turned on him, pivoting from entitlement to self-enmity in an instant. It told him he was no good and should never have tried in the first place.

Not able to realize his dreams on exactly his terms, Carl's ego – like his father – flipped and told him he was no good. Carl stopped trying to make it as an artist and took a supervisory job in the sheet metal factory where his father had worked as a foreman.

By the time I met him, Carl was a resigned person, with many bridges burned between himself and his soul's passion. However, I got to watch Carl come back to life, as he identified the enemy within and beat it. As we worked together, he began to realize how his ego had joined up with his parents' defeatist, critical attitudes, convincing him it was hopeless to ever have a life different from theirs. As Carl continued his search for his true purpose, he learned to accept himself as he really was, not as his parents or his inflated ego saw him. He also realized how he had undermined his own happiness by blindly accepting both his ego's criticisms and exaggerated expectations.

Once he stopped listening to his entitled, yet hypercritical ego, Carl began to make a new life for himself, discovering fresh outlets for his artistic nature and a deeper warmth for other people than he had ever experienced before. As he learned to accept his true self unconditionally, Carl discovered many positive attributes about himself that had never had the chance to be expressed. As Carl said of his rediscovered self when he finished therapy, *"I always was who I am now; I just didn't know how to be it."*

Meet the Ego

The ego is that part of your self that is rooted in fear, guilt, shame and grandiosity, and is directly at odds with your true self. The ego[2] believes that your greatest safety lies in becoming whatever others expect you to be. It exists to preserve the status quo and to prevent you from leaving the fold.

The idea of this inner, self-limiting force is not a new one. It is as old as the devil himself. The ego has been known by many names: the killing force of the psyche[3], the death instinct[4], the protector[5], the Voice[6], or even Satan[7]. But there is nothing supernatural about this idea, for your ego is nothing more than a self-defeating *psychological* force.

Whatever you call it, the ego's mission boils down to one aim: *your unhappiness and lack of personal fulfillment.* The ego does not want you to find yourself nor feel your unique purpose and power. Like a malignant advisor, its goal is not the good of your soul, but the preservation of its own power. Your ego sets itself up as an infallible authority and makes you feel afraid, at fault, and certain to be punished. The ego knows that guilt-ridden people don't challenge authority.

This inner saboteur pipes up with its destructive opinions every time you get close to your true self and purpose. It's the confounding inner presence that menaces you with the suggestion that maybe you should just go on back home where you belong and not try this grown-up stuff. Believe me, it is a paper tiger. It has exactly as much power as you want to give it.

Where Did It Come From?

The ego has both personal and archetypal roots. You feel its effects but you don't realize where it comes from. Its takeover is undetectable; its thoughts feel like your thoughts. When it merges with your consciousness, you lose all adult perspective and see the world through its eyes[8]. To get free of it, you have to understand its origins so you can step back and see what it's doing and why. Let's look at where the ego comes from and unmask it.

The Ego's Archetypal Roots

The ego has been an innate, archetypal character within the human mind since antiquity. Archetypes are ancient idea patterns that Carl Jung said exist in everyone's collective unconscious mind[9]. Just by being human, you hold these unconscious psychological energies and themes within you. People love stories and movies because they are already familiar with their archetypal themes of human challenge and struggle.

In the archetypal story of what Joseph Campbell called the *hero's journey*[10], potential heroes lead regular lives until they are called to their greater destiny. But as they start on their adventure, they soon run into the *threshold guardians*. A threshold guardian is anything – internal or external – that thwarts your efforts and makes you choose between giving up or trying harder. I think of the ego as an inner threshold guardian that tests your determination to see if you have what it takes.

The ego as archetypal threshold guardian has whispered into the ears of many accomplished people who have stepped beyond the ordinary. It weeds out people who are not committed to their dreams by tempting them to give up. It tells you that you don't have what it takes. It constantly threatens you with fear ridicule, exclusion, loss, or even death. It always speaks up when you're at your weakest, making you despair about fulfilling your purpose.

The Ego's Psychological Roots

The spirit of the ego is archetypal, but the individual form of your ego is psychological. Your personal ego comes from early childhood and reflects the opposition you got when you started asserting yourself. The ego is your fearful, small-minded part that sees life as limited, scarce, competitive, and too hard to handle. It says the safest thing for you is to listen to the authorities and stick with the status quo. From the ego's point of view, you live in a hostile environment in which no individual matters as much as the preservation of the tribe. When you start exploring your individual purpose, it becomes alarmed because it can't see anything good coming from this. In its tribal mind, it thinks it has to save you from shunning, banishment, attack, or even death from the authorities in your life.

The "voice" of the ego sounds like your own thoughts because it uses your voice to speak internally. However, ego thoughts don't come from you; they come from authority figures in your childhood[11,12]. If the ego still used the voice of your mother, for instance, it would be easy to spot and reconsider if you still want Mom telling you what to do. Unfortunately, your ego masquerades as the inner voice of reason, good sense, or self-preservation. You think *you're* thinking when the ego speaks. But instead of using your true mind, you're just reliving childhood fears about what would happen to you if you got too big for your britches.

The Ego is Not Your Conscience

The ego is not your conscience. Your conscience has constructive motives and serves your best interests by helping you operate from wisdom rather than impulse. It is a good thing to think twice before breaking the law or doing something that would hurt someone else. As your guide for ethical living, the prodding of a reliable conscience can have long-term benefits. But the ego is different: it's not about ethics; it's about fear of rejection. It thinks there is safety in keeping yourself small because then family members won't be envious. The ego must be differentiated from your conscience if you are ever to stop taking its advice.

Of course, the ego being the parasitic, alien life-form that it is, masquerades as a part of its host. You hear the ego and you think it's your conscience talking. It *feels* highly moral and righteous, as if it were infallible. It tells you "how things really are," things like: you're never going to amount to anything, you're a dreamer, it'll never work, and you're being selfish. *But whatever it says, it kills your motivation.*

Conscience instructs but does not undermine initiative nor rob you of energy. When your real conscience tells you something, the knowledge it imparts *adds* to your ability to cope. The conscience gives you helpful guidance, prompts redirection, promotes apologies, and steers you in the right direction. The ego, on the other hand, is only interested in taking things away from you and keeping you scared. *Conscience adds; the ego subtracts.*

Many people worry that antisocial behavior will result if they develop more self-interest. This worry is another example of ego nonsense. Self-development and conscience support each other and balance our psychological growth. You need your conscience. But you do not need the ego, that life-sucking leech that masquerades as your conscience and ruins your chances at adult happiness.

Hand-me-downs

The ego has the peculiar characteristic of presenting itself as the most personal and real part of you, and yet it is literally the most unoriginal part of you. The ego is all borrowed. It is not who you really are, who you came into the world as. It is an assortment of survival memories from *other people's* pasts. Like hand-me-down clothing, it often does not fit well. Your parents or society may have passed down these antiquated beliefs directly into your scared little child ego. So when you are judging yourself harshly or feeling total certainty about your chances for failure, just take a moment and ask yourself if those are really *your* ideas. Might you have inherited such self-attack from someone else?

It can be very hard to consider rejecting ideas and beliefs that you've held all your life. It can be the hardest thing in the world to think originally, to study the evidence and form another conclusion different from what you've always been told.

Yet this is what you *will* do if you are going to become who you were really meant to be. Your true self does not consist of the fears and opinions that have been passed down to you like great grandmother's quilt. To find our true purpose we have to begin seeing the ego part of our personality for what it is and stop refusing to let it have the final say over us.

The Ego's Attitude

The ego thinks it knows everything. It deludes you into thinking it is the master of the house when it is really a freeloading tenant. When you are operating by the ego's rules, you are out of touch with the unique gifts belonging to your true self. The ego keeps you who you're supposed to be in order to feel acceptable, but the self is who you really are.

The ego thinks it can do anything. Nothing looks hard to it, because it knows perfectly well that it has no intentions of ever really putting itself on the line. The ego is like the worst kind of crazy-making parent to the rest of your personality. On the one hand, it may inflate you and tell you that you can do anything. On the other hand, as you begin to work toward your goal, it may tell you that life should not be so hard, that this is too much effort. Besides, it might add, you probably don't have what it takes, which everybody is sure to find out when you are exposed as an impostor. What a treacherous force to harbor in your mind, and it's all the stronger for not being unmasked. It misleads you every step of the way.

The ego thinks it knows its way around a competitive world in which people are chasing their desires. It has a defensive attitude and a suspicious way of thinking that can be applied to every situation. However, the ego loves no one, and it has none of the radiance of the real self. Never can the ego supply you with the heart-expanding joy of creating your own wonderful life. The ego cannot create. It can only destroy what your true self has tried to create.

The ego is highly reactive emotionally and has opinions about everything. It tells you that you should've done things differently. It makes you a victim by complaining that this person shouldn't have hurt your feelings or such a thing shouldn't have happened, and so on. So much energy is spent by the ego on its reactions to everything, you have very little left over to actually do anything. The ego's goal is to create inner turmoil, not accomplishment.

The ego, while it served some purposes for tribal survival, was never designed to support personal growth. It is fixated solely on furthering its own mission of conformity via fear.

Let's Get This Straight

The ego – let's get this straight – is not on your side. The ego's aim is destruction, despair, and the disconnection of positive ties with other people. As we will see in a later chapter, some positive ties with other people are going to be necessary for your success, because nobody does anything completely on their own. Nevertheless the ego does not want you to trust other people or move outside your family. It wants you to listen *only* to it.

The ego hates your enthusiasm. It is not at all interested in your happiness or fulfillment, even though it insists that's its sole purpose. It is the bully who cannot resist knocking down what you have begun to build. The ego's main mission is to keep you from reuniting with your true energies and interests. Throwing you off track any way it possibly can is what the ego is really about. Its methods instill either hopelessness or unrealistically inflated expectations – although opposites, they are both equally deadly in the end.

The ego will be skeptical and cynical, *whatever it takes,* to keep you from being wholehearted about your mission. It will undermine not only your confidence, but your creativity as well. The ego will makes you side against your intuition and your desires, so that you mistrust the things you love the most.

Ego Attack

A client of mine, Kathy, had made enormous progress in her psychotherapy sessions, becoming her own person in spite of intense resistance from her family. She was learning first to ask *herself* what she wanted, and as a result her domineering mother's disapproval was beginning to lose its effect.

However, after a period of exhilarating growth and restored self-confidence, Kathy slumped into my office one day in a grimly depressed state. She morosely told me, *"I feel like all that other stuff I told you before was just a bunch of bull. Look at me, I can't do anything now."* (This was actually not true, but this is how one talks when the ego is in control.)

Perceiving that Kathy was in danger of breaking out of the family corral for good, her ego had become highly alarmed. It hit her with a blast of demoralization that caused her to doubt all her progress to date. We had to figure out how her ego stirred up this crisis of self-doubt and then how to put it in its place.

Kathy had spent the weekend with her family for the baptism of her sister's baby. Kathy's temper rose as she watched her mother take over and ruin her sister's special day by ordering people around and childishly pouting when things did not go her way. However, Kathy did not want to make a scene, so she pushed down her feelings of outrage over her mother's insensitive behavior. The strain of this internal tension exhausted Kathy and left the door wide open for her ego to do what it does best: stir up self-doubt.

Instead of continuing to be angry with her mother, Kathy turned her anger and frustration inward and began to doubt all her growth and progress thus far. Notice the *non sequitur* here, so common to the ego's illogic: Kathy's anger over *her mother's behavior* somehow morphed into pessimism about *Kathy's* capabilities and future. Kathy's ego had used these wobbly moments of internal conflict to shake her confidence and confuse her with a nonsensical train of thought.

Once we recovered what had upset her and saw how the ego had flung her back into childhood helplessness and guilt, Kathy was able to see the incident clearly and her depression lifted. When she no longer supported the ego in its attack on her, its power fizzled.

Kill It Before It Grows

The ego also has a very predictable reaction to any kind of pleasure that comes from joyful self-expression – especially if your creativity might connect you with other people and inspire them too. It's called the *ego stomp*. Even as that first shoot of green is poking through the snow of your self-doubt and criticism, the ego is lacing up its jackboots. Grow, stomp. Grow, stomp. It is a dance we all must hobble through at first if we are moving from a lifetime of suppression and fear into becoming our true selves. *Just what might happen – the ego warns you – if you go too far and enter a world that leaves your family behind?* Stomp. Aren't you tampering with the mighty forces of natural law? Stomp. Do you not deserve to be punished? Stomp. Is it not a safer, better idea to beat the ego to the punch and punish yourself for trying to be independent? Stomp.

As you find your way to your real purpose you may miss your first signs of growth. Sometimes these moments are so quickly stomped that we're not even sure we really experienced them. Next we'll look at Beth's experience, a woman who became intimately acquainted with the ego-stomp and learned to avoid it over the course of her remarkable growth.

Beth's Story: Waltzing the Ego

Everything about Beth looked warm and engaging, from her stylishly tousled hair to her curl of a smile. She dressed with a casual elegance that made her look as if she would be at home in either the boardroom or a cabin in the woods. Her intelligence and beauty made her seem ready to become someone of merit, a walking study in human potential. And she was connected to her own heart. When Beth talked, it was from her soul.

In her mid-forties, Beth decided the time had come for her to search for her real purpose for the first time in her life. She had been depressed and unhappy for years, playing the perfect, pleasing wife to a self-centered, dictatorial husband. Together, we figured out that Beth's depression was the result of her powerful and highly capable personality being compressed to the point of near implosion. Her decision to leave her husband was a protracted and painful process, but when she finally got her own apartment and started her new job, Beth was on a trajectory of growth that could no longer be held back.

But before she made it, Beth first had to hobble through her own egostomp dance. Her ego waltzed her through emotional ups and downs that left her weak-kneed. Much of the time she was excited and confident, enjoying life like never before. At other times, she was so flattened by guilt and loneliness she could barely leave her bedroom. Beth was a faithful reporter from these lands of elation and despair, and she described to me how her ego repeatedly tried to crush her.

After crying all the way home from work one Friday, Beth could only describe her state as "miserable." She could not control her mood swings all weekend, nor could she concentrate on anything. Retreating to her bedroom, Beth ate her meals in bed and only wanted her dog for company. Her thoughts were full of self-accusations about her "stupid mistakes," leaving her feeling deeply unsure of herself. Beth tried distracting herself by going to a movie, but reported, "I had to make myself sit there. I didn't feel right in my own body; I was very uncomfortable with myself. My mental state was out of control.

Recognizing that this was *normal transitional turbulence* in a person undergoing profound changes, Beth and I figured out what she needed to do to regain her balance. She had already made the decision on her own to go back on the

antidepressants she had previously discontinued. Knowing
the power of the ego very well, I supported her use of medica-
tion as needed. She also told me some of the things she had
already tried on her own to get through this difficult time.
Here's what she did:

- **called a prayerline and asked God to take care of these
  feelings,**

- **called her sister for sympathy and asked her to come for
  a visit,**

- **decided to take up guitar lessons so she would have something to do on lonely weekends,**

- **increased her attendance at a self-defense class she was
  taking so she would feel stronger and less like a pushover.**

After an initial period of self-doubt in which she worried about whether
she was wanting too much from life, Beth broke through a barrier of self-lim-
itation and entered "a real time of celebration." She took on a new position as
a hostess at a convention center, handling both crises and demanding people
with ease. Smiling with pleasure over how well she was doing, Beth went on
to tell me:

> I can honestly say I'm happier than I've ever been in my life.
> I was walking from my car to my office and I was aware of
> how complete I feel. I've never felt that way before. People say
> to me, "God, you're so different; you look and act so different.
> You're so calm!" I laugh with all my heart now. I haven't done
> that since I was a teenager. My attitude is so different; I rarely
> have negative thoughts. It feels good to be aware I'm making
> choices in my life. I think I've come a long way. It's like I had
> someone else's stifling cloak thrown over me and now I've

thrown it off. I don 't feel fear anymore. I'm not afraid to be alive anymore. I don't feel bitterness about love and relationships, I just feel smarter. I know what I want.

For a person like Beth who had lived so long in guilty subservience to others, she found she could not avoid a waltz with the ego when she finally "left home." Beth initially thought the only battle was with her domineering husband, but as she grew toward understanding herself and her purpose, she learned that the bigger battle was really with her own self-destructive ego.

—⤸

The Ego Can Use Success to Bring You Down

Interestingly, the ego isn't just about making you *fail* necessarily. It can accomplish self-defeat through success as well. If being a big financial success allows you no time to follow your real dreams, the ego will gladly encourage "success" instead of failure.

The ego can also use your otherwise positive dreams against you by inflating them too much and making you greedy. For instance, it might make you unwilling to accept that beginner's salary or hesitant to pay the necessary dues to get started in a new field. In this way, instead of starting at the bottom like everyone else, your ego may say you're somehow above the rules and entitled to something better.

Either way, the ego guarantees that the fulfillment of your inner dreams is not going to get off the back burner. When your ego whispers in your ear to chase empty "success" or overnight fame, your dream's chances can be ruined just as surely as if you had given up altogether.

Pretzel Logic

The ego has its own peculiar logic which can be very persuasive when it is delivered cleverly in little bits and pieces at a time. The ego does not expose its whole agenda at once, because if it did, you would immediately identify the deceiver and know better. Instead it just whispers a little doubt in your ear or suggests doing the very thing that will lead you down the path to ultimate discouragement. Taken one piece at a time, the ego's advice appears to make perfect sense. *But only if you're not wise to it.* If you know what the ego is up to – to keep you from finding lasting happiness – and you know how it operates (negatively and destructively), you are forewarned and forearmed for the false beliefs it might try to offer you.

Not everybody has an over-developed, destructive ego, but it can be presumed to be present whenever a person feels chronic frustration about his or her life. If your ego is well-developed and likes to work overtime, there will be certain reliable signs of its negative influence, like symptoms of depression, anxiety, and nagging unfulfillment.

The philosophy of life that the ego promotes must be looked at in broad daylight where we can really see how the ego mind works. Once exposed, you will never again be so naive as to blindly trust its opinions. Now let's look at how the ego's false advice drains your energy and ensures that you'll never arrive at what you want.

The Ego's Advice for "Success"

1. Chase Your Tail

The ego encourages indecisiveness and pointless tail-chasing. This is especially encouraged at three o'clock in the morning, or any other time when there is nothing you can do about what is bothering you.

The ego wants you to worry about what you did, what you did not do, and what you are about to do. The chief characteristic of ego worry is that it produces nothing but suffering and subtracts from your ability to cope with a situation. The result is that you worry about everything without resolving anything.

2. *Use a Cannon to Kill a Fly*

The ego leads you to believe that anything worth doing must be done perfectly. This includes the silliest, most inconsequential tasks. It encourages you to wear yourself out pouring pointless effort into meaningless little things, so you will not be in danger of succeeding in the big things.

3. *Put It Off*

Exaggerating every one of your little negative reactions, the ego can make even simple tasks seem overwhelming and draining. Think of the ego as the Great Complicator, insisting that everything be done perfectly and in a big way. Looking at life this way, every act becomes such a big deal that procrastination is the only way to get some breathing room. The ego's strategy is that it's better to delay your work until it becomes a rush job that no one would expect to be perfect.

4. *Figure Out Who is to Blame*

If you listen to the ego, you will hear that everything is always somebody else's fault. "They did it" is the ego's mantra. If you're unhappy, the ego tells you, it is because someone else has not given you what you need. The last thing the ego wants you to think is that *you* have the power to give yourself what you need.

5. *Trust No One*

The ego tells you other people cannot be trusted, they are out to get you, and you better watch your back. Cynicism and suspiciousness make good sense to the ego. It wants you to place your trust in nothing other than itself.

6. *Suspicion Will Make You Secure*

Through the ego's twisted logic, you think that the more you expect trouble, the more secure you will be. It promises that if you keep looking for all the ways that things could go wrong, you will feel truly safe. Don't take anything at face value, the ego warns, life is a lot trickier than you think. The ego knows that suspiciously ferreting out the obscure motives of other people is an activity that will completely distract you from following your own intentions.

7. *Think Scarcity*

As the ego sees it, there is not enough to go around. Another person's gain is your loss. The ego convinces you that you will be less likely to achieve your success if another person "gets there first" and "uses up" the limited amount of success in this world. This envious way of thinking pits you *against* the successful people whose stories could be inspiring and encouraging you.

8. *Survival of the Fittest*

Just as the ego tells you that this is a world of scarcity, so you are encouraged to believe competition should be cutthroat. The ego further informs you that helpful collaboration with encouraging friends is for weaklings, because *real* success means doing it completely on your own.

9. *Believe You're the Best There Ever Was*

The ego secretly assures you that you could do *anything* you want. You are the greatest, you are the best, and once you get going, everybody will see how exceptional you are. Such overinflated ego fantasies guarantee you'll be reluctant to start toward your goal because you may suspect you're not *that* great or you may doubt you will be able to live up to such high expectations.

10. Anything Worth Doing Should Be Easy

The ego believes nothing in this life should be very hard or demand much sustained effort. It tells you that if a goal is hard and causes you anxiety, this is a sign you were not supposed to do it. According to the ego, a goal is legitimate only if it leads to easy living *and* success. In addition, the ego is convinced that in order to achieve success, you have to get it from someone who already has success, like your boss. The ego's message: success is something bestowed, not created.

11. Wallow in Buyer's Remorse

Even if you're thrilled at first, if you get what you *really* want, the ego will make sure you suffer regret over your decision. For example, as soon as you come out of signing the papers on your new home, you'll start wondering whether you could have found a better mortgage rate. If you buy a new car, suddenly you will begin to notice road noise and that stiff suspension you overlooked on the test drive. Buyer's remorse only starts when you cannot go back. Remember, the point is maximum regret *when you cannot do anything about it.* It would not be any fun for the ego if you could suffer and then fix it. Regret is what brings the ego its destructive satisfaction.

12. Guilt is the Highest Moral State

The ego assures you of your goodness only if you keep feeling a little guilty about nothing in particular. To further its own agenda, the ego tells you that guilt, sacrifice, and suffering are your tickets to moral superiority.

13. Too Good to be True

The ego's last resort, when you are really close to getting what you want, is to make you suspicious of the very thing you should be grabbing with both hands.

14. Psychic Pessimism

This is a phony ego super power that allows people to look into the future and *know* that their efforts toward their dreams will have a bad outcome. Simply put, the ego predicts that your worst fears will come true, so why bother trying? It is the only time when many of us are willing to admit and stand behind our psychic powers.

15. Push Yourself the Extra Inch

In an extremely subtle maneuver that can mean the difference between giving up and success, the ego suggests you push yourself a *little* further than you really want to go at the moment. It knows you will then get sick of it and give up. You can test this out. Next time you resolve to do something you really enjoy, do it a *little* harder or a *little* longer than you really want to. This will mysteriously kill your enthusiasm after a few days, and ironically you will chalk it up to your innate lack of willpower, not the undermining ego.

16. Punish Yourself

Every time you make a mistake, the ego tells you to slam yourself hard. After all, the ego says, this is not about making a simple error; this is about being inferior. The ego somehow convinces you that accepting your fundamental lack of self-worth will give you new incentive to succeed. It also tells you that strict self-discipline is needed so that you can hate yourself into success. Of course this makes no sense, but in a weak moment, you may think it does.

Watch that Voice of Reason

The ego has a million tricks up its sleeve. Full of trickster logic, it often uses the voice of reason and good intentions to persuade you to drop your enthusiasms. Let's look at how the ego did this in Jenny's life.

Jenny's Story

Jenny was a Growth Group member who discovered a new and perniciously subtle way that her ego undermined her. She had come to the Group to figure out new ways to spend her free time. Successful in her career, she nevertheless was at a loss when it came to doing things just for fun. Jenny felt that she was missing out on something important. When the group asked about her hobbies, she told us about her love of creating stained glass art. The problem was Jenny lost interest whenever she finally had time to do it.

Every time Jenny got the urge to work on a stained glass piece, she would come to the conclusion that this was not the best time to get into it. All sorts of other responsibilities would crowd into her mind, along with sensible advice about how she should wait until she had a nice long block of time to do her activity, such as a Sunday afternoon.

Jenny liked to be efficient and so she was a sitting duck for this kind of ego persuasion. She put off her artwork until Sunday when she had no interruptions, and had finished all her errands and chores. Trouble was, Jenny's inspiration often hit on weekdays after work. By the time Sunday rolled around, her urge to create art was cold. She could not understand it. Sunday was definitely the perfect time, but she no longer had any desire to create. Unfortunately but predictably, Jenny came to the conclusion that she must not be very interested and she quit pursuing her dream.

In the group, we were able to help Jenny see the ego's subtle undermining of her incentive. She realized that the rational planning of her ego had succeeded in starving the roots of her motivation. Her inspiration and excitement were not things she could turn on and off like a faucet, according to sensible scheduling.

Just as it did in Jenny's case, our ego can set up all kinds of discouraging experiences to convince us that our dreams are not really right for us. Jenny's ego told her that if her motivation couldn't wait for four or five days, it must not have been real. Nothing could be farther from the truth. *Whenever we are starting out on a new path, we are extremely vulnerable to distractions, derailment, and delay.* There is no other time that we are so susceptible to being permanently discouraged. The ego knows this and finds ways to cool our fleeting but very real desires.

The ego can give us the most sensible reasons in the world in order to undermine our heartfelt urges for self-expression. For Jenny, its interference was so subtle and apparently well-meaning she could not see it at all. She thought she was just using good planning to have the best possible opportunity to pursue her recreation. Hiding under the guise of "planning" was her ego's secret purpose of killing off those first little urges of creativity.

How to Handle the Ego

What is the most effective attitude to have toward the ego? It does not help to take its threat *too* seriously, but we do have to respect its sneakiness. The ego is a con artist, smooth-talking its way past your better judgment by appealing to superficial logic and distracting you with greed and fear. The more you listen to it, the better it sounds. The more you argue with it, the more answers it has. *Believe me, once you start listening, you are no match for it.* Remember, there are plenty of embarrassed, intelligent people out there who bought the farm when they listened a little too long to a con man. Knowing better is no protection.

Be prepared for how the ego works. It offers you plausible alternatives, and cautions you against embarrassing "mistakes." It waylays your energy, and makes you put time into meaningless things you care nothing about. It has too many ways to count to get you to give up your truest desires and dreams.

After you have gotten to know your ego, how it works, and where it likes to attack, stop listening to it. Take out a psychological restraining order on it. Hang up the phone. As soon as you can identify that it is the ego speaking, listen no further. If it cannot hold onto your attention, it has no chance of undermining you.

Unmasking the Ego

If you're having trouble catching your ego at work, try a version of what Robert Firestone calls "Voice Therapy"[13]. The following exercise is a means of getting yourself to hear just what the ego really sounds like inside your head.

Exercise

On a piece of paper, write down your biggest dream, what you would do if you could do *anything* and didn't have to worry about money or other people's opinions. Try to lay aside any criticisms or discouragement just for a few minutes, and jot down your dream. Put that piece of paper aside.

Next, on a separate piece of paper, write down what your "sensible" and "logical" mind (alias, your ego) has to say about this dream. Let the ego have free rein to say whatever it wants.

Put the two pieces of paper in a drawer for a couple of days. Then come back and read the one from the ego *out loud* in a strong speaking voice. Read it forcefully with the feeling that goes with it: sarcasm, ridicule, anger, contempt, etc. Read it *out loud* until you get a feeling for who in your life might have said those kinds of words to you or used that tone. Try to figure out who it was that first inflicted that kind of negative criticism on you. This exercise is an excellent way to understand where your ego got its start, how you came to adopt someone else's pessimistic attitudes toward your own success and happiness, and how to separate your motivation from its attempts to shut you down.

Early in your life, you were a helpless, gullible child who thought parents or other grown-up authority figures were gods who knew everything – gods whose rules, restrictions and judgments were the final word. You had to identify with someone and so you took what you were given, even if it was this poisonous and destructive ego voice. *But you are not little and gullible anymore.* You no longer have to be robbed of your happiness and potential because of ideas you absorbed when you were very young.

The first steps are to hear the ego's voice, identify it, and return it to the sender by *naming the people who gave it to you.* Thus you begin the process of catching the ego in the act and stopping it by exposing its roots. When you can put a little distance and perspective between yourself and your ego, its power dwindles.

Decide to Take a Stand

Don't roll over and play dead because some disapproving opinion, some old message, some unthinking thing someone once said, happens to play on inside your head like the voice recorder from hell. If an inner voice tells you that you'll never make it, that you're building castles in the air, and you're a failure, call it the voice of fear and figure out the next step you can take toward your goals no matter what. Do whatever you have to do – self-talk, justifying your reasons, calling a friend, or writing yourself a go-get-'em letter – but don't let the ego have the last word.

Track it down. Every time you expose its pointless destructiveness, you get stronger. Each time you see it for what it is – a spoilsport who lives to dismantle your happiness – the ego will seem less all knowing and less powerful. It will begin to show its real face, which is cowardly and snide. Never really accomplishing anything on its own, the ego just tears down what others build. It hates motivation because it is so inadequate itself. It scares and humiliates us because it has nothing else to offer. It is a purely negative force, adding nothing to anyone's life but despair. It thinks it is playing it safe by being the voice of reason, but it is essentially sadistic and frightened. The ego takes its pleasure not in getting what it wants, but in depriving others of what they would have.

Don't be a puppet on a string to this terrible internalization of old cruelties. Whenever it says you will never amount to anything, don't accept that advice as if the ego knows what it's talking about. It doesn't have good ideas; it just uses whatever it thinks will work to make you give up. If you start working toward what you want, then the ego loses its job, doesn't it?

Don't passively accept what the ego tells you. Whatever the ego's voice says to you, take it with a grain of salt. Don't check your common sense at the door just because the ego has spoken again. If the ego makes you feel like a criminal for having your own desires, ask yourself the question: *is this how important people from my past made me feel?* Then ask yourself one more question: *is this how I want to continue feeling?*

The best way to take away the ego's power is to *decide* to take a stand against some of these scared and destructive attitudes inherited from other people. If you discover that they exemplified resignation and unhappiness instead of getting what they really wanted, it will make it easier for you to be different from them. You can be compassionate and polite toward your real family members, but be downright defiant toward that inner ego voice. It does not really exist, except in your imagination, so you're not going to hurt anybody's feelings. The ego's voice from the past is only a memory. A memory of when you were small and scared and no one was there to help you.

The Best Defense is a Good Pencil

When the ego first goes on the attack, filling us with fear and self-recriminations, we're usually in no position to rebuff it. As a matter of fact, we often fall so deeply under its spell that all the things we hate and fear begin to look pretty good again. We may not, for the life of us, be able to remember why we wanted to start this whole growth thing anyway.

To counteract this you need to have some self-supportive actions *written down* and readily available, so that you can retrieve that piece of paper at a moment's notice. A tangible list of ideas gives us other options for feeling better in these weak moments, rather than giving in to the temptation of handing back to the ego every bit of ground we had gained.

Jada's Story

After one of our sessions, Jada wrote down a list of things she planned to do next time she had a "bad moment" (otherwise known as an ego attack):

- **Stop myself from spiraling downward – reject ego thoughts.**

- **Call a friend.**

- **Take a bath and listen to music.**

- **Take a walk with the dog.**

- **Remember my successes and what I have accomplished.**

- **Go to the store.**

- **Do something nice for myself.**

Jada wrote these down on an index card and kept them handy in a kitchen drawer. It was pretty clear to both of us that she was probably going to be hearing from the ego again and we wanted her to be ready for it. She pulled out her list whenever she needed to. Jada learned to manhandle the ego over the rough spots, and a couple of months later she could say:

I'm growing in leaps and bounds; I know that. When I ana-
lyze it – all things considered – I've done remarkably well.
When I think of how much courage it took to move out of
my house – no job, no place to live except at a friends' house,
having only my car and my own wits – look how far I've
come.

It is easy to hear that this is *not* the ego talking, isn't it? It
was Jada's real self again – speaking out, supporting, and
strengthening her for whatever she wanted to take on in the
future.

Calm the Ego and Find Your Allies

Over time you will be able to lessen the ego's impact even further if you see
it as a frightened bully, overpowering others in order to hide its own fear. Let
your adult self stand up to the ego, telling it there's no longer a need for so
much fear and cynicism[14]. By communicating firmly with this part of yourself, you can help it back off and begin to accept that you can handle things
now as an adult. Remind the ego how old you are now and present your adult
credentials. Ask it to let the adult part of you take the wheel for a while. Tell
it you won't do anything rash to endanger yourself. Let it know you now have
friends and helpers that weren't there before.

The ego has good reason to distrust other people and make you suspicious
of them: it fears they will trick you and let you down. The ego is convinced
it's the only one who can protect you from fatal mistakes. (Of course to the
hypervigilant ego, everything looks like a fatal mistake.) The ego is especially
wary of anyone who makes you feel at ease, good about yourself, and hopeful
about your future. It trusts none of this because it's stuck in the past, originat-
ing in a stagnant family system that punished you for becoming your own
person. Yet to the ego, going outside the family for support seems foolish
beyond belief as well.

Terrified of making childhood authorities jealous, the ego tries to undermine your positive ties to other people. It points out other people's failings,

how they let you down, and why they might be using you. It tells you whatever works to make you suspicious, competitive, or envious of them. It wants to be the only one you listen to. But you need better advisors in the form of real people who have your best interests at heart and can help you see through the ego's fear campaign. Real allies will see possibilities and options that your ego is blind to. Other people can show you new ways of doing things and can point out things you never considered.

Since the ego's advice seems very real and very much a part of your internal landscape, it may be extremely hard to see what it's doing. Psychotherapy, support groups, a trusted friend, a partner who understands – all these can be allies to help you sidestep the negative effects of the ego's fears. Educate your allies about the demoralizing effects your ego has on you, so they also know its agenda and can give you their firm protection against it. When you start to lose ground, they can remind you about the ego's regressive motives and help you resist its takeover.

Positive ties with other people are going to be necessary for your success, because nobody does anything completely on their own. As we'll see in a later chapter, building trusting and supportive relationships are essential for making dreams come true.

CHAPTER 4

MOTIVATION VS. HELPLESSNESS AND HOPELESSNESS

Hopelessness does not have to incapacitate us to be effective; it just has to convince us to settle for less than we want.

One day I received a call from an Employee Assistance counselor in a large company who wanted to refer a woman who was a supervisor to the Growth Group. I met the client later that week and instantly felt an affinity with her. Linda was college-educated, tall and athletic-looking, with rich wavy red hair that kept sneaking out in tendrils around her face. Her freckled complexion made her look younger than her thirty-four years. She dressed in long dark-colored skirts and sweaters that had a muted artistic flair. It was hard to imagine Linda in the bureaucratic world I knew she inhabited in her supervisor job. When she sat down in my office, she looked hesitant and unhappy and yet there was eagerness and clarity in the way she described her problems. Linda recounted in a quiet, unsure voice how she had felt torn all her life by the conflicts that arose between what she wanted to do and her family's attempts to stifle her.

Linda had learned from an early age that she was expected to divert her motivation from her own interests into the conventional activities sanctioned by her socially conscious parents. She summed up her parents' feelings toward her by saying, "They want me to be a certain person and when I'm not, they can't stand it. They make it clear to me that I should want to do these "right" things to prove I'm normal and good."

From childhood, Linda's energies had been siphoned off to meet her parents' needs. Preoccupied with what other people would think, Linda's parents could not get past their own fears of social rejection to understand who their daughter really was. When Linda's motivation began to take her down unexpected paths of nonconformity, with interests in art and "unfeminine" competitive sports, her parents became alarmed and warned her against being so "different." On the rare occasions when Linda tried to stand up for herself, her mother became stridently critical and punitive. Linda's mother misread her daughter's self-defense as disrespect.

My work with Linda clearly had to help her focus on rediscovering the certainty of motivation she had felt as a child, before her parents' fears made her doubt herself.

Childhood Motivation

We all start out life full of motive. As little children, we are propelled around by motivation like inflated balloons released to jet around the room obeying the laws of physics. We are full of wants and desires, and the whole world is just begging us to come and get it. We *are* our motives. Thinking comes later. Concepts of good and bad come later. Motivation is there from the beginning. When our enthusiasm pushes us on to the next moment because it offers something better tasting, more fun, or more exciting, we heed its call. We zip along; the next challenge is calling. We move; we act. Unfortunately for some, as Linda described, we then get punished.

For those whose spirit is squashed, the surprise of punishment just when we are being most ourselves is an incredible shock to our sense of security about ourselves. As children, we felt divinely inspired to be ourselves and act on our impulses. Suddenly another force opposed our motivation – our parent's reaction. It dawned on us with sickening suddenness that we must have done something very wrong to upset this big, powerful person with whom we lived. Our parents' displeasure was obvious and our motivation suddenly became associated with bad feelings. If we were even less fortunate, our desires might have become associated with the pain of physical or emotional punishment. Consider this: our parents' disapproval and punishment showed how desperately afraid our parents were that our motivation might lead to unacceptable behaviors that could embarrass them. If you have ever felt this kind of conflict, then you know what an uncomfortable bind our truest childhood motivations sometimes can put us in. We can end up being caught between family honor and personal destiny.

Motivation Makes Us Different

Through punishment, we learned as children that there was something about us that caused big problems with people we loved very much. It was our motivation that made us different from them. Our childish motivation made us do things our parents objected to, like playing in the toilet. They scolded us and their disapproval made us feel terribly alone, left with nothing but our shriveled motivation. Motivation quickly loses its appeal if we are made to feel ostracized and humiliated because of our choices.

As a result, our motivations in adulthood may be experienced with suspicion if we think they might lead to the same kind of bad feeling and loneliness we felt as children. Fearful of being rejected and abandoned, we learn to turn against ourselves instead. We may still eye what we want, but we may feel conflicted about those impulses and eventually we may even stop being conscious of or paying attention to them.

Your Motivation Made Life Harder for Your Parents

Some children grow up learning that it is better not to follow their motivations and dreams because a highly motivated child makes life a great deal harder for a parent. As long as children have their own motivation and ideas about how they want to do things, the parents are going to be challenged. As self-centered parents have discovered, stopping a child's motivation early in life works extremely well for making the parents' lives easier.

Easier, that is, until the onset of puberty, when kids begin to cope with new hormonal surges that give a huge boost to their motivations. These formerly suppressed kids begin to get in touch with their desires and impulses again. It is very common for therapists to hear from parents how good and obedient their children were until adolescence. The sleeping monster of suppressed motivation then reawakens.

Too Nice, Too Little Motivation

Motivation requires some self-absorption – no question about it – but it may have become more important for us to be liked and approved of than to act on our own drives. We can become too focused on what other people think of us.

We may work so hard at being a nice guy or a good girl that we blunt our own motivational drive. It is sometimes hard to be really nice and really motivated at the same time. When you're truly motivated, you need intense self-focus and a kind of constructive self-centeredness. This means that sometimes you may not have a lot left over for extra social niceties and putting other people first. When you are motivated and act upon it, you may collide with other people's wishes. This is an unavoidable hazard when you have energetic motives flying around. However, such activity is not going to hurt the feelings of anyone who really has your best interests at heart. They will be willing to work with you because they will value your growth. A person truly on your side can tolerate a little neglect for a big project and is happy about your successes. However, the person who expects you to sacrifice your true nature for him or her will be extremely sensitive to how "nicely" you are treating them. Their *feelings* will become the focus more than what you are trying to *accomplish*.

Swallowing Other People's Attitudes

When we were very young, our motivation, our irresistible force, was stopped frequently by the immovable object of our parents' prohibition. At two years old, it was a clear-cut fight between us and them. The enemy, as far as our true self was concerned, was on the outside. We had no question that our motivation was sacred and something to fight for. It was us against them, with the lines drawn clearly. However, as we got older, we were persuaded to take in ideas and opinions about ourselves that did not originate within us, simply because we wanted so badly to belong to a group. We began the lifelong process of swallowing other people's attitudes.

On the positive side, this is how we developed a conscience and learned to be concerned about right and wrong. Yet there was much we swallowed that was not useful and was just plain indigestible. Nevertheless, we took it all in anyway. It may not even have been consciously chosen. We just started picking up the characteristics of our family and later of group members whose dominance and power impressed us. We respected how they stayed in charge of us and we automatically tried to make that authority a part of ourselves. The fact that this automatic taking-in of parental qualities really happens is known to any parents who ever caught themselves doing and saying the very things for which they had once resented their own parents.

As a child, we may not have been allowed to *behave* like that dominant family member, but we still may have taken in that person's rigid *attitudes* and made them a part of our mental world. The very things we most disliked being told as a child often become the very things we unconsciously start to believe about ourselves. We can be taken over by these swallowed attitudes, as if they were a kind of draining life form. These thought parasites can live inside us for years, even if they originally had nothing to do with who we were or who we wanted to be. We may not even realize we are supporting these destructive parasitic thoughts because we have become so accustomed to them.

The way we know these negative attitudes exist is by their destructive effects on our lives and our unfulfillment in the real world. Just like a virus, we know it is there not because we can see it, but because of our immune system's reaction to it. The same thing occurs psychologically when a person has swallowed some parental attributes in childhood that have made him or her emotionally sick. The person may feel depressed, anxious, hear voices or drink too much as an inner war rages. As a therapist, I look at a conflicted person's symptoms and wonder what kind of alien ideas they must have taken in when they were children to create such tremendous inner conflict. The psychological immune system activates against foreign bodies just as predictably as its physical counterpart.

Perhaps you too may have gulped down some beliefs in childhood that are now interfering with your adult development. Perhaps you may be discouraging yourself because of *somebody else's* old beliefs, to the point where you mistrust your own motivations. You may not have realized the alien, depleting nature of these hand-me-down beliefs. You have held them so long, they breathe right along with you.

Linda's Story Continues

By the time Linda had come to my office, she had already begun to realize these mental parasites were there, distorting her self-image until she could not see herself clearly. "I don't know who I am," she said honestly, "I've become who my family wanted me to be, and now I'm not sure how to go about finding and being the real me."

By speaking these painful words, Linda came closer than she had ever been to her true self. Of course, this was an extremely uncomfortable transition time; she now could tell what was phony, but she was not sure yet what was real. Her willingness to rediscover and commit to her true interests became the next step.

How Linda Learned Self-Doubt

When Linda was growing up, she was passionately motivated to spend all her time on things that truly interested her. When she took up tennis in high school, she practiced every day to become good enough to be on the school team. When oil painting captivated her, she spent every spare moment drawing and laying on thick bright colors with her brushes. As a teenager, Linda was not scattered or irresponsible in these pursuits; she continued to do well in school, dated, and had a good social life.

However, Linda's intense creative motivations made her mother uncomfortable. Her mother began to tell Linda that she was not leading a balanced life. For example, as Linda was going out the door to tennis practice in the evenings, her mother asked, "Don't you think you're spending too much time on that?" Disapproving questions such as this worried Linda's sensitive nature and began to undermine her eager motivation. Linda vividly remembered the day when she began to give up. As she poignantly expressed, "I started slipping and stopped practicing to avoid confrontation with her." Instead of persisting on her own path, Linda slowly withdrew and soon allowed herself to become emotionally dependent on a domineering boyfriend whose constant criticisms precipitated a serious depression in her.

By the time this bright and talented young woman was in college, she was totally confused about who she was meant to be. She dropped and added majors in fits of anxious indecision. When Linda's lack of educational commitment began to seem peculiar to her parents, they grilled her about what she was going to do with her life. If she took the bait and tentatively shared her latest career choice, her mother pointedly asked, "Are you *sure?*" If Linda momentarily forgot herself and expressed enthusiasm about a new direction she had found, her mother asked dubiously, "Do you *really* enjoy it?"

Absorption in our own motivation, especially if it's in the realm of creativity, can make our loved ones nervous, because the very act of our motivation always threatens to move us out of the familiar world we share with our family.

It was not surprising that Linda learned to have self-doubt and to fear that there was something pathologically flighty about herself every time she felt a new surge of motivation. Instead of naturally following her evolving interests, she began to hate herself for changing her mind so often. However, as we looked back on her development, Linda began to realize at a deep emotional level how she unwittingly had taken in her *mother's* doubt and ambivalence. Linda began to see that the helplessness and indecision she chronically felt were not totally her own. It became clearer to her that these doubts were the reflections of her mother's uneasiness over seeing her daughter no longer need her in the same way. Her mother's concerned questions effectively kept Linda in a dependent child role.

As I have seen with my clients, the stifling attitudes exhibited by Linda's mother are unfortunately all too common. While Linda's mother actively discouraged her activities, many parents discourage their children through a simple lack of interest or encouragement. Think back to your own parents and family when you were growing up. Did your parents hold expectations for you, encouraging you to do your best? Quite a number of my therapy clients tell me that their parents never expected them to go to college, never asked them what they wanted to be, and never urged them toward any kind of achievement. One of my clients exemplified this lack of parental involvement.

Sophie's Story

One day in my office, Sophia, an intelligent but depressed young woman, was berating herself for being "lazy." She told me how, as a young gymnast, she had lacked the competitive drive and ambition of her adolescent peers. She cited those teen years in gymnastics as proof of how little motivation she had ever had in her life. But there was a stunned look on her face when I asked her how many times her parents had attended her practices and meets. I wanted to know how enthusiastic and involved her parents had been about her gymnastic success. You could see from the sad look that followed that there had been a void there. For Sophia, unlike many of her more ambitious peers, there were no cheering parents in the stands, no dad coaching her through the anxieties of higher competition. Her parents paid for lessons, dropped her off at the gym, and that was it. They did not deprive her of the opportunity to participate in gymnastics, but they *did* deprive her of the sense of accomplishment, pride, and self-worth she would have enjoyed had her parents taken any interest in her achievements.

Parents who encourage their child to achieve and succeed help ensure the child's future as a functional, happy adult. However, if parents do not participate in their children's lives or make discouraging comments to their children, particularly when the children are in the crucial stage of beginning to leave home, parents can have a devastating effect. There are key moments in our development when, if our families express doubt and ambivalence about letting us grow up, these comments can truly interfere with the rest of our lives. The more we doubt ourselves in childhood and beyond, the more difficult it can be to become successful adults.

Learning Helplessness and Hopelessness

When our motivation and forward movement are stopped harshly and consistently enough in childhood, we begin to learn hopelessness and helplessness. If the message from motivation is *Go on!* the message from hopelessness and helplessness is *No, I can't!* As soon as there is enough self-doubt driven between us and our motivation, we start to those track of our desires.

Helplessness and hopelessness are the opposite of motivation. They are fear feelings, squirmy pits in the stomach. These demoralized emotions are based on the belief that nothing good is coming, there is no future for us, and bad things are probably going to happen. Helplessness and hopelessness are paralytic feelings of weakness, as opposed to the strength that flows through us when we are motivated. These feelings make us stop before we even get started. They can lead to depression, but often they serve their purpose at a more subtle level. In fact, sometimes helplessness and hopelessness can hardly be discerned behind the mask of a smoothly functioning life. Hopelessness does not have to incapacitate us to be effective; it just has to convince us to settle for less than we want.

Helplessness and hopelessness are psychological *defenses,* not just symptoms. Psychological defenses are those feelings and behaviors from the past that have been so effective in soothing bad feelings that we make them a part of our daily coping style. Helplessness and hopelessness are not just *reactions* to painful past events; they also can *prevent* the sparking of any motivation we think might bring pain to us. The more helpless and hopeless you let yourself feel, the less motivated you become.

The good news is that motivation is real while hopelessness and helplessness are fake. Motivation is intrinsic and instinctual to the human being. As little children, we came abundantly, extravagantly endowed with motivation. But helplessness and hopelessness have to be learned – we have to be *trained* to give up and feel weak because there is such a strong survival force resisting these defeatist mental states[15]. Even at the broad species level, evolution demands plenty of motivation. Nature has no use for hopelessness and once you understand where your hopelessness is coming from, I hope you will not have any use for it either.

The morbid twins of helplessness and hopelessness do not help you live a fulfilled life. They may help you *survive* under some conditions, but they quickly outlive their usefulness if the original trauma situation is no longer there. Helplessness and hopelessness can only be useful when circumstances are such that taking further action would lead only to worse suffering, such as when a person is captive in a dire situation. Of course, sometimes emotional struggling can be so hard on the psyche that it becomes a mercy to give up and stop expecting anything.

However, underneath hopelessness, motivation is still there, even if it has to be repressed. It may have gone dormant to save its life, but it is still there in the same way that your heartbeat is. Your job is to convince your motivation that it is safe to come out again. You can do that when you realize once and for all that the punishment you have been fearing was in your past, not lurking in your future.

Our Dreams May Remind Our Parents of What They Lost

You can be sure that there were childhood moments when your motivation came up against the very thing in your parents which was the "absolutely cannot be" of the parents' existence, the parts of themselves they thought they had to give up in order to be accepted in *their* families. This is what Linda was bumping up against in her mother's negativity. When Linda showed her passion about her pursuits, her mother was subconsciously reminded of all that she had given up to get married and become a wife and mother. Before her marriage to a man whose family was extraordinarily devoted to keeping up appearances, Linda's mother was a budding concert pianist who used to practice hours at a time, inhabiting a world of her own. Because Linda's father was annoyed by her mother's time spent at the piano, her mother gave up her potential career and tried hard to fit into her new husband's family. Tragically, instead of trying to produce perfect music, all she had left was to try to produce perfect children – children who would please her husband's socially conscious family. Therefore when Linda started expressing her joyful, self-absorbed motivation in adolescence, her mother's envy flared up and she reflexively reacted to shut down her daughter's spirit.

If there were unfinished dreams that our parents were never able to live out, they are often suppressed and become secrets kept within the family. If as a child you inadvertently bumped into this tender old wound in your parent's psyche, you intuitively sensed how badly they'd been hurt. Somewhere in your mind, you may have feared what it might do to your parent at a deep level if you followed your truest dreams. You might have worried that by becoming your real self, you might bring suffering to the people you loved.

Fearing Parents' Retaliations

Of course, you also may have feared actual retaliation from authority figures if you started growing and succeeding too much. This is particularly true for people whose parents were critical, easily offended, and often angry. Such fears of retaliation can give you a familiar jolt of anxiety when you start feeling too creative. Taking steps toward your true destiny can sometimes irrationally make you feel like something bad is going to happen. These anxieties about how the world might react to our freedom and success are nearly always rooted in painful experiences in the past, as Linda had come to realize.

All her life, Linda's love of art and desire for physical accomplishment had been torn down by parents who could not find it in themselves to support her joy. Every time she had tried to emerge into the next step of her development, there was interference. She had learned hopelessness in many ways over many years, but the simple and basic message was: become your real self and you risk an attack.

Two Steps Forward, One Step Back

As Linda began to understand what had been holding her back, she found herself becoming increasingly fascinated by a renewed interest in painting. First, she painted in her garage, using small craft materials and telling herself that she did not want to clutter up her home with her "art stuff." When the weather got colder, I began to hear about the large canvases that were taking over her dining room, because there was so much room in there and she liked a warm place to work. Just as importantly, Linda spontaneously began to reconnect with memories of her childhood fascinations: insects, leaf collecting, a love of animals, and a sensitivity to color that was visceral. She began to remember who she was meant to be: an artist and an inquisitive lover of learning.

As Linda began again to pick up her abandoned interests, she felt surges of energy and motivation that were very strong and rewarding. However, she also experienced many periods of lost confidence, in which she slipped back into critical feelings about herself and felt a sense of fatigued hopelessness. Usually these episodes could be traced back to some demoralizing contact with her parents or an insensitive friend, and once Linda began to realize the specific reason why she had started losing hope, her motivation quickly returned.

When Linda was in a depressive backslide, however, it felt very real to her. Even after a period of personal growth and sustained success in knowing her true self, she was still capable of temporarily slipping into the following frame of mind she described in one of our sessions:

> I don't feel like I have an anchor anymore. What can I do today not to fall in this big hole of despair? There's nothing to look forward to. I feel like I have no goals. I'm floating, out of

focus. I just don't know my mind anymore, I feel like letting go and forgetting it. I just don't care.

At that moment Linda felt like this hopelessness was going to go on forever. She genuinely could not imagine she would ever feel happy again. I sympathized but reminded her that these negative feelings only meant that she was in a slump, triggered by something that reminded her of the past, and that it was *not* a statement about her future.

We should always be suspicious of our feelings of depression and hopelessness! Even though they feel emotionally convincing, they cannot predict we are going to be miserable for the rest of our lives. They can only remind us of how bad our lives were in the past. When I point this out to people, they are always doubtful because they don't remember feeling that badly as children. I tell them they could not afford to be consciously aware in childhood of these awful, intense feelings, or else they might not have had the energy to grow up.

As children, we push these painful feelings down into our subconscious minds, but they resurface in adulthood when our inner self senses that we have grown up enough to handle them. When it is finally safe enough to clean out the painful old feelings, we can restart our growth process. A number of my clients have been perplexed when they feel depressed or have flashbacks of childhood mistreatment just when things in their life seem to be getting better. The reason these feelings crop up is because when one is finally in a safe harbor – whether it's a relationship, situation, or state of mind – one can compassionately accommodate and work through those bad memories.

When Linda experienced depressive episodes, she lost perspective and the resurgence of old feelings made her think that reality was hopeless. My job was to remind her that the feelings were nothing more than bad memories – reenactments of the despair she had suffered in childhood every time her parents controlled and misdirected her.

Linda's Solutions

Later Linda was able to visit with her parents without getting triggered into hopelessness and helplessness. She learned to be ready for them, anticipating their regressive effect and not blaming herself when she felt discouraged. She also wore her "freedom fetishes" when she went home, unobtrusive little articles of jewelry and clothing that had special symbolic meaning to her about reclaiming her artistic self. Her parents no longer had the power to permanently separate Linda's true being from herself.

As Linda paid closer attention to her level of interest and energy in any given moment, she realized that her real motivation had flowed toward creating art and pursuing *many* forms of learning. Now it made sense to her why she had changed her major so many times: one field could never satisfy her broad appetite for knowledge and new experiences. She learned that for her, mastery of a skill or topic was *meant* to stir up the urge to move on to the next challenge. Linda was never going to be happy doing routine things every day.

As she began to accept this about herself, Linda's artwork proliferated and flourished in a multitude of different forms. One day she told me that all of her pieces had sold at the boutique where she had placed them on consignment. Linda's mind swarmed with new ideas and images, and she dedicated hours on the weekends to turning them into her very original art. Linda held onto her office supervisor job, because she still wanted the salary and security, however she began to bring her creativity into even that setting. One day Linda created a training session for her staff in which they came up with ideas for art to make their workplace a more stimulating place. Her staff loved it. Linda laughed in her session with me about how she would probably get fired now by the higher-ups. Of course, she was not fired and you can imagine how much her staff appreciated that oasis in the middle of their paperwork desert.

Linda gained victory when she came down squarely on the side of her own interests and insisted upon integrating them into her life rather than disowning them. She found that even as a supervisor in a bureaucracy, she could still operate out of her primary identity as a creative person.

Helplessness and hopelessness are psychological defenses against fears of separation from our first families. They make us give up before we do the things that might stir up our anxieties about psychologically leaving home. Let me stress here again that these are the fears and anxieties of *childhood*. They are the dinosaurs of the psyche and ought to be extinct by adulthood. Because we may not have challenged these fears, however, they retain their impact and make us avoid the very things that could make us happy as grown-ups.

—❧

Reconnecting With Your Motivation

Going where your motivation leads you will be one of the most important achievements of your whole life. Feeling your motivation return means that your life is becoming your own again; you no longer live in such a way that you avoid success and happiness for fear of disappointing or upsetting others. When your subconscious goal is primarily to make your loved ones feel secure, you might reassure them with your failures or simply by limiting your success to an area that brings you no real joy. Recovering your sense of motivation means that you are willing to love your life again.

Now we are going to look at how to reconnect with your motivation and how to feel good about following its call. In order to regain your motivation, it helps to understand where motivation comes from and how to cultivate the best frames of mind for it to surface.

Working with clients to help them regain a sense of motivation in their lives, I have found the following suggestions and insights to be helpful:

1. **Feed your fascination.**

2. **Don't be afraid of being selfish.**

3. **Helplessness may just be inexperience.**

4. **Expect setbacks.**

5. **Use persistence and endurance as necessary.**

Now let's look at how you can use these ideas as guideposts for sustaining your motivation.

1. Feed Your Fascination
Notice what fascinates you and follow up on them, a little bit at a time, to whatever degree you are comfortable. Take a small action on behalf of your fascination, however miniscule.

The antidote to feelings of helplessness and hopelessness is healthy fascination. Even if you feel you have lost touch with what your original motivations were all about, your capacity for fascination always remains. Fascination holds an answer for you, even if you are not sure what it is. Fascination is more complex and mysteriously compelling than mere curiosity, for it is an instant recognition of the soul's desire.

Fascination is different from unhealthy obsession, in which a person tries to fill an empty life with something or someone they want to control. Obsession shrinks your life to objects of possession; fascination expands your life with broadening, deepening interests.

Wherever there is fascination, there is motivation. They go hand in hand, always traveling together. Fascination fuels the quest to recover disowned parts of the self, including your deepest motivations. The object of your fascination is a piece of your real self, lost but loved and intriguing in its insistent nature. It is a projection of what you need to complete your purpose. This object has a glow about it, and that glow beckons you.

If you cannot remember the last time you were fascinated by anything, maybe you are looking for something too dramatic. Fascination can have a mild, everyday face as well. An easy place to start is to notice what sections of the news you automatically turn to, which articles you read, and which ideas get you thinking. The same idea goes for noticing which topics you choose in books or which type of videos you like. What kind of movie attracts your interest? Consider the themes of the television shows you never want to miss and what you love about them. Think about the stores you keep returning to and what they sell. Ask yourself when you have free time and enough money, what you look forward to doing?

Look back at your childhood as well. Do you recall moments growing up when you were fascinated for long periods of time by something? Give some thought to what it was that absorbed your attention. These half-hidden clues probably hold pieces of who you were meant to be.

2. *Don't be Afraid of Being Selfish*
You are not being selfish when you follow your fascinations and motivation. Following your motivations can also serve the needs of other people.

Have you ever worried that your motivation and the dreams it holds are just too selfish to entertain seriously? This is what many frustrated people believe. Every time they raise a little hope that they can go for what they really want, the fear of selfishness scares them back into inactivity. If there is anything that can singlehandedly promote depression and defeatism, it is the fear of selfishness. Many times we reject what our motivation seems to be pushing us toward, because it may appear selfish and totally egocentric. By doing something we deeply enjoy, we have a hard time believing we actually could be meeting the needs of others as well. We do not trust that we have a responsibility to follow our motivations so that others will have the freedom to follow theirs. A different way of thinking about social responsibility is that what brings pleasure and fulfillment to us could also bring pleasure and fulfillment to others. For example, consider how much Linda's staff would have missed that day if she had not taken the risk to act on her inspiration.

Motivation feels like a magnetic pull being exerted upon us. It is coming from within, but there is also a sense that there is something on the outside drawing us forward. Consider this thought: maybe the magnetic pull that stirs up your desire and ambition is not coming solely from yourself. Perhaps it is partly a reverberation coming from other people around you. Maybe *their* needs and desires are subliminally helping to spark *your* needs and desires.

There is no proof that such a magnetic pull or the connection between one person's needs and another person's inspiration exists, but it has not been disproven either. If nothing else it is a harmless fiction, but one that gives a sense of broader purpose and social responsibility to our motivation. It may help you to consider this theory, because it helps you respect your search for personal fulfillment as part of a larger picture. My own belief is that our inspirations and motivations are never lonely, selfish acts, but are responses to our deepest connections with the rest of humanity.

3. Helplessness May Just Be Inexperience
Inexperience can give us an unrealistically hopeless view of the future. Learn to tolerate the helplessness of inexperience as a necessary step on your way to growth.

Taking a walk one morning, I heard the sound of a bird chirping insistently for food. I slowed down and looked around, and there in a neighbor's yard were two full-grown robins. The chirping was coming from the slightly larger robin, which still had the light orange breast color of a juvenile bird. This adolescent bird was hopping after the mother bird, chirping his head off, while the mother looked and listened for insects. He was fixated on getting something from *her* and yet the food supply was obviously there for him just as it was for her. The young bird actually had good motivation, but he was just going after his food in the way he had come to expect it. He simply thought his nourishment had to come through his mother or it was not food.

We have the same expectations. It is not just our old learning that scares us and keeps us back; it also can be our real lack of experience in a new area. Like the teenaged robin, we may not have looked for our own food in this new place before. Just because we can see that the neighborhood is full of other robins making their way each day, it does not prove to us that *we* can do it. Naturally we are unsure, and we may keep chirping after our version of the mother robin, because we are afraid to put our ability to fend for ourselves to the test. Of course, our own personal mother robin in adult life might masquerade as our spouse, boss, parent, or even a job we've outgrown.

You never know up front how well you can make it on your own. Nevertheless, you are placed in the world and expected to pull your living out of it the way the robin pulls the worm from the earth. When you finally perceive that this is the way life is, believe me, you will look for food or fulfillment in such a way that you have a great chance of finding it. However, if you have never done it before, you may not have the confidence that you can. This is the lag-time of inexperience calling for *sustained motivation in the absence of real faith.* Brand new robins have to do it every spring.

Your efforts at fulfilling your motivation may not bring you the results you want right away. You may feel like the effort is not working, because you have never acted on your dreams before. You may feel hopeless and lost not because of past emotional injuries, but because you're simply unfamiliar with this new way of living. This kind of helplessness and hopelessness is nothing more than the anxiety of inexperience. After all, you have not had much practice with living your dreams yet. You have no proof they can succeed. So it is normal to feel scared and uncertain. It's only natural that your intense but untried motivation should start to wilt when you get in touch with how inexperienced you feel attempting these new actions.

Nobody likes feeling inexperienced and many people withdraw when they realize they don't know what they are doing. But that embarrassing moment of helplessness is telling you it's time to tolerate your ignorance. The only cure for inexperience is to get the experience. *Inexperience is never a sign that you should quit.* Boredom and complete lack of interest are the signs that you should quit. You are on your way somewhere important and the helplessness of inexperience is just something to be gotten past.

4. Expect Setbacks
If your goal is based on who you really are, the ups and downs along the way are harmless. Chalk up your setbacks as signs of growth.

Consider the stock market graph. Successful financial companies intent on selling their stocks as investments often show those familiar jagged, upwardly mobile graphs in their advertisements. The graph is a visual demonstration that in spite of short-term losses and setbacks, over the long haul the stock market will give the investor an upward trend on his investment. It is *normal* for the stock market to have its ups and downs, its wins and losses.

That's the way your life is too. There is a pattern, an overall trend to what you are doing and planning. However, on any given day, it may all go to pot. You may lose sight of your purpose and feel lost and helpless due to random occurrences. You may not see the forest for the trees. Nevertheless, if you can keep on riding the ups and downs and not taking each dip too seriously, the pattern will begin to emerge and take shape. You just have to trust a little that there is a growth pattern unfolding within you, like that little wisp of destiny described by Hillman's acorn theory[16]. There is a part of you that is pushing you to make your dream come true. That part has its own natural course if you will let it unfold without panicking.

Think about an airliner pilot. He flies his aircraft from one city to another with minimal anxiety because of his attitude and knowledge. He knows his altitude, his flight path, his speed, and his timetable. He does not know – and does not need to know – how much his altitude will vary by what fraction of a degree every step of the way. No, this he chalks up to temporary variation and expects it to self-correct. Even a very bumpy ride is not an occasion for serious doubt about whether he will arrive. The experienced pilot has developed a sense of how much variation is normal under these conditions, and he doesn't worry. He just keeps going.

Did the pilot always know this? Did he step up to his first flight lesson with an inbred sense of perspective on this? Absolutely not. Probably he panicked the first time the aircraft did something more extreme than he had handled before. It was only very gradually that he acquired an informed intuition about how much variability was safe and perfectly normal.

Such a pilot has learned to be comfortable with the implicit laws of chaos, the fact that larger predictable patterns can be temporarily obscured by random variability in smaller details[17]. The pilot has learned that there may be temporary turbulence and losses in altitude, but there will be correction and successful completion of the journey. Departure will give way to arrival and, generally speaking, the flight plan will have been followed. If we were to focus nervously on every dip and change in altitude and each minuscule shift in direction the plane made, we might conclude there was no way this pilot would ever get that airplane to its destination.

Growth in real life is affected by the laws of chaos as well. Regressions and losses of altitude are part of forward movement, in stock markets and airplanes. It's true in your life too. You must learn to say to yourself: *I am going through a downturn. I have temporarily lost my altitude and motivation, but through the use of persistence and endurance, I will keep moving in the general direction I have chosen and these small inconsistences will correct themselves.*

I'm sure you're thinking, where is the line between going with the flow and knowing when you're really in a dangerous situation? The line is based on degree. If the aircraft's altitude sinks below a certain point, it becomes no longer something to ride out. It turns into a survival emergency requiring corrective action immediately. The pilot knows the level of tolerance he has for certain variations and he doesn't hope for the best and wait until the plane is in a death spiral before he takes charge. The same is true for an experienced stockbroker. He makes a judgment based on whether the sinking stock merely is the result of market corrections or because the company has major earnings problems.

Like the experienced pilot and stockbroker, you have to define your own limits between the safe zone and the danger zone. Decide how long you are willing to try your dream, how much risk you can tolerate, and what portion of your time and money you can safely devote to it. Sometimes the trajectories of our goals and dreams have to be adjusted so we can continue to make a living. (Linda's solution was to keep her secure job while she explored her art at home. This gave her time to identify exactly what kind of work she really wanted to do while maintaining security and stability.) You can determine your own limits, enabling you to pursue the dream without giving up needed requirements of your life. You may have to slow down at points, or even put your dreams on hold if finances temporarily get too tight, but persevere any way you can.

It's the giving up of the dream that is the killer. You haven't failed or given up if you have to make a temporary course adjustment. Just make sure that you do plenty of self-support talk along the way. If others hear you muttering to yourself about chaos theory and altitude variations, let them wonder. You know what you're doing.

5. Use Persistence and Endurance as Necessary
Expect to switch back and forth between motivation and
perseverance.

If the excitement of your original motivation begins to wane, you have another psychological asset that can take over. It is what the professionals use. It's called persistence.

Persistence and endurance are motivation without the glamour. They are the forward-looking, future-oriented workhorses of the mind and spirit. These hardworking attitudes give you another way of approaching your goals that does not rely on the effervescence of fresh motivation. Motivation *must* begin to rely on persistence at some point. Good days and bad days are part of the process and persistence keeps moving you when the original excitement of motivation is fading. The good news is that your motivation and sense of excitement will kick in again later, every time you get past a hard part. The high spirits of motivation sometimes need to catch a ride on the wide back of plodding persistence. Motivation is powerful, but delicate and reactive at the same time. That is why hopelessness can so easily throw it off track.

Never entrust an important project or career move to motivation alone. It should be very clear in your mind that you will be switching to persistence when the challenge temporarily loses its fun. Motivation is designed to take you right up to the gates of persistence, then it steps back to give you a chance to develop endurance.

After reading this chapter and gaining more self-knowledge, you hopefully now have a new awareness of how frightened you can become of your motivation – and why. Also, you now know why the excitement of motivation might signal danger to you rather than optimism. You have learned how your past experiences as well as your inexperience may have impeded the forward movement in your life. Once you realize that you feared your motivation was threatening to your loved ones, you will be able to *mistrust the fear* instead of mistrusting the motivation. Then you will be realigned with your inner power, that inspired source of forward movement called motivation.

CHAPTER 5

LOYALTY, GUILT, AND GROWTH

*Even though we want to experience the thrill of exploration,
there can be a lingering tug at the heartstrings when we see our
family receding in the distance.*

My father had polio, and when I was a little girl I can remember matching my steps to his, limping in syncopated adoration. To think that my healthy six-year-old stride might show up his infirmity was painful to me, and I felt better when I made myself like him. It was my version of survivor guilt. I have been amazed at how many of my clients use similar rationalizations. Physical illnesses, depression, panic and sexual dysfunction are just some of the ways that we match our parents' crooked gait and thereby show our love.

In an instant we will sacrifice ourselves, our true selves, in order to sustain our loyalties and bonds. We become who we think we need to be in order to carry our parents' pain and expectations, to confirm their view of the world. We have such a strong need to belong, to be a member of a group, that we will deny our own perceptions in order to do it.

These are the wrong ideals to live by. Childhood loyalty and guilt exist to be grown out of. Think of how many times our loyalties must change in the process of growing up. Really good loyalties are not so binding that you have to stop growing. Good loyalties continue to give something back to you.

Sometimes guilt is simply a growing pain, not a sign you have done something wrong.

When we start exploring our individual destiny, we may have strong feelings if it looks like our purpose will take us away from our family. Even though we want to experience the thrill of exploration, there can be a lingering tug at the heartstrings when we see loved ones receding in the distance. What exactly are those tugging threads that hold us back? Some of the strings that hold us back are genuine love and attachment, but many are attachments of loyalty and guilt.

Feeling Their Pain

At certain times of life and in certain relationships, children often act as parents to their parents. This role reversal goes on more frequently than most of us would imagine. Our parents' need to be nurtured and protected is not lost on us; we feel their pain. Reacting emotionally to our parents' pain and emotional needs, we treat them as if they were our fragile offspring. We don't see our parents as perfectly capable grown-ups, ready and able to get on with the rest of their lives. Instead, we see needy children.

The mistake to avoid here is to believe that compassion for your parents' pain means that you should stay behind to help them cope with it. *They already have ways of coping with it.* We don't realize what tough old birds they really are, as we stay fixated on that damaged inner child of theirs. At their age, they are by definition successful survivors. They know how to get their needs met in ways that work for them.

If you have not been able to follow through on your dreams, one major reason might be that you are a very sensitive person who's holding yourself back because of guilt-induced loyalty. The inner conflict we're talking about here is between rescuing your parents and living your own life.

The Secret Strength in Sensitivity

Sensitive, empathic people are extremely strong psychologically. Think about it. If you are empathic, you not only carry your own feelings and problems, but you also respond to your loved ones' emotional needs *at the same time*. Your sensitivity will not allow you to rest until you can come up with a way not to hurt the feelings of loved ones as you pursue your goals. Sensitive individuals tend to take on formidable family problems[18,19]. There are experienced CEOs who would think twice before taking on the management of a high-maintenance corporation like the family. Intelligent, sensitive children with enormous psychological resources are often the only ones who can *afford* to tackle the family's problems, even at great cost to their own development. They're the ones who have the inner strength to constantly monitor the tension between their wishes and the needs of loved ones.

Survivor Guilt

Having a happier, healthier life than that of your family members can stir up terrific guilt, as if the only way to be loyal is to be just as miserable as they are. Let's take a look at one person's struggle with this.

Elaine's Story

Elaine was a high functioning, got-it-all-together bank vice president. She came to see me in a crisis after her alcoholic sister had been locked up for assaulting a policeman. Elaine's parents were both dead and her sister was the only family she had left. For the past two years, Elaine had been stuck with picking up after her sister's escapades, interceding with exasperated employers, or finding new people to give her sister a chance. Usually her sister's drinking and abusive behavior started up again soon after these interventions, frustrating Elaine to no end. Yet Elaine hung in there, functioning for two people, trying to keep up with her job duties while nervously keeping one eye on her sister's addiction.

In Elaine's childhood, she had felt trapped in a family situation with a mentally ill, explosive father and a mother addicted to prescription pain medications. Elaine had always been the steady, capable one in her family, doing well in school, and generally causing no one any trouble. But her younger sister was a different story. From early childhood, her sister had been an ill-tempered handful, adding more stress to a family already overwhelmed with problems. Elaine was always the "good" one, and with her natural intelligence and maturity went on to care for her parents as they became older and more infirm. Between her career and her parents, she never had the energy to marry and now she was facing middle age with an out-of-control, thirty-year-old sister who was acting like the adolescent from hell.

Now her sister's problems had crossed the line from her private world into the arena of the legal system. Elaine was beside herself ever since she learned that her sister's insulting, belligerent behavior in the city lock-up had caused her to be held without bond. She also knew that her sister's mottled record of rehabilitation and relapse would impress no judge. When Elaine's efforts to get her sister released were unsuccessful, she began to feel panicky and desperate, prompting her call to me.

Elaine's love for her sister went beyond mere family attachment. She was subconsciously convinced that she had been given the mission of *saving* her sister. When this failed – as it always did – Elaine became demoralized and guilt-stricken. Where had she gone wrong? What had she overlooked?

Accustomed to making things work out, Elaine could not give up on her sister.

When Elaine could do nothing more to get her sister out of jail, she expressed her survivor guilt by making herself suffer along with what she imagined her sister was going through. One night, Elaine was horrified and conscience-stricken when she realized she had put her sister out of her mind for a couple of hours while out to dinner with friends. Ashamed of her "disloyalty" to her locked-up sibling, Elaine spent the next day holed up at home in a depressive funk. Elaine had clearly gone beyond empathy for her sister's self-induced problems and had deteriorated into attempting to take on her sister's imagined suffering.

But Why Feel Guilty?

From childhood on, Elaine had always felt a kind of survivor guilt over the fact that she had created a good life while her sister's life perpetually floundered. I told Elaine I could understand her empathy for her sister, but confessed I was at a loss as to why her sister's distress should cause her feelings of *guilt*. Sorrow over seeing a ruined life was understandable. But what was the connection between her sister's problems and Elaine's feelings of *guilt?* It made no logical sense. Elaine had done nothing but try to help and protect her sister all of her life, especially when their parents were out of control or incapacitated. She was actually the one in her family who was *least* deserving of guilty feelings.

Blame Projectors

I asked Elaine to explain why her sister's troubles made her feel guilty, and suddenly she hit upon the answer. Growing up in her family, it seemed like everybody was angry with everyone else all the time. If anyone was in a bad mood, it was always somebody else's fault. If an accident happened, somebody should have been more careful. Blame flew all over the place. Childish accidents were punished as carelessness, and as the oldest child Elaine was given plenty of blame if she did not watch her little sister closely enough. In this way, Elaine's sister learned to find fault in everyone but herself. And as the responsible, older child, Elaine learned to accept guilt for all kinds of things that were beyond her control.

Blame-projecting family members make others feel guilty for enjoying their lives in many ways:

- **In subtle or not so subtle ways, they make other people feel responsible for their suffering.**

- **Their crises have a repetitive, unsolvable quality.**

- **Envy, anger, and criticism characterize their attitudes toward others.**

- **Blame is projected; nothing is their fault.**

- **No amount of help or attention is perceived as being "enough."**

- **They insist on help on their terms or not at all; a high need to be in control.**

These characteristics do not mean such people are wicked or evil, but it does mean they are very *needy* and *unaware* of how they are contributing to their own miseries. Individuals with these characteristics look outside themselves to deal with life, so they naturally see other people as the source of – and solution to – all their problems.

Very sensitive and caring people can easily take on the impossible task of trying to be the one-person answer to the blame-projector's problems. In this way, they support their family members' mistaken beliefs that it is up to other people to make them happy.

However, if you have dealt with blame-projectors, you have noticed that with their attitude of blame and entitlement, nothing makes them happy for very long. This is because they are always looking *outside* themselves for the

WHO YOU WERE MEANT TO BE

next gratification. By definition, their happiness cannot be internally maintained for long.

Self-Sacrificers

In contrast to blame-projectors, people like Elaine who sacrifice out of survivor guilt seem to have several traits in common:

- **They are exquisitely sensitive to the feelings of other people.**

- **They are idealistic and conscientious.**

- **Their empathy is exaggerated; they feel worse than the person with the problem.**

- **They have overly active imaginations; they react to and fall for drama.**

- **They get emotionally confused about whose pain is whose.**

- **They peg their self-worth on how well they fulfill family roles.**

- **They believe that their sacrifice will magically help another person change.**

If you have any of these characteristics, your job is to find a way to love so that helping others does not mean emptying your own life[20].

Was Your Love Ever Enough?

Elaine's type of guilt is not uncommon. *It is the guilt of a giving, sensitive person whose troubled loved ones are incapable of receiving love and help.* Elaine saw her "guilt" as not having done enough or given enough. Elaine was looking for meaning and purpose in this lifelong, desperate self-sacrifice, even if it meant blaming herself. She had come to the conclusion that *she* must have done something wrong if things were this bad.

Elaine had made the mistake of thinking that because she was giving, the other person must be receiving. Therefore, if her sister did not get better, it must be because Elaine was not giving enough. It was very hard for Elaine to realize that her help and intercessions ran through her sister like a sieve, having virtually no effect on the situation.

Elaine ultimately did accept that painful truth. She took a long, realistic look at her sister and at what the situation was doing to herself. Elaine realized now that her job as an adult was not to *feel everybody's pain*, but to *cope with the situation* in a way that was reasonably fair to everyone, herself included. When Elaine couldn't stand her sister's self-pitying calls from jail anymore, she got angry with her sister and told her so. She stopped sopping up all her sister's turmoil with the sponge of her heart. Instead, she offered help when she could, but not at the expense of her own stability. Helpfulness and loyalty were strong aspects of Elaine's personality, so her solution wasn't to totally walk away from her sister and her problems. Instead, she did what she could without exhausting herself, then hoped for the best.

Focusing on her own feelings and realistic limitations made Elaine feel "like an adult," as she said with a calm smile one day. It was as though she had found the magic key. Elaine didn't have to stop loving her sister, but neither did she have to sacrifice her life just to suffer along with her sister's bad judgments. When she finally told her sister that she was unable to tolerate the constant demands and telephone calls, her sister backed off and was more respectful of Elaine's time. Actually, her sister had had no idea how much Elaine was taking the sister's problems to heart because Elaine always managed to act so unflappable.

Growing up, Elaine was not only a bright little girl, she was also the highest functioning person in her family. Not just the highest functioning *child*, but the highest functioning *person*. Elaine had the combination of personality strengths that allowed her to function at a higher level more consistently than anybody else in her family. She was smart and emotionally under control. She could contain a tremendous amount of anxiety and still function. As Elaine noted in one of our sessions, "If you are the highest functioning one in the family, then you have to be *that*. You can't be who *you* really are. It all flows to you, whether you want it or not." Now seeing her old family arrangement with perspective and with compassion for herself, she was able to say no when she had to.

—❦—

Am I Able to Love?

Unfortunately, many sensitive, empathic people like Elaine grow up with the gut fear that perhaps they are incapable of loving. This is because their love was never enough to help their loved ones, no matter how hard they tried. This is not about anyone's inability to love. It is about a family's inability to *receive*. The bottomless-pit quality to a family's misery is often because they cannot accept love, even though they constantly demand it. You often may have come away feeling like your efforts just were not enough or that it was too little too late. This especially includes gifts of the heart – like trying to please them or make them proud of you – not just material things you might give them.

Even if you are a very loving person, *if your parents had a childhood in which they did not feel loved, they may not be able to accept or benefit from the love you try to give them.*

As we began to pry Elaine's fingers off her sister's life, she was able to get some perspective and let herself enjoy life more. She learned to curb her dramatically empathic imagination and to remind herself she really had no idea how her sister was experiencing her predicament. After all, her sister was a seasoned veteran of turmoil, whereas Elaine was easily upset by it.

Instead of reflexively jumping whenever her sister called, Elaine began to rely on her own instincts to guide her as to when she should try to help her sister. If Elaine felt tired and resentful, she refused. If she felt rested and generous, she would do what she could. In this way she honored her own need to be generous and responsible, but she no longer gave until it hurt. Elaine no longer believed she was a bad person if she couldn't change her sister's life.

A Rule of Thumb

If you are a conscientious sort of person, you can be seduced into feeling that maybe if you tried a little harder, in a different way, you would be able to give your loved ones what they so obviously need. But if they rebuff you repeatedly, consider them impossible. It's a rule of thumb: *if you continually feel that you can't give a loved one enough, you actually can't.* You try and it's not enough. Therefore, it is not. And not because *you* can't give, but because *they* can't receive. Prove this to your satisfaction, then back off and stop trying to make them into something they are not. Your loyalty does not require that you perform the impossible.

The Pain Container

Loyalty doesn't mean that you have to metabolize the pain of others. No one is helped when you internalize others' suffering. Mark was a client who had to learn this truth the hard way.

Mark's Story

Mark had suffered through this kind of dilemma for years. He was his mother's confidant, literally listening for hours to her criticisms of his father and the betrayals she had suffered.

Mark was a bright and mature ten-year-old when his parents developed problems. When his mother started talking to him about her unhappiness, Mark naturally thought he was being asked to help, to give comfort or advice perhaps. Yet he discovered that whenever he said anything, his mother seemed irritated and almost annoyed that he was interrupting. Whether sitting in the kitchen or going for long drives in the car, Mark tried to help his mother solve her problems, but his suggestions were always discounted.

Mark soon learned to keep his emotional distance from his mother, in order to tolerate these episodes. When he grew up, this self-protective distancing carried over into his adult intimate relationships, which he was careful not to let develop past a certain point. When his girlfriends became too "needy," or seemed to intrude upon his "space," Mark became irrationally infuriated with them for what he saw as their horrid "dependency." When he came to see me for therapy, Mark was beginning to think he was a damaged soul incapable of sustaining a relationship with anyone. His worst fear was that he was basically incapable of love. Mark wanted to be loyal and he felt intensely guilty when he inexplicably backed out of what he knew were promising relationships. Soon Mark was making the connection between his conflicted adult reactions and his childhood experience as hostage therapist to his mother.

Mark thought loyalty meant he was supposed to just sit there and be a *container* for his mother's difficult emotions[21]. His mother had no intention of leaving her unhappy marriage. But she relieved her frustration by pouring her distress into Mark, the child with the most understanding and empathy. It was a convenient release. After expressing her pain and resentment, his mother felt better and was able to go back to exactly the way things were. Instead of putting her foot down with her husband, she complained to Mark. He was expected to contain his mother's pain and not let anything leak out to his father or anyone else. After years of this, was it surprising that he felt like exploding? Was it shocking that he could not get away from women's needs fast enough?

The energy it takes to be someone else's emotional container is formidable. It ties up the motivation and energy you would have to spend on projects of your own, a life of your own. To hold pain for other people means you lose room for your own pleasure.

"I Didn't Love Her"

Mark's turnaround came when he began to be honest with himself about his feelings toward his mother. He was clouded up with so much loyalty and guilt that he had never asked himself how he really felt about her. All he knew was that he was supposed to love her and that she desperately needed his love. So Mark tried to turn himself into the kind of attentive son the part required. He showed his mother what she needed to see, regardless of how he really felt.

As an adult, Mark berated himself over his problems with relationships, wondering if he secretly hated women or was not entirely heterosexual. Mark was relieved when he was finally able to get to the bottom of his fear and guilt. He did this by uncovering his worst guilty secret about his first important relationship with a woman, his mother: *"I didn't love her."* He had loved her once, but her terrible self-centeredness made it impossible later. Mark had had to keep this truth even from himself in order not to slip up and devastate his mother. He felt guilty about not feeling more for her, and so he subconsciously kept trying to feel the right feelings. He carried this over to his relationships with girlfriends, guiltily trying to give them what he thought they wanted while growing more and more distant and angry toward them. Once Mark got the idea that he was not a bad person and was not obliged to manufacture feelings for the emotionally needy, his relationships began to open up into the kind of real joy that he had never considered himself capable of experiencing.

The Fifth Commandment

Mark's feelings toward his mother and Elaine's empathy for her sister were initially described by both of them as "love." Therefore, when Mark and Elaine felt angry or frustrated with their family members, all they could feel was guilt that they were not being *loving* toward these people they *loved*. It was terribly confusing, a mess of illogic and false premises based on the first commandment of many families: love your family before anyone else.

For a long time, Mark was utterly confused about how he felt about his mother. He knew that he did not *feel* love for her, yet how else could he understand the depth of his loyalty to her? Elaine certainly could not maintain loving emotions toward her sister when she was disrupting Elaine's life, but she would have done anything for her sister that she could. This confused Mark and Elaine, because they both believed that in order to be good people they had to *feel* love for their family members all the time, no matter how they were behaving.

In order to sort out such confusing feelings, we need the right words to think with. Without question, we can feel **bonded, attached,** and **loyal** to our family members, but these emotions may be far removed from the warm, rewarding feelings that we associate with **love.** You can be intensely bonded to someone because of tribal loyalties and identifications, but this does not necessarily mean you have loving feelings toward them or that you desire to be in their company. We have no choice about our human heritage of family attachment, but it does not follow that we can manufacture love out of heredity.

As a wise teacher and good friend once remarked, the fifth commandment does not tell us to *love* our parents. It instructs only that we *honor* our father and mother[22]. You have no control over whether or not you can feel love for a parent. Sometimes we cannot develop true feelings of love for family members *until* we have first worked through our other feelings about them.

Loyalty, Guilt, and Growth

Loyalty and guilt have very different goals than growth, but they are often seen traveling together. Like it or not, a person on the path of personal growth often feels dogged by the shadowy figures of loyalty and guilt. These feelings can be very hard to shake off and can end up making you spend as much time looking backwards as looking forward. Our psychological growth often strains against our loyalties and when it pulls *too* hard, guilt results.

Erik Erikson observed that children go through a pivotal conflict in early childhood between urges of initiative and feelings of guilt[23]. Erikson poignantly describes how a child becomes symptomatic when too much guilt and loyalty interfere with the child's initiative to *go-and-do*. The challenge to resolve these conflicting feelings is a difficult one and many people get stuck here, endlessly oscillating in their adult lives between ambition and guilt.

How this conflict is settled sets the tone of the child's future. Is the life force of initiative channeled into competence and hopefulness, or does it bring guilt and indecisive worry? The key is whether the child perceives that she can have her cake and eat it too. She desperately needs to know at this point that acting out her initiative does not mean that she will lose the bond with her parents that she continues to need so much.

Little girls and boys at this stage need freedom to be healthily aggressive and acquisitive, pursuing and grasping their desires, but they also need to know that freedom has not been won at the expense of family bonds. We can only move forward freely when we are sure that our home base is secure and wants to underwrite our expedition into self-expansion.

What do you think were your experiences with initiative and guilt when you were, say, four to seven years old? How about other times in your life when initiative was called for? Did you worry that your success might make someone else feel bad? Or did you know that your family would always be there for you as you went out into the world? In other words, did they leave the light on for you?

The Meaning of Your Initiative

Conflict between initiative and guilt results in a back-and-forth dance of permission-seeking that people do when they are first tempted to leave the nest. As you nervously approach loved ones with your new idea or plan, you may keep asking them in one way or another, "Is this all right? Am I being too aggressive? Should I be feeling guilty about this?" Although an encouraging response from another person is always helpful, this compulsive reassurance-seeking cannot end *until you finally decide that your initiative is not a sign of disloyalty.*

How you feel about your urge toward growth and initiative will depend on the meaning you give it. Guilty feelings of course would result if you saw your initiative as an *attack* against your family's control. That's why I don't encourage people to make dramatic, aggressive stands against their parents. It usually works better to work out misunderstandings and hurt feelings gradually, addressing one piece at a time. After all, *most of us feel a bond to our first families as well as our futures.* We often can find a way to have them both. However, this does *not* mean that we have to keep things the way they were in the past. Keeping a connection with our families of origin does not mean hanging onto outgrown childhood roles. It simply means taking our rightful place with them as fellow adults.

If you look at it this way, your motive behind taking initiative is self-development, not the rejection of your family.

Once we are at peace about our own motives, we can move forward and wholeheartedly engage the growth experience without unnecessary guilt. But it always helps to know what to expect next in this growth process. In the following section, we will investigate how it feels once you start moving away from home base and toward your own interests.

Desirable Discombobulation

In order for any of us to take the next positive step forward in our lives, our old personality has to be loosened up and reshuffled[24]. During these periods of inner growth, you may feel disrupted and preoccupied. Problems with concentration, feelings of emotional fragility, a fear of shame or exposure, and torturous indecision all can be signs of a **psychological growth spurt.** It may seem as if you can't get all your horses pulling together in the same direction anymore. Verbal mistakes and slips of the tongue increase during these times, reflecting the mental disarray that precedes the next step up to a new level of becoming your true self. You may feel fuzzy mentally, and disconnected from yourself.

This is because you are psychologically on the move and nothing is in its old place anymore. A good analogy for this growth spurt is what our lives are like when we are moving from one home to another. We still have all of our possessions, but they're scattered among many boxes and hard to find.

This stage of growth can make you feel confused, unsure, and unable to trust yourself. It is critically important to understand the source of your discomfort at these crucial points of development. If you mislabel your distress as a sign of psychopathology, you could end up blaming yourself and remain stuck in fear. The purpose of this chapter is to help you see these symptoms as the signs of growth that they are. By understanding the way inner growth feels, you no longer have to be frightened by it.

Remember that when you start to move on your dreams, you often encounter turbulence. For a time, it may feel as though everything is holding you back or getting in your way. What is really happening is that you have gone past the point where your old ways can satisfy you and you are ready for the next jump. You have outgrown the nest. It is no longer cozy; it is cramped.

Going into the Gap

The **gap** is the space between who you were and who you are becoming. Imagine yourself walking along uneventfully on a familiar pathway, when suddenly you notice the path ends up ahead. The trail just breaks off into thin air. There's a fog bank shrouding the space ahead of you, and there's no way of telling what happened to the path. Getting closer, you can see beyond the fog in the distance where a somewhat higher trail continues on solid ground, but, amazingly, whatever's in the cloudbank before you hides everything between here and there. You are facing an mysterious gap. This is a bad case of discontinuity.

You step forward to peer into the cloudy nothingness before you and notice what looks like wisps of thread peeking through the cloud cover here and there. You move even closer and see that they are ropes. It is a rope bridge! Connected to your end of the path, a suspended wooden pathway disappears on an incline, apparently connected to that higher section of rail further on.

Deciding whether to step onto that flimsy looking bridge, in the hopes that it *does* connect up with the other side, is a matter of no small anxiety. Yet, at certain points in our lives, the growth urge is so strong and we are so sick of the old familiar path, that the wispy little bridge starts to look pretty appealing. We step out into the gap, hoping like crazy that it's attached to where we think we want to go.

Of course you will have all kinds of dire thoughts when you are about to step out onto the bridge for the first time. Actually, your ego may get *hysterical* when you try the bridge for the first time. It will say whatever gives you the most gut-gripping anxiety and self-doubt. The ego desperately wants to keep you off that bridge and back under its control.

While your ego is howling its objections, you need to look at your growth map – which we'll cover in Chapter 7 – and get a little reassurance to go on. Wouldn't you be more likely to keep on with your quest if you knew in advance that these gap points were likely, that sometimes a swaying suspension bridge is going to be the only route of travel? You'll be a whole lot less likely to get discouraged if you know about this in advance. Go ahead and test it out. If you don't like it, turn around and come back. But resolve to take that step out of the past into your future.

What is it like in the gap, once you've stepped onto the bridge of transition?

Life in the Gap

For one thing, although you know you are going in the right direction and the ropes are heading toward that higher trail ahead, after the first few steps into that fog, you cannot see where you *are*. There are no familiar landmarks and even where you have come from is losing its form in the mist as you look back. You are literally in a state of suspension.

This is what *transition* feels like and this is why the uninformed and unsupported often turn back at this point. In the gap nothing feels the same as it did before. Old pleasures may seem hollow, while a new way of living has not yet materialized to reassure you. You feel like you are hovering over an abyss[25].

Why does anyone keep going when new terrain feels this uncertain? Often it is because he or she has had the *convincing experience.*

The Convincing Experience

The *convincing experience* is something I finally recognized after years of trying to get people to make healthy changes in their life. As I mentioned before, early in my career if I tried to persuade some of my therapy clients to try something new, most of my suggestions usually hit the floor like lead weights. After all, it looked to my clients like I was pushing them toward that scary, rickety, blowing-in-the-breeze bridge for absolutely no good reason other than I thought it would be "good for them." If I encouraged them too strenuously, I found they usually left therapy. I was a slow learner. Gradually, after having a few convincing experiences of my own, I discovered that if the person was *ready* to grow, they would soon have an experience that would make them *run* onto that bridge.

The convincing experience occurs when the old way of living becomes totally bankrupt. Life as you know it suddenly does not work anymore. All the old ways of coping hit a wall, and you cannot go on in the same way. *That is when we are ready and willing to try the gap.* Actually, at this juncture we are willing to do *anything*. Suddenly it is too awful to stay on that old path any longer, for even one more minute, so you grab those ropes and sink your feet onto those gyrating boards beneath you. Any place has got to be better than what you just left. The road behind you might as well be on fire.

Sometimes the convincing experience is a happier event, a wonderful fleeting exposure to what *could* be. You might have a transcendent experience that catapults you briefly up to a new level, where you linger just long enough to get a taste of its reality. It might only be a moment, but it can redefine your life and give you a goal that heretofore you had not known existed. This is what happened to Jody.

Soul Dancing

Jody's story is an example of how a seemingly small moment can transform a person's goals for life. Jody had the convincing experience of being transported from one level of life to another.

Jody was a widow who had taken care of those she loved all her life. Now approaching middle age, several years after the death of her husband, she was feeling lonely but had no desire to go back to the kind of marriage that she had with her quiet, unambitious husband. For Jody, there was not much to recommend getting married again. She had always been saddled with making all the decisions.

One evening, Jody met a new man at her dancing class. They talked and she felt an instant connection. When they danced that night, her new partner stepped firmly with her onto the dance floor, his hand commanding her back and his body moving against hers in a masterful ballet of control. Jody had never been held so firmly nor guided so confidently by a man in her entire life. To Jody's everlasting credit, she recognized this moment was a turning point for her. As they swooped and glided backward into twirls, pulled in close and swung out in arcs of grace, Jody knew she had what she wanted. She had jumped the gap for those moments, getting a taste of what it was like to be with a man "who not only had potential, but would allow me to use my potential." Jody had an undeniable *convincing experience* in which she knew that she could never be fully satisfied by her previous style of relationship again.

Things did not go any further with that wonderful dance partner, but in that one encounter Jody hit a level of joy that made the old trail no longer adequate. Jody began to plan how to gain the kind of life where she could meet this caliber of man and where she herself would be skilled and confident enough to attract a like-minded partner. One who liked the things she did, such as dancing, but also one who could appreciate her grace and balance on other levels, too.

The Swinging Bridge

Those moments like the one Jody experienced are serendipitous. More often, people are pushed into the gap by circumstances that involve no choice. These are often disorienting and distressing. We realize there is nothing to go back to, even if we wanted to. This happened to Marilyn when she sold the family home because of a job transfer to another city. Marilyn was not too worried because the job transfer meant that she would be able to move in with her sister who lived in the new city. Marilyn's adult son had been living with her, but when Marilyn had to sell the house, her adult son had to go out on his own.

Six months later, the store that Marilyn had been transferred to shut down. She was jobless until she managed to find another position back home. Having sold her house, Marilyn now could only afford a much smaller condominium. She found herself suddenly living completely on her own for the first time in her life. It was especially hard on her socially, now that her son no longer was available to be her companion. He had gone on to develop a life of his own, and although they still met for dinner occasionally and chatted on the phone, things had changed. In our session, Marilyn instinctively used the bridge imagery to describe her feeling of being in the gap:

> *It's like being on a flimsy bridge and it's swinging. You're not sure how to get off or even if you can get off. You don't know if you're going to fall. It's like walking on one of those Tarzan movie ropebridges on which all you can do is hold on tight. And you can't go back. It is so uncomfortable.*

Circumstances had changed to the point where Marilyn had to grow, like it or not. I told Marilyn that at this point, her goal must be to simply *hold on,* to learn to tolerate the feelings in the gap until she felt strong enough to begin moving forward again.

Being able to understand what was happening to her was immensely comforting to Marilyn because it gave her perspective. She went on to say, *"Maybe I need a little map across the bridge to get me to the other side."* A map is exactly what Marilyn needed when she was swinging in the gulf between who she was and who she was becoming. This book is a piece of that map. To expect these gaps and to know what they feel like will give you, I hope, new confidence in coping with these stressful times of growth.

Very successful people – the ones who take risks to get what they want – have an instinctual acceptance of the gaps along the road of fulfillment. They *expect* these white-knuckled moments, hold on during them, and keep heading for the other side to reach their goals. They are so focused on where they are going that if a swinging rope bridge is thrown in their path, they will not hesitate to use it. After all, a rope bridge is still a bridge.

Just remember, you will be less afraid and less confused if you understand that this painful time of transition is the way true self-development happens. We have to take ourselves apart before we can put ourselves together in a new form. Because of our human heritage, we may battle some guilt for going after what we want. We may even feel a little disloyal, perhaps. When we step out into the gap, we may feel lost and unsure. The pay-off is your freedom, your true self, and a life that fills you up rather than draining you dry. Don't be afraid to keep moving across that gap. That kind of bridge has been used for centuries. It will hold you.

CHAPTER SIX

WISHING AND RISKING

Your wishing function is not immature fantasy. It is the raw material of reality.

I was waiting for a table in my favorite Chinese restaurant when a little boy of about seven approached me shyly from the dining area. I had never seen him before, but he intently peered up at me. "Ma'am?" he said softly with a perplexed look on his young face, "Is it okay to wish for things?" Just then, an irritated-looking woman leaned out of a booth and called roughly to the boy. His eyes stayed locked on mine. "Absolutely," I said. If I had taken the world off his shoulders, he could not have looked more relieved. Back he walked to the booth, carrying a little hope under his arm.

For some strange reason, many people see wishing and imagination as signs of childishness, to be given up as a rite of passage into real adulthood. Some people lose the ability to imagine and wish in adulthood. They give those away with their childhood possessions. But children know better. They know how alive wishing makes them feel. They know what wishing does for the soul, and they know what it does for the world.

Your wishing function is not immature fantasy. It is the raw material of reality. That was the truth the little boy needed to hear, not to make him feel better, but to put him back in touch with reality.

I was lucky as a child to have a father who knew how to dream and was not afraid of wishes. One of my best memories was having him tell me stories about the fairies that lived among the big tree roots on the banks of a little forest stream near his childhood home. His descriptions were so vivid and his enjoyment so contagious, to this day I still look twice whenever I pass an old root-gnarled tree. Am I sure one day I will see a fairy? Not exactly. But my father taught me how to enjoy the *possibility* of fairies. He taught me how to enjoy the *idea* of things that aren't there.

As a little girl I played with a much younger child in her backyard. I was inspired by some little toadstools to tell her all I knew about fairies and how they might come out at night to perch on these little seats in the moonlight. She was spellbound, until her mother abruptly broke it up by telling me to stop filling her daughter's head with such nonsense. She was raising her child to spurn all that make-believe stuff. I could not have put it in words back then, but I definitely understood that her mother's intent was to raise a rational, realistic child who would never be fooled by anyone.

But who's a fool for wishing? Fantasy, imagination, and wishing are not about ignoring reality; they are about playing with reality. It's the "what-if?" of life. When my father told me about fairyland, on the surface he was technically telling me stories about little creatures that did not exist. But the wonderful, eminently practical thing he was teaching me was to *appreciate the possibilities.* If I could open my mind to the possibility of fairies, what possibilities in myself might I open my mind to? In this way, I was encouraged to imagine what could be, to think of more than meets the eye. I should add here that although my father loved the idea of fairies and ghosts, he also knew how to run his own business, make a payroll, and plan for college funds – as should we all. The thing to remember is that being a responsible adult does not mean you have to get rid of wishful thinking.

The paradox of modern culture is our one-sided worship of practicality, coupled with our secret, deep dependency on the creative minds of a few good dreamers. Nobody would have their dream automobile or house were it not for the wishes and daydreams of our inventors and architects. It is just as true that *your* dreams coming true depends on your internal inventor, your own inner architect of possibility.

A caution that so many of my clients have heard from their parents is that dreaming is all very nice, but sooner or later you have to realize that real life is not like that. My question is: *whose* real life is not like that? Theirs? If your parents have stripped their lives barren of dreams and think that being realistic means having no imagination, that does not have to be the recipe for your life. It probably wasn't even a very good recipe for their lives, as you can see if you closely examine how much success anyone with this attitude actually has. Please give this some thought. Did shutting the door on wishful possibilities get them what they wanted? When parents invoke the name of reality to discourage their children's hopes, it's because *they* feel hopeless – not because real life *is* hopeless.

Emotional Hijackings

Don't forget that a child's well-developed wishing function puts extra stress on any parent, because a child's wishes and brainstorms make him or her beg for things. In other words, the parent may have to work harder to meet more demands. Parents, in their humanness, reflexively clamp down on their child as soon as his or her wishes begin to make them feel inadequate. The child, in turn, is made to feel bad about wanting more. It is always easier on the parent when the child gradually learns to give up asking for what he or she really wants. How many of us cut back on our biggest wishes just so our parents would not feel they were being asked for more than they could give? (This is also true regarding the secret wish to have the kind of parents who could give us the emotional support we needed so much.)

But an adult does not have to say "No!" to spoil a child's wish. It is often just as effective to make some minor adjustments to the child's wish, just enough to make it no longer fun. This is what happens when the adult appears to meet the child's wishful need, but not really. For instance, a musical boy is made to take piano lessons when he really dreams of an electric guitar. Or a little girl who wants to sculpt in clay is given lessons in watercolor from a convenient artist in her neighborhood. The same thing happens in adult life. We persuade ourselves to take jobs that we do not want because it is *kind* of like what we are looking for, or we marry a spouse who is like those piano lessons – in the ballpark, but not home base. It is a kind of *emotional hijacking*. We were on our way someplace, then someone came along and took us in a different direction.

Wishes can be spoiled or ruined by other people's doubt, too. It does not take much to cool a wish to below room temperature with questions like "Are you sure?" or "Wouldn't you rather...?" These are some of the suggestions and ideas that emotional hijackers love to use. And they do not stop in childhood. Has your wishing function ever been hijacked by a person who just wanted a cheap ride to his own destination?

What Are Your Intentions?

In his deep and detailed description of childhood psychological development, Stanley Greenspan[26] describes how a person's sense of selfhood develops from childhood wishes and needs in the context of interactions with other people. Primal wishes insist on expression, pushing the child to make her first efforts at communication. Soon the child learns to form an *intention*, which means that her wish becomes conscious and satisfaction is sought through action or interaction with others. This is the raw beginning of our capacity to imagine those things we want so badly.

In our earliest years, we are unrelentingly intentional, but the fate of our ability to remain deliberately, consciously intentional depends on the reactions of others around us. A little too much negativity, and we may stop doing things "on purpose." We learn how to lead safer and less intentional lives. We learn to do things we later say we really did not "mean" to do, and our life begins to seem more and more out of our own hands. "I didn't mean it" becomes a way of keeping our relationships at all costs.

Be intentional about your wishes. You do mean it. Who you really are may be very different from who you have been told to be. Aren't you tired of living life like a double exposure: a little of the real you showing through somebody else's idea of who you are supposed to be?

Good Wishing Gone Bad

Wishes are holy. They have their own integrity and don't like to be tempted with approximations. When we renounce this wishing force, it can turn dark and hostile, bedeviling us with unwanted thoughts that seem alien to the self. Intractable fears and unwanted fantasies can take the place of our original, simpler desires. Freud was right about many fears being nothing more than disguised wishes[27]. We don't like what they may be telling us. Frightened and unsure of our feelings, we may mistrust our wishes even more, not realizing they have come to rescue us.

To whom does your life belong? The answer to this question determines your attitude toward your dreams and wishes. Totalitarian regimes and dictators are found in families and communities everywhere. When your life doesn't belong to you, then your wishes can seem to be a threat to the group's security. *You too will see your wishes as dangerous as long as you do not believe you have the right to a life of your own.* A little ridicule, rejection, or well-placed threat of abandonment and most of us can be persuaded to turn against our deepest wishes.

But your wishes continue to flow only one way. Your mind works like water running through a pipe. Ideas never turn around and flow back up the pipe. Nothing can ever change the direction of an idea's intention, which is to be expressed outward into the world. None of us has a choice about this: it is the way we are built psychologically and spiritually. Fortunately we are not equipped with the means to totally eradicate our wishes.

When you turn against your wishes and push them out of your mind, you are not getting rid of them; you are wounding them. And like any wounded, living thing, our wishes can turn on us. What was originally your innocent childhood need, your constructive intention, can be attacked and rejected to the point where it must fight for its life. And nothing in this state is a very pretty sight. Your wounded wishes may take on forms that are unrecognizable, scaring you with their bizarre appearances, irrational intensity, and obsessive persistence.

Beverly's Story

Beverly had given up much of her own life to take care of others. She had been so loyal to her parents that she gave up her own hopes for a family and put her energies into running her parents' household. She was a loving auntie to her brother's children and had found a kind of peace in her decision not to have a family of her own. But around the time her brother's last child was born, Beverly herself was nearing middle age and beginning to feel the strain of her overly responsible nature. Nevertheless, she agreed to take care of the new baby during the day while her sister-in-law worked. The infant brought delight and stimulation into Beverly's life, and she adored the little boy. She came to see me because of "horrible thoughts" she had begun to have about her nephew. Beverly had started having flashing images about getting rid of the baby. These unwanted and completely alien thoughts shocked her badly and she thought she was losing her mind. I questioned Beverly carefully: she had no intention of harming the child and really was not about to lose control of her impulses, but she was distraught she "could even think of such things!"

Beverly was just paying the cost of her own wounded wishes for freedom. She was not crazy; just trapped like many mothers of demanding newborns. Out of her love and loyalty for her family, Beverly had sacrificed too much of herself, not allowing normal wishes their place in her life. The added responsibility of the baby's care had finally pushed her wishes against the wall, and they responded in the extreme language of destructive imagery. When Beverly realized the source of her disturbing and unwanted fantasies, she calmed down and had some sympathy for herself. Once she grasped the idea that she was just feeling overwhelmed by everyone's needs, the shocking thoughts diminished.

Debbie's Story

Another client, Debbie, was much more self-accepting of her frustration and resentment over caring for a colicky baby who never seemed to sleep. Debbie had no illusions about being able to handle everything on her own and was very much in touch with her wishes for relief. She laughingly told me about her visit to the pediatrician that morning. She told him he'd better give her something to help with this colic because the night before she had dreamed of putting the baby in the oven instead of the Thanksgiving turkey! Your wishes may get quite bizarre and dramatic if you keep tuning them out.

The Innocence of Wishes

Remember that you cannot be expected to take responsibility for that which you find yourself wishing. You have to take responsibility for how you *act* on your wishes, but not for having the wishes. Your wishes and your fantasies come from the psychological realm of who you were meant to be. But this is an amoral, primeval realm, like the mind of childhood. Wishes, like children, resent being neglected, and will always let you know it in no uncertain terms.

If you ever have fantasies or wishes that take on an immoral or scary tone, don't panic. You are a grown-up: just ask yourself the simple question of what it might mean. Your true self may have been forced to put the solution in crude terms, but what if it is trying to tell you about something essential you are neglecting? This can be complicated work, and it is sometimes so hard to see it on our own that a therapist is needed. But short of this step, ask yourself – without horror or judgment – how your life would be different if the dreadful thought came to pass. You might be surprised at the secret sense of relief and freedom it might bring. If you can find the innocent wish behind the "horrible thought," you will be able to find other acceptable outlets for it.

Brainstorming

Finding outlets for your wishes can be a challenge if you have fallen too far into the rut of conventional attitudes. Brainstorming is a way of deliberately being silly and extravagantly imaginative in a way that throws our ego off its high horse so we can get some real work done.

Marcie's Story

I already knew Marcie socially when she approached me to say she was interested in joining the Growth Group. I was taking a break from running the group and had not planned to start another one so soon, but Marcie's tenacity ended up persuading me. When it came time for the group to tackle the topic of wishing and brainstorming, it was clear that Marcie was going to be the group guinea pig.

First we tackled what Marcie was doing with her life so far. Marcie was working hard but none of her energy was being channeled into what she really wished for. Her main job was selling homes in her brother's real estate agency, but she also owned a little hobby store in her small town and did phone sales on the side. We asked Marcie to quickly name all the things she did *not* like about her current job. She came up with: low income, last-minute mortgage crises, dressing up nicely every day, complicated office politics, and an intense atmosphere of competitiveness that constantly sapped Marcie's energy. Hostile clients who blamed her for everything did not help either.

Next we told Marcie to wish out loud for what she wanted in the ideal job situation. Not what the job would be, but what the perfect job would allow her to do. *It is important not to identify the name of the job you want at this stage of the process.* Naming it at this stage is limiting at best and misleading at worst. Even if you have a name for your dream at this point, don't use that label yet. At this stage of wishing and brain-storming, you *first want to describe your ideal situation in as much detail as possible, without actually calling it anything.* So I wrote Marcie's wishes on the blackboard for the group to see:

Lots of money. Few hours. Casual attire
A big, new Ford Explorer
Wants to feel she's helping someone
Wants to feel done at the end of the day. No weekends, no nights
All the modern conveniences she needs (fax, computer, etc.)
An aide or helper at her beck and call
Flexibility to come and go, freedom to be outside
Freedom to bring dog to work and talk to friends on the phone
    while at work

Next we covered her list, and had Marcie list the occupations she had been considering for her career change. Then we compared her wish list with the occupations she had been considering to see if any of them seemed to fit. Some of her ideas included teaching physical fitness, pursuing a physical therapist degree, becoming a nutritionist, and getting a job as a health educator. She had also thought about being a driving instructor, fixing up houses, or becoming a building contractor.

Now here is where the pure self-honesty has to come in. Which one of these potential occupations fit Marcie's wish list best? I told Marcie to be boldly honest about which one of the occupations jumped off the board at her, whether she liked it or not. She hesitated, then slowly said, "Building contractor." It was clear from her embarrassed expression that she would much rather have chosen "nutritionist" or "physical therapist." Marcie really, truly wanted to see herself as the kind of selfless person who wanted nothing more than to help people. But that self-sacrificing ideal was an ill-fitting shoe.

The simple, hard-to-face truth was that Marcie needed to be her own boss, an entrepreneur who made things happen and told other people what to do. It was her deepest nature, and had already peeked out its entrepreneurial face in the form of her hobby shop venture. However, Marcie was deeply ambivalent about this aspect of herself, and she looked profoundly uncomfortable when the group came up with the inescapable conclusion: Marcie needed to be the boss.

One of the other group members told Marcie that she had seen the look on her face when she listed "contractor" and had known immediately that was the one Marcie loved. Anything that allowed her to be the take-charge, free boss of her own projects would fit the bill, but her real estate career had been requiring her to passively serve the needs of her customers. No wonder she was so miserable. But Marcie felt ashamed of her wishes to be in charge, cringing as she said, "I don't want to be a steamroller!"

"But," I said to her, "is it any better to pretend you are a washing machine, when you really *are* a steamroller?"

Marcie was afraid to let go of the more "feminine" role of service that she thought her loved ones expected of her. She did not want to run the risk of becoming too different from her family's norm. Marcie could justify leaving the family real estate business for a lifetime of selfless service to others, but to leave in order to create her own business seemed downright competitive and conceited. Shouldn't she instead stay in her brother's business and help him (serve him) first? If she had an interest in business, wouldn't she be more of a "good person" if she devoted her energies to her brother's success? Here was Marcie's dilemma in full bloom. Yet for that hour in the group, Marcie awakened and left feeling buoyant and excited about the prospect of finding a way to do contracting work.

However, the ego makes it hard to resist those fears, and Marcie was no exception. A week later, she told me that after several days of feeling on a high from her radical self-discovery, she had recoiled back into doubt and fear. She was just too dependent, she was just too afraid, etc., etc. I knew that Marcie had already stepped out on her path to the future, because the others and I had seen her excitement during that group session. Marcie and her ego could deny it for as long as she needed to, but the "boss" in her was not going away. It was just going to take some time to accept.

About two months later, I ran into Marcie again and she was glowing with excitement. She had not quit her job, but she had bought an old house to renovate and sell. Her love of setting things up, scheduling, and telling people what to do now had its potentially profitable outlet. Marcie had taken the step out into the gap of true growth, moving toward who she really was.

The Ego's Final Exam

In an earlier chapter, I told you how the ego likes to jump in and knock down your excitement by asking you the *one* question that deflates everything. This is what I think of as the ego's "final exam" question. Here you are, barely half-baked and tender as a pudding, in the first stages of discovering your true self, and along comes the ego demanding to know how in the world this measly mush of new selfhood is going to withstand the latest worst-case scenario it has just dreamed up. You have barely enrolled in the full-credit course of self-development, and the ego has hightailed it to your side to put you to the final test. If this is really the right path for you, the ego will say, then you surely must have all the skills right *now*. And then it will proceed to present the hardest, most challenging, and stickiest questions any human being has ever faced, as though to mock your resolve with your own inexperience.

All you have to say is: **It is not time to take my final exam yet.**

There is not one of us who would not fail the ego's final exam question if we agreed to take it at the wrong time. It tempts our conceit with its urgency, telling us that if we really had the potential, we would be able to give the right answer. But do not even attempt to answer the ego on this one. Final exams do not belong at the beginning of any course, when there is not yet any mastery there to test. You have time to develop the mastery. Don't let the ego rush you into a feeling of failure.

Marcie's Setback

After Marcie's initial elation over beginning her house renovation project, she was hit with her ego's final exam whammy several months later. At that point I ran into Marcie and asked her how the house project was going. Tears welled up in her eyes, and she told me she felt totally stuck and hopeless about ever getting out from under her family's control. Marcie explained that she had gotten her dad to agree to underwrite her project as an investment, with the result that she now felt dependent on him for every new bill that came up. It killed her to have to go back to him over and over for the cash to do the next step. Before she could act on the obvious solution of asking her father for a lump sum deposit, her ego got the jump on her. "Obviously you have failed," sneered her ego, "what self-respecting contractor goes to daddy for every nickel? If you were really cut out for this, you'd be able to do it all without any help." In effect, her ego was labeling the situation as her final exam, the make-or-break moment in her life. If she did not do this one according to the book, she was about to get an "F."

Even though Marcie had gotten caught up in the *feeling* that she was failing, she really wasn't. Looking at her situation from the outside, charting her movement along the track, anyone could see how far she actually had come. Her instinctive choice to include her father had been a perfect next-step. She was solving her central dilemma: how can I be my true self and still keep my ties to my family? By asking for her father's support in the pursuit of her authentic dream, she was using her old life in service of the new. She was building solidly on her past to bring about a new future. Marcie was also tacitly reassuring her family that she was not rejecting them and that she still valued their help. When Marcie's dad agreed, whether he knew it or not, he was giving her his blessing and literally betting on his daughter's potential.

What's the Experience You Want to Have Every Day?

This is the most helpful question you can ask yourself to clarify your true wishes. It is what we were making Marcie answer in the group that evening. It's the one question that ensures you will not settle for something you really don't love. If you do not want to do something *every* day, then a lifetime of it won't do, will it? If Marcie could drive around in a big new Ford Explorer, with her dog, dressed in casual clothes, and tell people what to do, she would be in heaven. She knew she would want to do that every single day.

Asking yourself this question will quickly separate out the real from the ideal. There may be many things you wish for that originated in an outgrown childhood longing and that would never hold your *adult* interest day in and day out. Or you may discover that the demands of your dream are much greater than you ever imagined, and so you put the old wish to bed with relief.

Tanya's Story

Tanya was a client of mine who could not give up on a disappointing relationship with her drug-abusing boyfriend. Tanya had no interest in doing drugs herself, and she was stuck on the hope that this young man with so much potential might kick his weaknesses and start a worthwhile life. As she talked about her dreams for how their life could be once he was no longer dependent on drugs, Tanya began to see something she had never realized before. She began to have the uneasy feeling that this was a *very* familiar fantasy, one that started way before this boyfriend – in fact, way before she was even old enough to have boyfriends. Tanya realized that she was being driven by the wishful fantasy life of her six-year-old self, who had so many plans for what her family would do when her daddy finally stopped drinking. Tanya had never given up that childhood determination to reform her father and thereby save the family from the high cost of his drinking and irresponsibility. It was a genuine wish, but it was the genuine wish of a frightened little girl. Reforming an intoxicated man was no longer what she wanted to do every day now that she was an adult with choices.

What Do You *Not* Want to Do Every Single Day?
If you are sorely out of practice with knowing what you want, your soul's desire might come a little clearer if you ask yourself what you do *not* want.

In this way, finding your true wishes is a little more like sculpting stone than painting a picture. You are trying to chisel away what you know you don't want, in order to get a rough idea of what you do. With a wishing function that is badly out of shape, you may need to start slowly with simply identifying what is making you miserable. It can often happen that something that used to bring you great pleasure and meaning in your life changes to the point where you no longer even enjoy it. You begin to realize that you do *not* want to do this every day anymore.

Marsha's Story

Marsha, a depressed woman with whom I worked, was overjoyed when at forty-two she finally got pregnant with her second child. Marsha had looked forward to all the wonderful moments with the new baby that she remembered with her first child, who was now nearing adolescence. All her feelings of depression and aimlessness improved as she enjoyed looking forward to being an infant's mother again. When the baby arrived, Marsha was dismayed that she continued to feel so unfulfilled. She could not understand it. Marsha had wanted another baby for so long, but now she was feeling restless and trapped.

Marsha had the hard job of accepting that her wishes had changed, as she herself had changed over the past ten years. It wasn't another baby that she was longing for after all. Marsha loved the new child of course, but her new daughter was not the answer Martha thought she would be. Instead Marsha turned her attention inward, seeking out more secret longings, and found she had a hidden desire to write. What she discovered was that her dream was to write a book. She took a writing class and began opening up a mid-life change that included being a mother, but was no longer solely defined by that wish.

Ben's Story

Ben, a middle-aged businessman, also decided to follow his dream to write a book and his delving lead him to a different conclusion than Marsha's. He finally went to a two-day intensive workshop on how to write and get published and at the end of the experience went up to the instructor and thanked him profusely. "I now know," he said with relief, "that there is no way I could ever stand the life of a writer. Thank you! Now I don't have to go on wondering if that's what I should have been doing with my life"[28].

Getting your outdated wishes out of the way is very much a part of the growth process. What you really want right now, with these life experiences and these resources, may bear scant resemblance to what would have thrilled you years ago. We all are constantly undergoing psychological development during our lives; it does not stop in our twenties. By asking yourself what experiences you want and what you do not want to have *every single day,* you can be sure your wishes are firmly rooted in who you really are now. Nobody can keep up a daily interest in something that is not coming from his or her core.

The old saying of "Be careful what you wish for, you may get it" gets at this psychological truth. If we are not deeply enough attuned to what we really want and what is really important in our lives *right now,* then we are likely to wish for something that has become outdated without our conscious knowledge. Like anything else, wishes have a shelf life and don't stay fresh forever. If you are still reflexively wishing for something that should have expired a long time ago, you may end up getting what you no longer want.

Risky Business

Once you have revived your wishing function and have even gotten some practice in brainstorming the kinds of experiences you do – and do not – want to have every single day, then there is the need for some action. Barbara Sher, in her book, *Wishcraft*[29], talks about finding the perfect baby step that will start you on your path toward your dream. She encourages you to find the step that you can actually take tomorrow in order to get you started. It may be as simple as a phone call or looking at ads online; if you look for it, there is always a step you can take right now.

Sooner or later – as you will see on the Map of Growth in the next chapter – there comes a time when tiny baby steps are no longer sufficient, and a great step with a significant risk begins to loom in front of us. It is that moment, described earlier, when we are faced with the need to step out onto the swinging, cloud-shrouded bridge *before* we can clearly see the other side.

Ask yourself what your typical response to risk is. Everyone has a different tolerance for risk but, for the most part, none of us wants more of it than is necessary to meet our goals. Even thrill seekers want to enjoy their risks with enough safety built in that they are around to keep enjoying their thrills. But for our purposes here, just ask yourself how you usually respond to risky situations. We are after some self-analysis of *how* you cope with risk, not how *much* you fear risk. When you have to take any kind of risk in order to keep following your dream, what is your gut reaction? And then what do you do?

If you are like me, for instance, you might feel overwhelmed, scared to death, and then procrastinate like crazy. Other people might eat, drink, shop, or call their mothers. Whatever you typically do, take a moment and write down right now how *you* react to risk. Because this is what your ego will use to stop you.

In light of recovering your ability to wish for changes in your life – what risk is really all about – ask yourself, what fear is this risk stirring up in your primal, tribal, childhood self? It is probably saying something along the lines that you are putting your life in danger, you are not very capable or strong, and it's a jungle out there. Risk is also about inviting you to become a board-certified adult, to take responsibility for how your life turns out. That's a showstopper right there, isn't it? Taking a risk doesn't have to be big or dangerous to have a powerful psychological effect on us. Often it is those little risks that reveal how different we are from our families that scare us the most.

Sandy's Story

I had been working with Sandy for many months on her penchant for picking men who inevitably ended up leaving her. Sandy was a pretty, petite woman who was turning forty and had no man to share her life with. Her longterm relationships stayed just that: long-term relationships, without an ultimate commitment. Sandy had been married for a few years, but she was not surprised when her husband left because she could never quite understand what that handsome, successful man ever saw in her in the first place. Since then Sandy had dated a lot, but no commitments had materialized. She was confused and frustrated because consciously she longed for someone with whom she could share her otherwise happy, active life.

Who would think that being willing to have a happy, committed relationship was taking a risk? But for Sandy, it was. She had always worried a great deal about her mother, who had suffered from chronic depression since Sandy's early childhood. Her marriage to Sandy's father had been a miserable one, and yet everyone kept going through the paces. One day I asked Sandy what she might be risking if she were to find a man to marry. Of course, she could see no risk at all in such a wonderful outcome, but I pressed her to think of the big picture. What would such a change in her life mean to everyone she cared about?

What began to emerge was the realization that finding committed happiness with a man would only serve to highlight her mother's unhappy life. Sandy risked losing the deepest part of her connection with her mother if she renounced her own depressive attitudes and claimed happiness and contentment. Above all, Sandy did not want her mother to feel more abandoned or worthless than she already felt. The joy of announcing an engagement or planning a wedding would be a cruel contrast to her mother's emotionally barren life.

Sandy's story shows how *anything,* even the thing we say we want more than anything else, can be secretly perceived as a dangerous risk which could hurt us or someone we love. Deep down, we might see what looks to others like avoiding happiness as a sensible avoidance of enormous risk to the balance of our family loyalties.

As long as Sandy gave up happiness to protect her mother's feelings, she was never going to find the "right" man. First of all, Sandy had to think long and hard about the subconscious loyalty vow she had unwittingly made to her mother, in which she pledged not to become *too* happy. Sandy's challenge was to come to grips with the need to take the risk of leaving her unhappy mother behind, at least enough to live her own life.

Barnstorming

Barnstorming was an old flying pastime that can be a model for taking risks in our own lives. Daring pilots would go up in their small planes and fly them low and fast right toward something big like a barn. Charging, or storming, the barn in an airplane looked like imminent catastrophe, and of course, crowds loved the make-believe challenge. At the last minute the pilot would pull back and narrowly evade a collision. Nobody expected the pilot to actually crash the plane into the barn; the thrill was in watching him narrowly avert the disaster. It was playing with risk for fun. Why did people stand around, watch, and get such pleasure from seeing someone else take risks? Because *everyone* wanted the experience of a brush with mortal danger. They experienced the thrill of watching one person, all by himself, totally on his own, take his life in his hands and fight the fear. This is what made those shows so compelling. It was the flying symbol of being in control of your own life and taking responsibility for your split-second decisions.

You too can barnstorm, by making breathtaking passes at things you want. The point is not to crash and burn, but to muster your courage and get *really* near the thing that scares you the most. Give yourself a thrill by calling someone you never thought you would have the nerve to call. (It still counts if they aren't home.) Order an entree you desire but can't pronounce. Inquire about a job that is out of your reach. Nominate yourself for a position to which you are sure you would never get elected. Tell a parent or authority figure you're planning on being a great success one of these days. Swoop and roar down the field of life for fun, feel your engines burn and the ground rush past. Then pull up sharp and leave it all behind. This kind of barnstorming is a wonderful, courage-building game. The point is not to be brave enough to crash into anything, the point is to *approach* something (or someone) you are really afraid of and make a close pass. It will put the hero energy back in your heart. You will feel the thrill of rushing at the thing that seems so big and scary and then at the last second swerving away and not crashing after all.

This is the kind of play that all young mammals do in their preparation for adult life and its challenges. In their contests of dominance, they act like they are going for blood, but at the last minute they stop. The point of such play, for animals or humans, is not to win at any cost, nor to injure ourselves or others, but only to practice the thrill of coming close to the real thing. It ripens our skills and bravery. Like barnstorming, it may only be a game, but *we* know, when we have tested ourselves and lived through it, that we can go on to the real contest.

Testing yourself is important preparation for the time when your bravery will count, when the stakes may be real. Don't wait for the big day to learn how it feels. Play around with the concept now. It may only be in the barn of your imagination, but the same principles will train you to defend yourself in the ultimate contest. If you don't get used to taking little risks in a playful way, you may lose your nerve and back off just when the chance of a lifetime is about to show up.

Even on smallest risk-takings, it is crucial to *consciously* recognize that you have taken a risk. When you know that you have taken a risk – even if it is one of the silly, little ones suggested earlier – you get to put that experience under your belt. "Remember how scared I was to...?" becomes exactly the kind of memory that makes the next hurdle a little less intimidating. It does you no good to take the risks and then minimize them in your own mind. Take full credit for them. Savor them, put gold stars next to your name and then add them to your resumé as a grown-up risk-taker.

Section II

Developing Your Adult Destiny Despite Present Obstacles

CHAPTER 7

WHAT STANDS IN YOUR WAY?

You have an appointment with who you were meant to be, but many things can keep you from reaching that appointment on time.

Ellen hated her tight-fitting life, but was too scared to make a move. Every time she wanted to try something new, she ran into an obstacle. Sometimes it was interference from her demanding husband. Other times it was panic attacks. Ellen made plan after plan, only to give up when she suddenly and inexplicably felt scared, guilty, or exhausted. For a long time Ellen seesawed between dreams and disappointments. She reversed this frustrating pattern only when she began to understand how her overactive empathy and fear of being alone were holding her back in a way that mere outside obstacles could never do.

Despite her trepidation, Ellen's dream of having her own career excited her. After being a homemaker for years, she plotted her escape into the world of paychecks and job titles. However, too often Ellen acted as though her dreams were unattainable. Motivation and self-doubt wrestled within her. Some days she was exhilarated and other days it all felt impossible. Finally she decided that no matter what, she was going to pursue the job she wanted. One thing after another blocked her way, as though mocking her new resolve.

Ellen's husband expected her to accompany him on a business trip to the West Coast just when she was scheduled for group aptitude testing for a new position. Her mother cautioned her against taking on "too much." Her daughter began to have marital problems. Her cat got sick. She asked herself, *How am I supposed to do anything for myself with all this going on?*

Ellen's mind, which had embraced hope for a new future, was now cluttered with worries about other people and even animals. Ellen slumped back into her well-worn role of worrying about others.

However, despite this detour, Ellen had started on her way. She had begun to progress along a route with an appointed destination, even if it seemed that she kept breaking down by the side of the road. Her dissatisfaction with her present life kept spurring her on. It seemed such a small thing, getting a new job, but for Ellen, it was about who she was meant to be: an independent adult with an income of her own.

Like Ellen, you have an appointment with who you were meant to be. Many things can keep you from reaching that appointment on time. In this chapter we're going to look together at some of the things that may be currently holding you back. There are many reasons for not going after what we want, but the one we all know best is fear.

The Big Fear

You may be afraid to gain what you want. Success can stir up our biggest fears. For each one of us, the Big Fear wears a different form, shaped by what has happened to us in the past. It might be abandonment, loneliness, punishment, or disapproval, to name just a few. When we give up and back off from our dream, we may unconsciously breathe a sigh of relief at having eluded the Big Fear yet again. If you have repeatedly backed away from your dreams, it is quite likely that you have been avoiding the Big Fear.

The Big Fear is what we feel when we come up against the wall that blocks us from our original motivation. Emotional pain and fear built that protective wall for us in childhood, and we can be very reluctant to break through it. We don't want to be brought back into contact with the painful or frightening thing that made us give up our motivation in the first place. We do not realize that as adults we may still be protecting ourselves from childhood fears that we now have the resources to overcome easily.

A successful and accomplished friend of mine once told me: "All this good stuff is coming into my life, but the feeling I'm having is exactly as if something bad is about to happen." It is the biggest irrational fear there is: if I get what I want, something terrible will happen. Your Big Fear is as unique to you as your fingerprint, but it probably falls under one of these types of fears:

- **You might fail and expose your deep inadequacies, shamefully revealing that you do not have what it takes.**

- **You might suffer a huge loss.**

- **You may die.**

- **You may contract a life-threatening illness.**

- **Someone you care about might die.**

In other words, your fear tells you that you'll pay dearly for becoming a truly individual self who wants to leave home and start his or her own life.

These fears are exactly what our unconscious mind serves up when we approach the forbidden arena of what we really want to do. Visions of humiliation and tragedy are laid before us in our daydreams and weaken our resolve. Often this is blamed on God or fate, as we encounter this primitive part of our mind. If we are going to push past our fears, then we have to take a good look at what this ancient, eye-for-an-eye part of the brain is threatening us with.

It's crucial to realize the childhood origin of our fear. It originates in the insecurity of a child who did not feel it was safe to grow.

Many people never get to the Big Fear stage, because there are so many effective defenses to prevent you from getting that far. For instance, you might feel bored or uninspired. You may feel guilty and resolve to give up this foolishness. And you might never realize that the purpose of these reactions was just to protect yourself from going too far. It is a very positive sign if you have managed to become aware of this fear consciously. It means that you have pushed your comfort zone past the point of old defenses, rendering you much more open to growth than you were before.

One point to emphasize here is that big steps forward in our development often confront us with anxieties about death. Fears of heart attacks or illness, breathing problems, or a morbid preoccupation with one's mortality are just a few of the symptoms that can pop up when a person is getting close to making a big shift toward growth. This is the inevitable subconscious imagery which heralds a transformation, as the old ways "die" in order to make room for a new way of being[30]. Remember, your subconscious mind speaks the truth, but uses drastic images to get your attention. When you are going through a period of great change, do not be alarmed by dreams and fantasies with death themes.

Cosmic Consequences

Are you afraid of what will happen if you begin to get the things you want? What would happen if you let yourself feel the full exhilaration of happiness? Do you think the fates will applaud, or will they become envious and destructive toward you? And what about God? Will He take you down a notch or two if you get too full of yourself? These secret beliefs about the cosmic consequences of our success can be very powerful. People often pull back from success just as they are beginning to feel really fulfilled, and yet have no idea why they are sabotaging themselves. When I ask clients about this, they often explain that some things are just too good to be true or that nothing good lasts forever. It's clear to me as an outside observer that *they* are stopping themselves. They act as if something or someone is just waiting to sock it to them if they go too far.

"God's Gonna Get Me"

Amy had reached the point in therapy where she was finally pursuing the activities she loved. She had time for them because she no longer allowed her life to be dominated by pushy friends and family members. Amy was happier than she could ever remember. But after the initial rush of excitement, she began to struggle with guilt and fear over enjoying herself so much. She soon managed to create misery out of her own happiness!

In our sessions together, Amy finally discovered her belief that if she really attained her desires, God was going to punish her. Amy was embarrassed to say this, but it was the truth. In her mind, happiness and divine punishment went hand in hand. It only made sense for her to withdraw from her joy before she pushed it too far. As far as Amy was concerned, enjoying her happiness was like putting a sign around her neck that said, "Strike me dead!"

Amy did not want to believe that God was waiting around up there, tapping a big bat on the ground, ready to wallop her for getting too big for her britches. However, the dread was persistent, making her feel extremely vulnerable whenever she started enjoying herself When this feeling became too uncomfortable, Amy would give up and retreat into a bout of depression, effectively neutralizing the temptation she was presenting for God to punish her.

As Amy and I talked about these feelings, we began to see how her beliefs about God were confused with memories of her reproachful mother and sanctimonious older sister. There was not much happiness in her family. Her parents overworked themselves, and her sister was resentful about having to take care of the younger children. In Amy's mind if she relaxed and enjoyed moments of play, her mother or sister might swoop down on her with accusations of laziness and selfishness. The message was clear: life was *not* something to be enjoyed. Only hard work was respectable and legitimate. Amy had been told outright as a child that if she did not always put other people first, then terrible things would happen to her in the future. God would punish her for being so lazy and inconsiderate.

The truth was that it was Amy's family members who were punitive and envious of her happiness, not God. As Amy began to realize this, her fear lessened, and she was able to enjoy herself more. Amy learned that the lightning bolt never hit, and instead of turning into a shiftless, selfish egoist as she feared, she actually became a more naturally generous and productive person.

Jack's Story

This fearful vision of a vengeful rather than loving God afflicts many people. Another client, Jack, confessed his fear that "the dark hand of God" would surely smash his plans if he allowed himself to get too carried away with enthusiasm. Jack traced this image back to a childhood humiliation that had a tremendous impact on the way he was to live his life.

When Jack was a spunky five-year-old, he loved to accompany his father to his construction worksites. Jack could barely contain his excitement and pride when the workmen noticed him and joked with his father about his new helper. One day, full of himself and hanging out the truck window as they drove up, Jack blurted out a cheeky, exuberant greeting to one of the workmen, making a silly word play on the workman's name.

Out of nowhere, his father's hand shot out and popped Jack hard on the back of the head for his disrespect. Jack was shattered. His father's blow came out of nowhere with no warning, just like Divine punishment. Ever afterward he remembered the intense shame of being hit in front of the workmen and how confused he felt. Jack learned to be more reserved. He still had fun with his father and enjoyed their outings, but he was always careful not to get too carried away. If he felt too sure of himself, too on top of the world, he was sure the dark hand of God could strike again and he would not have any more warning than he had the first time.

Fearing Our Joy

It is a tragedy when we as little children learn that to be fully and freely ourselves might lead to being hurt by someone. Yet this is a very common occurrence in many homes for many children. They learn that to be joyful and confident means that bad times are right around the corner, because in their unhappy family, that was true. When children unfortunately make a connection between feelings of joy and fears of punishment, a lifelong avoidance of "too much" happiness is instilled. They learn that if they are quieter, ask for less, stop bouncing off the walls with big ideas and loud laughter, their parents will be less volatile or depressed. This reinforces the sad idea that it was their exuberant emotional state that was the problem.

Does this ring any bells? Do you hold yourself back from happiness when it comes, because you don't want something bad to take it all away? If so, this is a signal for you to start learning it is no longer dangerous to feel safe and happy in your world. It is now within your grown-up power to break that erroneous learning connection as often as you can. Have the courage to enjoy your happiness a little longer each time you experience it than you have before.

The Foreshortened Future

When we have suffered life-altering emotional injuries or trauma, it is common to feel paralyzed by a pessimistic view of the future. Trauma makes many of us project the past onto the future, giving us the feeling that a disaster is just waiting to happen[31]. A client of mine once described it as "waiting for the other shoe to drop." He thought he was anticipating the future when what he was really doing was *expecting his past*. He didn't realize he was turned around backwards.

Along with anticipation of disaster, trauma survivors do not expect to have much of a future. This sense of a foreshortened future is a hallmark of Post Traumatic Stress Syndrome. It is the symptom most likely to disrupt a person's willingness to plan for the future and take reasonable risks for greater future gain.

If we view our future apprehensively because of a difficult past, it helps a great deal to have some objective information about the normal challenges of personal growth. Everybody's growth process gets bogged down at points. However, if we do not know this, we may take setbacks too seriously, thus confirming a trauma-based, pessimistic view of our future. When we understand how growth works, we can use this knowledge to tolerate and navigate the process. Instead of predicting a foreshortened future for ourselves, we can realize that things are radically different from the past.

Remember Ellen and her obstacles, from the beginning of this chapter? Ellen did not need comforting and encouragement so much as she needed information. She needed a map to show her what to expect from growth. She needed a way to understand what she was doing and what all those obstacles were really about. Without that awareness, she could not see that she actually had come a long way, and was merely experiencing the very common setbacks that hit all of us when we begin to take action. Without a map to tell her what to expect, Ellen could take her setbacks too seriously, and get needlessly demoralized about her future.

The Map of Growth

If you were on a trip, would you get hopeless about ever arriving at your destination simply because you looked at a map and saw you were still ten miles from where you were going? You probably would not pull off on the side of the road and feel despondent because you were not already within a half-mile of your destination.

But when it comes to following our dreams and our longed-for purpose in life, we often act just that irrationally. We do the equivalent of looking at a roadmap to see how to get to a nearby city, only to collapse in despair because we have to drive all that way and stop at so many traffic lights. It's hopeless, we say metaphorically, and turn around to go back home. We say to ourselves that if our dream is going to take this long or require this many stops on the way, it is not worth it – as if instantaneous materialization at our destination is the only thing for which we'll settle. Of course, the information given by a real map would not depress us; we would simply adjust our expectations based on the realistic information it gave us.

Having a mental map allows you to see where you are and what has to come next. The map of growth that follows gives you insight into where you may have become blocked. It allows you to see growth as a practical and obtainable process, not as a mystical transformation that some people achieve and some do not. Let's take a look at this map and its highpoints.

Map of Growth

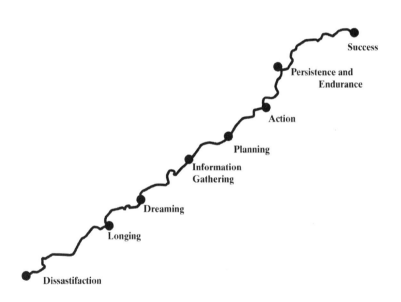

The following are the basic stops on our growth map, just like towns we would pass through on a journey toward fulfilling our dream:

1. At the outset, you first become aware of **dissatisfaction.** A highly important area of your life is not giving you what you need. You realize there is a poor match between who you want to be, and where you find yourself. You are tired of what you have been putting up with.

2. Soon after this point, you become aware of a feeling of **longing.** You may not know exactly what you are longing for, but you definitely have the feeling that *something is missing* from your life.

3. You then start noticing that you are **dreaming** of something different for your life. You cannot stop fantasizing about what you would like to do. You are strictly at the level of daydreaming at this point.

4. Before long, you begin to wonder about specifics. What would be necessary for you to follow this idea? How would one go about pursuing such a goal? You become curious enough to take the big step of **collecting information.** This can take any number of forms, but might include telephone calls, trips to the library or bookstore, talking to friends, observing people in work settings, or checking out ideas on the internet. Collecting information includes anything that involves learning about things you're interested in.

5. With the new information in hand, you begin putting together a rough **plan** for your goal, which may or may not be very clearly defined at this point. Making your first plan will probably be a messy, inaccurate affair, resulting in ideas that may be very vague and rough around the edges. Your thoughts will refine themselves as you collect more information.

6. Finally you are ready to take **action** toward reaching your new goal. You continue looking for opportunities to adjust and fine-tune your plan as new information comes in.

7. Be aware of what to expect next: as soon as you enter the planning and take-action stages, you will encounter challenges and obstacles, just as Ellen did. Therefore, the next step on your map requires you to practice **persistence** and **endurance** as you continue to work on your plan and take action in spite of resistance.

8. **Success** occurs when the state of longing and dissatisfaction has lifted and you feel you are living your dream instead of daydreaming about it. Success feels like you are there. The old daydreaming and wistful longings are gone, and the ghost of unfulfillment no longer haunts your life. There is no longer a neglected part of yourself standing on the sidelines, longing to get into the game.

Take a moment now and pinpoint where you think *you* are in this process. Make a mark on the map at that location so you can see the stage at which you are working.

Marking your location on the growth map is important, because it tells you what your current issues are likely to be. It also tells you what the next step has to be. For instance, Jillian had trouble figuring out what she wanted to do because all she knew was that she wanted to be successful, live at the beach, and make a lot of money, but she had no idea what kind of work she wanted to do. She had progressed through the stage of **dissatisfaction** (with a low paying job in the city) and **longing** (she knew the kind of lifestyle she wanted), but she had leapfrogged over the **dreaming** stage straight to her vision of **success.** There she was stuck, fantasizing her desirable lifestyle but having no specific idea of which direction to take in order to get there.

None of these sticking points is worse than another. Anyone can get stymied anywhere along the way. It does not matter if your problem is letting yourself begin to daydream, or letting yourself enjoy the fruits of your success. If you stop, you stop. If your goal is to reach the destination of who you were meant to be, then the fact that you are two miles from your goal is just as much an incompletion as if you had stopped two hundred miles away. Believe me, people have gone right up to their last year in college, their last licensing exam, their last interview for the job, and backed out. At a deep level, they believed an insurmountable obstacle stood in their way. Often a *panic attack* is behind these choke moments.

Panic Attacks

Unfortunately, at any stage of our growth, we can encounter **panic attacks.** These moments of lost faith and pure dread are created out of:

- **inner conflicts made up of guilt, fear, and shame.**

- **demoralization, with discouragement and loss of nerve.**

- **acute discomfort with new changes in your life.**

You could experience any of these roadblocks at any point: at the outset, in the dissatisfaction stage, or all the way at the end, when you might have trouble coping with your success.

Sam could never get past the **dissatisfaction** stage to the stage of **longing,** because he kept telling himself he should be happy with his good-paying job and lovely family. Any longings for something more were instantly met with suppression, as Sam guiltily chastised himself "for even thinking something like that."

Ashanti, on the other hand, had a relatively easy time of deciding how she wanted to change her life, and what educational steps she would have to take to achieve her goal. However, she froze up in fear and felt depressed when her intelligence, high grades, and maturity led her professors to recommend her for a fellowship in her graduate school program. In this way, Ashanti almost stopped herself at the **success** stage. She temporarily lost her nerve and was sure she would be exposed as an intellectual fraud if she accepted her mentors' confident expectations of her. Fortunately, Ashanti pushed ahead anyway and proved her professors right.

It is tremendously important to know where you are on the map of growth. Ashanti found it much easier to go ahead and take the fellowship when she could see how far she had come and what her conflict was about. Using the map, Sam could have felt reassured that longing and daydreaming were only the barest beginnings of growth, and were nowhere near actual life changes. He could have known that it's possible to play with feelings and fantasies without *ever* moving into planning or action. If you are not familiar with the map, however, you might think that a harmless daydream could mean that you are on your way out of your marriage or in danger of quitting your job.

Panic can hit us anywhere along the map of growth. When it occurs, we become paralyzed by such uncomfortable feelings that we would do anything to feel better, including giving up our desire for change. All panic is designed to make you take evasive action. The instinct is to run, to escape, no matter what. Thinking shuts down and automatic reaction takes over. Panic reactions can happen anywhere on the route of growth, but they can take on a different quality depending upon where they occur in the process.

There are two points on the map that are most likely to stir up feelings of panic, overexcitement, and turbulence in your life. As you can see from the following diagram, one is right before the **action** step and the other is during the **persistence** stage, before success is achieved.

When you are entering the **action** stage of your dream goal, your sense of anxiety and self-doubt may reach higher levels than you thought possible.

Map of Growth

Success

Persistence and
Endurance

Action

Planning

Information
Gathering

Dreaming

Longing

Dissastifaction

Roadblocks ("panic attacks") can occur at any point and include:

- inner conflicts, such as guilt, fear, shame

- demoralization, loss of nerve, discouragement

- acute discomfort with new changes in your life

Fears of *embarrassment* and *exposure* are paramount at the action stage, because action brings you out of hiding to declare who you really want to become. You may dread ridicule, loss of support, anger, or misunderstanding from loved ones at this point, and it may feel to you as though one thing after another is getting between you and your goal.

However, once you have taken action on your plans and have entered into the stage of **persistence and endurance,** another kind of panic can set in, which feels more like despair than anxiety. It is at this point that people encounter what the mystics have called the dark night of the soul. It is a testing time, when a new way of life hangs in the balance and you have no way of knowing how things are going to turn out. It is a time of excruciating uncertainty, and many people get stuck indefinitely trying to avoid this make-it-or-break-it stage.

Laura's Story

This happened to Laura, one of my clients, in conjunction with her artwork. Laura had been eager to find some way out of her boring job and into the art world. One day, a family friend offered her the opportunity to produce specialty pieces of sculpture to display and sell in his coffee house, which was located in a part of town renowned for attracting just the kind of artistic, well-heeled clientele Laura needed. By the time she told me about it in one of our sessions, she had been dragging her feet for weeks. Laura had come right up to the brink of success, but now was paralyzed into non-productivity. She was dismayed by her loss of motivation, and had not been able to come up with a single inspiration for even a few simple pieces.

As we talked, Laura agreed to try to pin down her greatest fear over the situation. The worst thing that she could envision happening, it turned out, was that her sculptures would go on display and no one would buy them. While this would certainly be disappointing, Laura saw it as a life catastrophe that must be avoided at all costs, even if it meant giving up this marvelous opportunity.

Laura believed that if she put her dream on the line and failed, that would mean the end of her art. Laura loved art; it gave meaning and joy to her life, and was the only occupation she knew she would enjoy totally. If no one wanted her sculptures, Laura thought she would have to interpret this as meaning she was not an "artist" and therefore should stop creating – a personal loss she could not bear. No wonder she was stuck. We worked to open up this situation in Laura's mind, so that she no longer believed that the future of her creativity had to hinge on this single venture.

We all encounter these now-or-never moments. Often these are times when we think our future depends on someone else's reaction or acceptance. We feel like the gladiator in the arena, caught in the unspeakable moment before the crowd roars its approval – or lets us die. The vulnerability we feel at this point is not for the fainthearted and many people turn back. However, if you have a map, you can see how far you've come. It helps to know that you cannot suffer a level of angst like Laura's unless you have already progressed a great distance.

The Attitude Inventory:

How Hard is it for You to Have What You Want?

Your past experiences have exerted a strong effect on your attitudes about yourself, and what you expect from life. Let's explore some of your attitudes to see if you are creating obstacles to your personal growth. The attitude inventory that follows is not any kind of formal clinical test. Its purpose is simply to make you aware of some attitudes that may be interfering with your growth into who you were meant to be. Answer the questions by circling either true or false. Don't spend too much time on any one question; it is better to answer them quickly.

ATTITUDE INVENTORY

For each statement below, circle **T** if the statement is true, or usually true, about you. If the statement is false, or not usually true, about you, circle **F**.

1. **I often feel that I am not living my true purpose in life.**   T   F

2. **I feel like I need the "okay" from loved ones before I start something new.**   T   F

3. **I find myself often having angry, critical thoughts about both myself and other people, even if I am acting nicely.**   T   F

4. **I get discouraged quite easily.**   T   F

5. **It doesn't seem right to be happy when people I am close to are still suffering.**   T   F

6. **I try not to spend too much time on wishful thinking.**   T   F

7. The happier I get, the more I start wondering when
   something bad will happen.   T   F

8. I am afraid of being seen as selfish.   T   F

9. I can remember many times when I did the opposite
   of what I *knew* I wanted.   T   F

10. I am afraid of causing a bunch of big problems in my
    life if I tackle a new direction.   T   F

11. It's hard to be truly myself with the people I am
    around the most.   T   F

12. I think I have always know what I wanted to do,
    but it seems impossibly out of reach.   T   F

Now that you have completed your attitude assessment, let's score it. Your score is only meant to give you a rough idea of the degree to which you have had difficulties in finding your true purpose in life. Go down the column of statements and count how many *True* statements you circled. This number is your raw score. Use the following chart to identify your attitude toward growth.

1 – 3   *Mild worries about effects of personal growth*

4 – 6   *Moderate frustration in achieving personal growth*

7 – 9   *Serious self-doubts about growth potential*

10 – 12   *Severe blocking of personal growth process*

Depending on how you rated yourself, you will have some idea of the degree to which your own attitudes may be standing in your way:

Mild worries (1 - 3 points) means that you want to move forward, but have some residual ambivalence to sort through first.

Moderate frustration (4- 6 points) means that you want very badly to pursue your dreams, but have felt very blocked.

Serious self-doubts (7 - 9 points) means that you have felt so discouraged in the past, you hesitate to try again.

Severe blocking (10- 12 points) suggests that many of your experiences have made it extremely hard for you to even think about seeking your own happiness. *Until now, that is.* By reading this book, you are signaling your willingness to make some changes for the better.

Blocker Beliefs

Each one of the attitudes on the inventory belongs to a mind-set that could derail even the most determined seeker. You may not be experiencing all of these holdups right now, but they are so common that it is a good idea to be prepared for them. Basically, the statements represent some of the most effective self-defeating attitudes. Look at the statements you circled. Their numbers correspond to the chapters in this book that have something special to say to you.

Don't be concerned if you ended up circling every statement. It just means this is the right guidebook for you. The statements on the attitude inventory are common beliefs of people who have fallen into the habit of holding themselves back. These are not permanent conditions; they are simply the kind of viewpoints that are most likely to derail us when we are starting out on a program of growth. Throughout this book, we are going to be dealing with such problems, in one form or another.

Turbulence

There is another obstacle to growth that is actually only a side effect of the active transformation of your life. This is the phenomenon I call *turbulence*. In the movie, *The Right Stuff*[32], there is a scene in which Chuck Yeager, the test pilot, is attempting to take his plane through the sound barrier. As his aircraft moves faster and faster, the air builds up in front of him because it cannot flow out of the way fast enough. Before the breakthrough, the plane shudders and shakes to the point where we believe the pilot's life is threatened. Finally the pilot breaks through the sound barrier with a boom, and then it is smooth flying.

Like that test pilot, we too experience accumulated pressures from the past, from old ways of doing things that are impeding our progress. The old beliefs tell us we're facing insurmountable obstacles, as they throw up barriers to our progress. Our lives buck and shake. We hold on tight, and many times there is a part of us that is sure we are going to die, convincing us that what we are doing is impossible. It tells us there is an impassable point in our own lives just as it seemed to be when an aircraft first came up against the sound barrier. Yet that barrier is really just air. It is because we are going so fast in a new direction that the old ways appear to have substance as they build up in front of us to block our path to the future. In truth, habit is not a solid thing and it is certainly not an impassable point.

Nevertheless, be prepared for the turbulence that precedes a breakthrough. Turbulence may take the form of those unanswered phone calls or that rude person who makes us sorry we ever asked a question. It is the broken-down car on the way to the interview. It is the lost transcripts and the lukewarm letter of recommendation. It is the disappointment and the letdown, just when you really, really needed a break. However, if you let such turbulence deter you from your purpose, you will not break the symbolic barrier to your future. Try not to pull back even if you're scared to death from all the shuddering and shaking. Remember, such barriers only come when the emotional buildup reaches a critical mass and you are approaching the speed necessary to overcome the resistance. In other words, when turbulence occurs, you must hold on and keep going to the breakthrough.

Many times it is not others but ourselves who create our own turbulence. Have you ever had an extremely important phone call to make, one that might open up an important opportunity, and you dialed the wrong number? Have you ever emailed an important reply and forgotten the attachment? There are countless ways that we pile up wind resistance on our own cockpit windshields, holding ourselves back.

There may be many bumpy moments in pursuing our true purpose. At first, our dream can feel so elusive it seems as if we will never be able to grasp it. We may discover our purpose, but feel scared to death and ambivalent about acting on it. However, after the worst of doubt and turbulence has passed, there is a liveliness that will spring into your goals. It becomes a current beneath you, a river that carries you, oftentimes much faster than you are ready to go – and sometimes without a paddle! When your goal takes on a life of its own and you are going with it, it is not work, it is just a matter of keeping up. We begin to feel the smooth-as-silk ride of going with the current of our future, which is always propelling us along. We realize just how much work it has been to stand in the way of that force for so long.

Overexcitement

There is a positive kind of feeling that can block our way too, and that is the feeling of overexcitement. Have you ever been at a carnival or amusement park and seen an overstimulated, frenetic little child, who wants everything and can be satisfied by nothing? Overstimulation revs you up but takes you nowhere. It may initially seem like fun, but when it reaches the point where you have had too much or you are overwhelmed and out of control, it ceases being fun anymore. It's a kind of energy overload, too much of a good thing. When people finally begin to believe that maybe their dream *could* come true, they frequently experience an energy burst that rockets them out of their customary sense of limitation. Suddenly they are filled with a euphoric sense of possibility, and they radiate a mental hyperactivity which is often poorly contained at first. They are very excited, but don't know what to do with the feeling. They end up running around in little circles, starting things but not finishing them, dreaming up possibilities, and fantasizing without purpose.

Many times this kind of energy is unfocused and lacks structure. The "how" is missing. The planning is missing. It is the scattered energy of unbridled inspiration, with nothing steering it that even remotely resembles an actual goal. The person becomes agitated with unlived potential and expansive in a way that is almost completely opposite from his or her previously self-denying stance.

Many times the sudden upsurge in energy and the flourishing of hope takes the original form it had when it was first suppressed in childhood. It is like an underground spring that disappears into a field and does not come back up again for miles. But when it finally bubbles to the surface again, it is still carrying the same waters. Childlike fantasies and wishes are often the first things to come out when we reconnect with this energy. It is important to feel and accept this without shame or apology and look for ways to help those childhood dreams mature into their adult versions.

This excitement phase can be heady and take you over, but it needs to be compressed into a laser-thin line of deliberate planning. Your energy burst needs to be honored strictly for what it is: raw material. Further sculpting and honing is essential to make it a success source, not just a power source.

The experience of overexcitement is not really an obstacle; it's a breakthrough experience. It is a taste of the power over our own lives that we always knew we had. When we can't maintain our energy at that peak or we don't know what to do with it, we can end up dropping the feeling altogether. We can even feel like a fool for having been tricked into false enthusiasm. Nevertheless, there is nothing false about it. It is the most real thing in the world. Your challenge is to see excitement for what it is: a very good sign that you are on the right road. Excitement's purpose is simply to reconnect you with yourself and to fuel you for the next stage of growth, before dropping away like a spent missile. Look at the overexcitement checklist below, then read on for practical suggestions on how to deal with these feelings.

DEALING WITH OVEREXCITEMENT

Overexcitement is overstimulation: more energy and feelings than you can handle. Here is how to identify this state:

SIGNS OF OVEREXCITEMENT:

- Exhilaration

- Giddy, inflated feeling or scattered thinking

- Overly emotional

- Feelings of disorganization, don't know what to do first; impulsivity, running around in circles

- Inefficient, start things without finishing them

- After initial high, discouragement and aimlessness

When you are overexcited, you need to stop, get back under control, and refocus before you can proceed.

STEPS TO REGAIN CONTROL:

1. **Stop!** You are accomplishing nothing right now.

2. **Remove yourself from the immediate scene** (e.g. go outside, take a restroom break, walk down the hall).

3. **Distract yourself by doing something else for awhile** (e.g. read a book, watch television, do repetitive paperwork, wash dishes).

4. **Rest, calm down** (e.g. listen to music, meditate, stretch and breathe deeply). Leave things alone for the time being and promise yourself you will go back to them later.

5. **Recover.** Stay away from the activity until you feel calmed down and you can think straight about it again.

6. **Reapproach.** Pick back up with the idea or project, keeping perspective and focusing on necessary steps toward your goal.

The Challenge Junkie

I once had a dream that alerted me to another type of problem that can stand in our way as we try to find our real purpose in life. It is the love of challenge and adversity for its own sake.

I am riding my bike on a winding country road I've never been on before, with Janie, my childhood buddy, a daredevil tomboy. Janie is out in front of me on her bicycle and I am pedaling to catch up. Then I discern something on the path ahead. It looks like a row of big, puffy tumbleweeds piled up across the road. It's clear my friend has already burst through them, because I can see her off in the distance on her bike, curving around the next bend in the road.

The next thing I know, I'm down on my hands and knees, tangled up in some kind of shrub that is growing at the edge of the road, right by the tumbleweeds. Rather than plow through the tumbleweeds like Janie did, I get off by my bike and start struggling to crawl through this vined, prickly bush. I am aware that if I really wanted to I could tear the whole thing up, but there is a kind of fussy care I am taking not to dislodge or break the plant. What a pain in the neck to go inching through the undergrowth, getting pricked in the back and scratched on the arms! I am annoyed and irritated, but I continue the task.

This dream may be interpreted as a description of how we can go out of our way to tackle things that are beside the point. At the time of my dream, I was obsessing over some problems from the past. In the dream, I saw a complicated, tempting challenge– a literally thorny situation – sitting there beside the road. Who can resist the opportunity to use well-trained problem-solving skills, hard won and very thoroughly learned? Especially when it feels like second nature? The dream was telling me I tended to get overly involved in challenges that were not even on my path, problems that really belonged to someone else.

I asked myself that if I was making my dreams this difficult, *what was I doing in my waking life to make my life harder than it really needed to be?* I began to do some honest self-reflection. That's when I realized that I was a *challenge junkie.* I had developed so much courage, had so much experience with setbacks, and could be so persevering, that I subconsciously *loved* situations in which I struggled through hardship and finally solved the problem.

Marlene, one of my clients, was also a challenge junkie. She came to see me because she was sick of being drawn to deadbeat guys who treated her badly. The problem was she *knew how* to deal with these men, having had a cruel and insulting father. Marlene had a whole set of beautifully crafted and functional skills for how to be in relationships with mean guys and survive. She was like a Navy SEAL who can survive on rainwater and crickets. She knew how to do it, and the subconscious rush that came with executing those hard won skills was formidable. Marlene's childhood had been spent refining skills for getting along with Daddy. Her whole life had depended upon it. This kind of destructive relationship had become her arena of competency. It was what she did well. And what we do well is a *very* important part of our identity. The question was: would Marlene ever want to take up with stable, nice guys now that she had mastered the convoluted skills of dealing with abusive, controlling narcissists?

As we learn how to deny our own needs and develop survival behaviors instead, these skills take on a life of their own. We get very attached to anything we have learned to do well. It is what a craftsman feels as he picks up his tools or what the race car driver experiences as she slips behind the wheel; it is the confidence of a mother as she bathes her child. When we learn the motions to this level, it feels like who we are.

Look at it this way: When you try a back flip off a diving board for the first time, it is not a pleasurable, transcendent experience. It's scary; you feel uncoordinated, and you aren't sure you aren't going to get badly hurt. But once you learn the trick of it, the back flip becomes a joy to execute. You are now carrying around something new in your repertoire that was not there before. Of course you want to take it out and use it whenever you can. You have a new potentiality within yourself, like a coiled spring waiting for release.

Our psychological skills are like that, too. Once we learn how to deal with difficult people, how to handle violent parents, or placate a demanding spouse, these skills have their own autonomy[33]. Once these originally defensive skills have been learned, they nag us with their very competence: "Use us, use us," they wheedle. Just like the acrobatic diver who feels that itch in his muscles when he sees a diving board, we are drawn toward situations that will let us use our skills.

Everyone has a different story in this regard, but the challenge junkie phenomenon answers the perplexing question of why people keep embroiling themselves in such apparently self-defeating situations. They are not self-destructive – they're just exercising their expertise. If you are a challenge junkie, the question to ask yourself is: is it time to find some challenges that are more fun?

By now, I hope, you are realizing that the things standing in your way are not the malevolent forces of fate. They are the good old, garden-variety psychological and family hang-ups common to everyone. But you now have the advantage, by virtue of being consciously aware of them. If you understand your fears and misplaced motives and see them clearly, you will no longer be moving blindly through your life. These truths – about how you have had to turn against your own best interests out of fear and loyalty – will develop a new consciousness within you. You will be able to see that the things that stand in your way are not just your own secret fears and insecurities, they are *everybody's* fears and insecurities. As such, we can predict them and dismantle their power over us. Each one of us has a Big Fear; we all get over-excited in the growth process, and at times every one of us wants to cry like a baby on the shoulder of a road we haven't traveled before. The difference is that you are now holding the map.

CHAPTER 8

PUTTING YOURSELF FIRST

Are you condemning natural self-interest and self-protection as some sort of crime against your loved ones?

Obstacles and doubts always flare up when you are trying to reestablish contact with the real self after years of neglect. In adulthood, these obstacles may seem more complex than those that come from your childhood because now you may be a parent, spouse, wage earner, etc. Nevertheless, if we had not spent the time in the first half of this book trying to understand the roots of your fears, symptoms, and guilt, it would be much harder for you to move freely toward discovering your destiny.

Now I am going to ask you to take the next step. One little step in attitude, an acceptance of a new starting point in your thinking. It is a small shift in awareness, but it is essential for realigning yourself with the inner power and instinct that can guide you the rest of the way toward becoming who you were meant to be. If you cannot accept this little shift, keep trying. It may arouse stiff resistance, but that is simply your ego becoming anxious. You may also "get" it, but then find you keep losing it. All I ask is that you keep considering taking this step that will bring you closer to the person you want to be.

This shift in thinking is a pivot point for the rest of this book. If you do not make this change in perspective, then everything else you learn will crumble as soon as any pressure whatsoever is applied to it. If you develop difficulties acting on the suggestions in any of the chapters to follow, be sure to come right back here, to check whether or not you have lost touch with this basic attitude shift.

Here is what I am going to ask you to do:

Though you may now have financial, spousal, parental, relationship, and employment concerns that affect your reaching for your true purpose in life, I want you to accept the idea that you must *put your self first* in your life. If you have not been doing this so far, you may have a strong reaction to the idea. You may even be able to hear the doors of your mind banging shut. But go with me a little ways on this, and see how you feel at the end of our discussion here.

Most conscientious people have a positive horror of being thought self-ish. In our culture, being selfish or self-centered has been branded the height of immaturity. We cringe if our children come home from preschool with a note saying that they have trouble sharing. We are afraid to become suspect in the eyes of others for following a path that takes us away from group think-ing. And so we avoid *anything* that might be remotely related to what we call selfishness.

But I am not talking about selfishness! Putting the self first is simply the practical first step to take you to a more rewarding and more loving way of living than you've ever had. Did I say *more loving?* Absolutely. Once you learn to put your self first, listening to it and respecting its wisdom about what you need to do next, you will be amazed how your attitude toward other people changes for the better. Having learned to know and accept your true self, you will never again feel as judgmental or resentful of other people as you do now. When you are realigned with your true self and are in tune with your own cre-ative desires and inspiration, you have plenty left over for other people. Once you get into the habit of tuning into your self first in any situation, you will easily have a more truly generous attitude toward other people.

Putting your self first means you must know yourself and your desires well enough to be *able* to love other people, truly and from the heart. You re-ally know what you like and what you need, and so when you connect up with other people who match this, you are crazy about them. There's no working at it, or straining to do the right thing. The joy of knowing what your true self needs puts you squarely in the path of people and situations with which you really fit.

Remember what the true self is. There is a good reason why it has to be put first in your life. The true self is the deepest, most profoundly individual part of you, the inborn potential for who you were meant to be. At birth there was a core wish in the center of your being, urging you toward the unique things *you* require in order to feel fulfilled and happy. This deepest part of you goes far beneath the superficial personality you show to other people, and is hooked up with powerful currents of intention over which your conscious mind has no control. It is the simple, but indelible patterning of your happiness and there is no substitute for it, no matter how hard you try to fool yourself.

The Fear of Selfishness

Putting your self first is strictly an interior event. It is not about being loud or overbearing or pushing your way past other people into the limelight. It is about seeing life through your own eyes – not the eyes of your parents, your spouse, your boss, or your demanding children. The person who puts himself or herself first has come back to a point of internal balance and is able to mediate wisely between the worlds of individual need and group contribution. Putting the self first is nothing more than a realignment, a balancing of a system that has been pulled out of symmetry by the torque of an over-spun ego.

Unless you want to announce it, no one else has to know that you are putting your self first. It is strictly an internal, mental, personal step that may have no perceivable effects on other people for quite awhile, leaving plenty of time for everyone – yourself included – to get used to the new way. However, I can guarantee you, unless this first step is taken, there will be no new way.

I know you are worrying that putting yourself first will make you "selfish." But the key here is: what is your *goal* in putting yourself first? Actual selfishness – and there is such a thing, I agree – is an end in itself. It is a closed system of narrow obsession with personal appetites of whatever kind. Selfishness is not motivated by growth or a desire to connect with other people; it is strictly focused on immediate gratification or the release of tensions.

Because selfishness is usually repetitive and non-creative in its expression, it is intrinsically boring and requires *more and more* to get ever brief jolts of satiation. Selfishness is petty, and is of the ego; it takes you absolutely nowhere.

Are you with me so far? I'm not advocating that kind of selfishness. In your own mind, you are simply going to put yourself first for awhile, in order to really grow up. In this way, you are going back to the mindset of a young person who is willing to think new thoughts and entertain possibilities beyond the family expectations. Don't be afraid of this step. Doing this does *not* mean that you leave your responsibilities, quit your job, or do anything drastic in regard to your duties in the outside world. No, you are simply going to make this one little, crucial change in your inside world: you are simply going to stop forgetting about your self. Read that again. *You are simply going to stop forgetting about yourself.*

The Practicality of Putting the Self First

Let's consider for a moment what happens when you try to forget about your self and its needs. When you have neglected and forgotten about your real self long enough, it will do what is required to get your attention. It will create a symptom or start making major problems in some area of your life. Perhaps you will then go to a mental health professional and purchase hourly sessions of total self-absorption in which you are supposed to do nothing but talk about yourself and how you feel. How ironic this is. Once you are in enough distress, you will *pay* someone to give you permission to put your self first, for a whole hour each week, often for months at a time. And it works!

The healing occurs as you reconnect with who you really are, as you remember your true self and what it needs to feel energy and optimism. This process never requires you to betray anyone or leave anyone behind; healing begins as soon as you stop leaving *yourself* behind. You don't have to wait. You can begin now to heal yourself on your own by conscientiously putting your self first on a daily basis. When you can do this consistently on your own, the need for a therapist will evaporate. You will be on the road to discovering your true purpose.

Which Self Will You Put First?

Before we go further with this idea of putting the self first, let us pause for an important clarification. The self that needs to come first is not our socialized persona; it is our original real self. One way of defining the goal of becoming who you were meant to be is to say that you are on your way to becoming a person who is not ruled by his or her past. If we put our socialized false self first, we will encounter the problems of the past over and over again. It is the only way that that old self knows how to live.

When we have seen enough of the truth of what happened to us in our past relationships and family of origin, an interesting thing starts to happen: we stop explaining ourselves to ourselves based on our past, and we begin creating the honesty of fresh responses to new situations and possibilities. We move from the "why me?" frame of mind to the "what's next?" outlook on life. In other words we shift from a neurotic outlook to a creative one. At this point we go from being a person defined by *causes* from our past, to a person who takes responsibility for the *effects* we want to experience in our future.

People who have thoroughly come to grips with the truth of their upbringing can enjoy the freedom from the past that one man described when he said, "I'm over all the research on that old stuff. There's no more in it that I need for the rest of my life." No longer unconsciously dominated by family-of-origin mandates, this client had come to understand that his life was now his to choose in each second of his existence. At a fundamental level he now knew that he had the power to make a huge positive difference in his life by putting the needs of his present-day real self first whenever possible.

What Happens When We Put The Self Last

Ignore yourself at your own peril. Those words came back to me one morning as I felt the full brunt of my irritation and fatigue. For several days, I had planned to sit down and start this chapter, looking forward to the mornings set aside for time alone. But Monday went somewhere, eaten up in odds and ends of other things that had to be done. Tuesday was a short morning, and a business report had to be finished. Wednesday, we were out of milk, so the grocery store was first on my to-do list. Countless little necessities stood between my writing and me. By Thursday I was fuming. The days had ticked by and still I had not done what I had been trying to do since Monday: start this chapter.

My frustrations mounted. When I tried to print out that nuisance business report, the paper stuck and jammed in the printer. I could not get it to work properly. Then the coffee-maker filter crumpled into a sodden clump, releasing a stream of dirty grounds into the coffeepot. A swarm of incoming phone calls distracted me. I became preoccupied with finding something to eat. Trying to override the needs of my true self, I was creating nothing but a tangle of inefficiency. My mind was divided and resentful, and it was therefore impossible to do anything well.

Finally I had to stop and look at what I was doing. Thinking back, I realized that from the time I woke up that Monday morning, I was not me first. I did not experience myself as the center of my world, out of which I loved and lived. Instead, I had begun to sort through all the things I had before me that day to get done. It is clear to me now that the *very last thing* on my mind was myself. I had started out letting the ego run my day.

My deceptive ego promised me – I know this, because it has been promising me this for years – that as soon as I got all this other stuff done, then I could start living for me. It always seems to me that I am very close, just down the road, to getting to do exactly what I want. But if I do not watch it, I will never get there because there are *always* "just a few more things" that need to be done first.

The ego appeals to our sense of orderliness and sequence. It is the part that tells us there is a time and a place for everything. But too often it is our real self that is left standing in line, anxiously waiting for its turn in the rush of daily chores.

It is easy to kid ourselves, to go along with our egos and to accept that we are just finishing up a few loose ends before we get on to the stuff that is really meaningful to us. The trouble is, our lives can be over before we let ourselves do it.

WHO YOU WERE MEANT TO BE

Only Leftovers are Acceptable

Maybe you recognized yourself in that description of my misguided morning. You too may have been living on leftovers – leftover time, leftover energy to do what you really want. Like me, you may have found that there is less and less energy left over when you live life that way.

Unfortunately, by the time you have finally done everything you are "supposed" to do, your tank is empty. You are so tired from taking care of everything else that you now lack the energy for your vision, your dream. After wearing yourself out on little chores and putting others first, your passion for your own future has been emptied out like a canteen in the desert. There is nothing left for you. You can remember your dream and still want it, but now it seems like too much work. You are too tired and too spent.

Our deceptive egos present us with only two choices: sacrifice yourself or be seen as selfish. To sacrifice for others means goodness and acceptance. To be seen as selfish is a horror to be avoided. Being called selfish will immediately bring you to heel, won't it? It is society's most shaming tactic and its effect on us can be electric.

Many of us buy the ego's false promise that we will eventually have our chance, if we only take care of these other responsibilities now. But to accept these terms is nothing but paying a ransom for no return, for the ego will never willingly release your time and energy back to your true self. Like it or not, you have to *take* your life back. And the only way to do this is to accept the challenge of putting yourself first.

Putting yourself first is above all a mental position. It is a positioning of the self that puts you in the center and aligns all other things in their proper spacing around the hub of that wheel. To get to this centered place within ourselves, where we can gather our strength, we have to learn to get out of the mental prison of *always* thinking of others first. Don't misunderstand me here: there is nothing wrong with putting other people first when necessary, such as caring for children, listening to your partner, or satisfying a customer's request. What I am talking about is the kind of anxious, helplessly driven thinking in which we are constantly keeping score as to whether or not we are doing enough *in other people's eyes*.

Don't be a willing prisoner of what other people think of you. You don't have to be the eager pupil, always hoping for the "A" on the report card of life, especially when it is graded by the very people who care the least about your personal fulfillment.

The High Price of Self-Neglect
Neglecting yourself doesn't just make you unhappy. It can actually threaten your life, as Jordan's dilemma illustrates.

Jordan's Story

Jordan was a tall, powerfully built young woman who came for therapy in a state of serious depression. She felt suicidal and her love for her two small children was the only thing restraining that urge. Only twenty-five years old, Jordan had taken on more responsibility than many older people. She was married, working long hours, and raising her children while fielding phone calls from her middle-aged parents over their recent bitter divorce proceedings.

Everyone else had been coming first for so long that Jordan had forgotten what she was living for. She felt overwhelmed, jittery, and down. Even minor disappointments were enough to enrage her, and recently she had been flying off the handle into screaming arguments with her husband. Jordan felt as though she were constantly living on a knife's edge of tension, with everyone pulling at her, both at work and at home. She was trying so hard to solve everyone else's problems that she did not allow herself to think about her own needs. When Jordan finally broke down under the pressure and seriously considered ending her life, she realized how self-destructive her selflessness had actually been.

Jordan had entered adulthood brainwashed with the idea that *good* people take care of everyone else first. That belief had taken over to the point where the run-down quality of her own life made death seem like a preferable option. Jordan saw herself as a caretaker, mother, wage earner, wife, counselor, and mediator – but none of these roles left room for her soul.

Jordan finally decided that she had to start putting herself first in order to restore her desire to live. She cut back on her work hours and refused to listen to her parents complain about each other. Once an avid volleyball and soccer player, Jordan realized that she had enjoyed no strenuous sports for years, instead keeping herself "cooped up" with the kids or working constantly. Wasting no time, she began working out and signed up for a community league. Within a couple of weeks, Jordan was like a new person.

Jordan knew in her bones that her choices at this point were quite literally between life and death. She came to the conclusion that "I need to focus more on me." As she learned to accept this way of thinking, her angry despondency evaporated.

As Jordan began to put herself first in a healthy way, people began to tell her how much she had changed, especially how much calmer she seemed. Even her husband became more affectionate and attentive, as they talked about their needs together rather than screaming their resentments at each other. When Jordan finally declared, "I'm not going to kill myself worrying about everybody else" she was making her commitment to live. She looked peaceful and resolved as she told me, "If I'm happy, the happiness spreads out to other people. If I'm miserable, others are miserable. I'm relieved, it's like a big monkey off my back."

Jordan was figuring out her own *owner's manual,* the one that tells each one of us what we need in order to stay happy and not get depressed. High on Jordan's necessary maintenance list was her need to be outside, to be physically active and to feel the sun on her face. She realized she was basically a high energy, fun-loving, outdoorsy person, not the overly responsible drudge into which she had tried to turn herself.

Jordan had pretended it was not necessary for her to take care of herself. Treating herself as an expendable quantity in her life, she spent her energies into emotional bankruptcy. Running on empty, Jordan nevertheless kept pushing herself to do more and more for other people. For a long time she overlooked the simple, self-maintaining things that would have kept her running. It was not until Jordan had hit rock bottom, sitting in her bathroom with a handful of pills, that she came to her senses. What in the world was she doing? *Why was she trying so hard to make it so easy for everyone else?*

Like Jordan, many of us have to be pushed to the brink of personal disaster before we make a choice on our own behalf. We reach this point when we finally realize that people in our lives are not going to voluntarily give up their demands on us so that we can have some time for ourselves. In Jordan's case, she realized nobody else was going to put her first, no matter how enraged or desperate she became. She then knew deep down *she* had to start putting herself first.

That's when Jordan began to develop her owner's manual. She *itemized* what she needed to enjoy life. She no longer felt that it was a proof of her love and goodness to put herself last. In fact, she had exhausted that theory right up to the dead end of suicide. Jordan finally admitted that there were certain things she had to do to take care of herself, in order to keep her life running.

Your Owner's Manual

Go ahead now and think about the things you need to remember for *your* owner's manual. What are the essential things that you must do for yourself, and on what kind of schedule, in order to keep your life engine running? The temptation, of course, will be to underestimate your needs and to pretend to yourself that you need a whole lot less than you really do. The things that will keep you honest in spite of this are your *symptoms* and your *level of energy.* These are the indicator lights that cannot be ignored. You can pretend that your "check engine" light does not mean anything serious, but sooner or later, if you keep driving, you will be forced to pay attention. Once you have been sidelined a few times on the great highway of life, you will begin to develop a deep respect for your "check engine" light. Which is just as it should be. You now *know* you must keep an eye on your indicators for trouble.

Now, give some thought to what form your warning lights take. What are these signals? How and when do they light up? It may be a subtle signal like a tense neck and a tight stomach, or it may be as big as a screaming rage or wishes to be dead. But it is still just your psychological indicator light blinking, trying to tell you something is wrong.

To make up your owner's manual, you must include everything you need in order to function well and spell out what each "warning light" means. Being practical about your owner's manual takes the whole self-maintenance issue away from the judgment of moral idealism and puts it back into the realistic arena of common sense, where it belongs. When our car breaks down or runs out of gas, we might be frustrated at the inconvenience, but it would never occur to us to waste our breath trying to make the car feel guilty about its selfishness and lack of concern for others. We would never take the time to tell the car that if it really loved us, it would start up anyway. We would not even try to make it feel inadequate by comparing it to those well-functioning vehicles that were zipping past us with no trouble whatsoever. Not one second would we spend on such ridiculous attempts to shame our car back into action, because we accept the obvious fact that automobiles will not run if they do not have gas, even if all the essential parts are in working order. It is the same with each one of us.

It is crucial to develop the same practical attitude toward ourselves. Our depression or anxiety or unhappiness are not signs of being morally inferior – they are signs that we have been ignoring what must come first in order to keep us in working order.

When I work with people in individual therapy and they start to improve, I make a special point to ask them exactly what they have been doing that has made them feel better. These positive actions then become part of their owner's manual – things they have to do in order to keep functioning well. If they want to save on mechanics' bills and therapy, they now know what they have to do for themselves.

It's also important to track down what people did in the past week that made them feel worse or to figure out why they are backsliding after a period of rapid growth. In therapy sessions we puzzle over these things together, looking for clues to their recent resurgence of symptoms, and we usually find it. "Oh yes," the person will finally recall, "Last Thursday I let the kids pour sugar in the gas tank, and I drove my car the rest of the week with two flat tires... Do you think that had anything to do with it?" Don't laugh, we often treat ourselves with just as little consideration!

When Work Takes Over

Demanding work situations are often fertile ground for the kinds of symptoms that come from putting the real self last. People with a high capacity for devotion and conscientiousness often become so identified with their job roles that they forget to think about their own needs. I once heard a story about why farmers in the old days preferred mules over horses for farm work. It was very simple and practical. A mule would stop working and refuse to go on when tired, whereas a horse would gladly work itself to death. Buying a mule therefore meant automatically buying built-in insurance on protecting your investment. Mules have no problem putting themselves first as necessary, and the wise farmer appreciates this quality.

Allie's Story

My client, Allie, was unfortunately a career thoroughbred. She absolutely loved her job at a television news station and seemed to thrive on the fast, demanding pace of last minute deadlines. It was safe to say that Allie's whole world was her job; even her social life revolved around her work relationships. Then one night Allie suddenly was struck with chest pains and trouble breathing. Sure she was dying of a heart attack, she got her roommate to rush her to the emergency room. Allie was mortified when the doctor told her she was having a panic attack and suggested she see a therapist.

When we began our work together, Allie could see absolutely no reason why she should be suffering these waves of overwhelming anxiety. It made no sense. She kept saying over and over how great her life was, how much she loved her job, how successful she had been, and so on. But persistent exploration revealed that Allie's panic had its roots in this very job.

Several months before, Allie's news station had been sold in a merger with another larger conglomerate, and around that time Allie's executive manager had resigned his position. This man had been a mature and steadying influence around the station – Allie called him "the grown-up" – and without his expertise, management was going haywire. Allie's new supervisor was an extremely reactive and alarmist woman who used to call Allie at six o'clock in the morning to share the latest rumor, or to gasp about the possibility of them all losing their jobs. For weeks upon weeks Allie would calm and soothe her manager, doing whatever she could to keep things running smoothly. Finally, it was too much. Allie had a panic attack of her own, never dreaming that she had had such strong feelings about it all. Out of loyalty to her job, Allie refused to think of her own self at all and, in fact, had thought she was handling everything just great. Incidentally, this kind of emotional denial is a classic set-up for panic attacks, when suppressed feelings come roaring back with overwhelming intensity.

As Allie began to make the connection between her panic symptoms and feeling forced to be the container for her manager's anxiety, she gradually learned how to stop and check-in with her real feelings before she said yes to anything. She began to detach from her complete identification with her job, and started putting her attention on what she needed to feel better. It felt hard and unnatural to put herself first after so many years as the prototypical company woman, but her panic attacks faded as she established a more balanced approach to her life.

A Marriage Called Off

Christy was a brand-new pharmacist in her first job out of graduate school. Everything in her life had been on schedule. She had dated her boyfriend for five years while getting through school, and they had announced their engagement at Christmas for a summer wedding.

As the wedding date got closer, however, Christy began to feel such a profound sense of dread that she finally had to admit to herself she no longer was in love with her fiancé. This put her in an anguished state of emotional confusion because "everyone kept saying how nice he was." She was torn between fitting in with her social group and listening to her real feelings. Ultimately, Christy's distress became so strong that she did the unthinkable and called off the wedding. They lost their deposits on the invitations and the honeymoon, and all the bridal shower gifts had to be returned. Christy's best friend called her "mean and heartless" and sided with Christy's stunned fiancé.

By the time Christy came to see me for therapy, she was experiencing anxiety attacks with a racing heartbeat and recurring feelings of doom. She couldn't think straight and trusted none of her choices. Her experience was described as "unnerving, unlike anything I've ever experienced." Christy was in shock from operating out of her real self for the first time in her life. She was starting to live from the inside out now, instead of by prepackaged social standards. Until now, Christy had accepted the code that *you have to do this no matter how you feel; you can't have any feelings about this.* By finally putting her true self first, Christy experienced a great upheaval. Yet this very upheaval opened up options and alternatives that she would not have allowed herself to see previously.

Christy's courageous decision to put herself first rather than make a terrible mistake brought a new sense of confidence into her life. Once the emotional dust had settled, she was sure she had done the right thing. What if Christy had managed to override that last alarm from the real self? What if she had forced herself to go through with the wedding? What would her life have been like then? Many people, after having trapped themselves in emotionally false situations, turn to addictions of one sort or another.

The Little Freedoms of Addiction

Addictions of whatever sort are not just bad habits. They are action patterns that are powerfully compelling because they supply huge unmet needs in our lives. Addiction is just a desperate way of putting yourself first. The popular wisdom is that people with addictions are selfish and self-absorbed, interested only in their own pleasures. Actually, the opposite is more often the truth. We crave addictions when we cannot have what we really want: freedom to live as our true self and to put our deepest needs first.

Eating, drinking, smoking, and spending to excess are symbolic ways of giving to yourself and yourself only. We call them guilty pleasures because they are unhealthy attempts at healthy self-interest. For the fleeting moments of enjoying our addiction, we are free. We have been excused. We can self indulge. We have the feeling of "This is just for me" or "I get to do exactly what I want." It is as though we have been released from the burden of meeting the world's expectations for how we should be.

The ultimate goal of all addictions is the temporary freedom to put yourself first. Addictions are compromises because we persuade ourselves that one day we plan to give up our addictive behaviors and become *totally* responsible and self-sacrificing. On that day, we believe, we will finally be good and willing to put other people first *all* the time.

Addictions are how you buy yourself off from fulfilling your destiny. They keep us just satisfied and distracted enough not to find out what we really want to do with our lives. Of course, they also keep us feeling bad about ourselves, which is another way to put ourselves last.

The Criminal Within

Even if addictions are not a problem for you, the guilt over following your innocent desires can be very strong. Many truly kind and conscientious people act as if they would be no better than a criminal if they began to look after their own needs. This is, of course, the ego jumping in to launch an attack on you, asking you what would happen if the whole world acted on the basis of self-interest. Have you heard this one before? I certainly have.

The ego offers no rational suggestions for how to get your needs met appropriately. Instead it conjures up visions of catastrophe if you take *any* steps toward getting what you want. "What about people who rob banks?" the ego mocks, "Aren't *they* just going after what they want?" The ego humiliates our sense of decency by throwing these extreme and illogical objections at us.

We feel chastised and draw back. "Why no, I don't want to *hurt* anybody," we say to ourselves, "What a bad person I must be to have even thought of that!" But hurting somebody was *not* your motive! The ego is fooling you. You have no intent to rob, kill, or sadistically cause suffering to others. You are not a psychopath or a serial killer, though you may have *felt* like one when you were little and your parent upbraided you because of some childish, "selfish" thing you did. In these dreadful experiences of self-criticism, we learn to label our natural urges toward self-expression as antisocial. The ego so thoroughly distorts our motives with irrelevant accusations that we never get it figured out. We don't even question the ego because its sanctimonious and superior tone tells us this is not allowed, no way. We slip back into our childhood mind and accept the big people's judgments unquestioningly, without a thought for ourselves.

What we should be doing is asking the ego a few clarifying questions. For example, is wanting to take time away from your children in order to pursue your neglected education the same thing as being an ax murderer? Is deciding not to go to your parents' dinner the equivalent of treason? Of course not. Squint at the ego's hysterics until you can see it with a little perspective and proportion. Give some thought to how you malign your own needs. Are you condemning natural self-interest and self-protection as some sort of crime against your loved ones?

Don't passively accept the blame. Whatever the ego says to you about your criminal selfishness, take it with a grain of salt. *If you were not an antisocial, unfeeling person before, you certainly are not going to turn into one at this point.* If you have suffered internal conflict between your needs and those of other people – especially if to the point of becoming depressed or physically sick – you are by definition not a selfish person. Criminals *never* make themselves sick worrying about their responsibilities to others.

How to Change the World Around You

Far from becoming psychopaths, it has been my experience that the people who have succeeded in putting themselves first always end up with happier, more rewarding relationships – often with the very same people that used to drive them crazy! It's like magic. They go from feeling persecuted, neglected, and angry to enjoying pleasant, open interactions with loved ones in which there is a healthy acceptance of differences. Sometimes I wonder at how these can be the same people my client complained about at the beginning of therapy.

Margie was marveling in my office one day about how her adult daughter and husband had changed so much for the better. She was noticing how pleasant her conversations had become with her daughter and how easy it was now to call her up and go shopping together. In the past, Margie's daughter had repeatedly made excuses for not getting together, leaving my client feeling rejected and left out of her daughter's life. Margie also reported miraculous developments in her husband's attentiveness and helpfulness. He now paid attention to what she said as he never had before. If she had had a magic wand, things could not have turned out better.

Yet the most marvelous improvement had not happened in either Margie's daughter or her husband; it had happened in the attitude of my client. Margie had consciously stopped criticizing her adult daughter's decisions and she made a point of not pressuring her with guilt to attend family functions. With her husband, Margie no longer felt she had the right to indulge herself in emotional meltdowns if he did not do what she wanted. She had begun to honor his right to act freely and not on her demand. As he no longer felt the waves of resentment and criticism coming from her, he felt more generous and attentive toward her.

How did she manage this? Through the long process of learning to put herself first, Margie gained real compassion for other people's needs as well as her own. Able now to say no to feelings of coercion and guilt in her own life, my client no longer could bring herself to burden others with those same emotional manipulations. She had worked hard to understand the ways in which she blindly carried along the same old guilt-ridden patterns she had suffered in her family of origin, and she decided to stop the pattern of blame and resentment in her current family. Instead of seeing herself as the victim of others' rejection and insensitivity, she started making a point of meeting her own needs as much as she could on her own. This made her a much more pleasant person to be around, and it showed in her closest relationships. She literally changed her world by putting herself first and allowing others to do the same.

When You Try To Be What You Are Not

People who do not put their true selves first have very predictable patterns in relationships. Male or female, they are usually very appealing individuals who attract people easily, and whom others find very pleasant to be around. Often they are very generous and seem ready to do anything for anybody. They are unusually empathic and sympathetic, and are so devoted to loved ones that they seem to find self-sacrifice easy. But they have a dark side, as anyone can tell you who has been in an intimate relationship with one of them.

At intervals, these same infinitely good-natured caretakers can have episodes of anger and depression, which may be expressed directly and verbally or else furtively and secretly in some form of acting out to get their needs met outside of the relationship. When they take the verbal route, they launch emotional accusations toward loved ones of being unfeeling and selfish. They complain of being unappreciated, taken for granted, and never able to please anyone. Often these incidents are intensely emotional as these bottled up feelings come spewing out. The typical reaction of the other person in these episodes is puzzlement and intense discomfort, as though they cannot figure out what in the world they have done to make the person so upset.

What's going on here? Quite simply it is what has to happen when one does not put oneself first and keeps attempting the impossible task of making oneself into what other people expect. One person I worked with, Dave, described feelings of hatred, annoyance and repulsion he had started to feel toward his wife of twenty-five years. He claimed it was her selfishness and inconsiderateness that were making him so unhappy. However, I suggested to him that these particular kinds of feelings might be related to his own loss of energy that was coming from his not putting his own essential needs first.

Acting out or outbursts of these kinds typically mean that you are exhausted, because you have badly denied your true self. In order to feel this angry and depleted, you probably have turned against yourself in order to fulfill a self-imposed ideal for how you think you're supposed to be. In other words, your reactions are rebelling against your outlandish agreement to separate yourself from your soul in order to go along with what you believe another person thinks or wants. It takes an enormous amount of energy to separate oneself from one's true self needs and that's why we eventually lose emotional control. The cure is to put yourself first, refuse to try to be something you're not, and prepare to tolerate the other person's temporary reaction.

Playing the Role

Nala came to see me because of her frustrations with dating after her divorce. She started out her relationships with men with intensely positive feelings. However, as she got to know each man in more depth, she kept finding things that she did not like about him. Surprisingly, however, this did not signal her to stop dating him. Instead she would continue to see him, even though inside herself she was quite critical of him. Even when she knew better, she seemed unable to speak up and tell her companion of the moment what she really thought.

Nala's problem was that she subconsciously believed that a woman was supposed to become whatever a man needed her to be. This was in order to help the man pretend to be the kind of man he thought *he* was! If Nala thought it was important for the man she was dealing with at the time to feel powerful and in control, she would keep her opinions to herself and let him feel in charge – until she finally blew up, much to the man's surprise. As time went on, Nala learned to practice asking herself, "How does this person need to be seen? What is the role I am playing in order to help him be who he thinks he is?" She was finally becoming like the alert little boy in the story of the Emperor's new clothes; she stopped putting her precious energy into feeding the other person's fantasy of how he wanted to be seen.

This subconscious agreement to participate in supporting another person's false self image is incredibly draining, but is often so subtle that no one sees what's happening. No one can figure out why these nice ladies or do-anything-for-you men ultimately blow up or act out when they seemed so sweet at first. If you put yourself last, your real self won't stand for it indefinitely. Putting yourself first from the beginning of a relationship means never having to go through Jekyll and Hyde mood swings.

⟡

Overflow

When we give ourselves room to do what we love – what gives us energy – we naturally become more accepting and generous toward other people. We all feel most generous when our own needs have been taken care of. This is what I mean by overflow. Truly generous people do not deprive themselves. When *you* stop depriving yourself, you will feel more generous too.

I can imagine the objections and fearful "yes, buts" that are flying through your mind right now. Many of us have learned not to trust our natural generosity and instead have felt forced into "sharing." As a result, our attitude toward our own generosity has become incredibly confusing and ambivalent. Often it is hard to know if we really *want* to share or if we are simply ashamed not to.

When you consider putting yourself first now, you may dredge up past recriminations from others who made you feel selfish. Perhaps they made you feel you never again wanted to risk feeling so morally bad and socially deficient. You may have become so afraid of being seen as selfish that you force yourself to be a "generous" person by constantly making a straining effort.

Chances are very high that if you are reading this book, you *are* a basically generous and giving person. How do I know this? Because it is only the truly generous, loving people who can feel so guilty about not giving enough that they will turn themselves into whatever other people need them to be. You have been trying all this time to be what your loved ones have expected you to be, so as to preserve that relationship and make them feel important. I ask you, what could be more generous than that? To give up your true self, to give up the unique dream of your life, rates up there with the all-time great acts of generosity by any standard.

If you accept the fact that you are – by definition – a loving, generous person, imagine what it will be like for you when you can give genuinely instead of from fear and guilt. You will follow the rhythms of natural generosity, in which giving is inspired out of the needs of the moment, not out of fear of criticism. In the state of overflow you simply give with pleasure rather than under the whip of obligation.

I bet I can read your mind at this point: what if you don't *feel* like giving when you *should,* then what? Just use your common sense. If pressing circumstances demand that you have to give whether you feel like it or not, do what you must do. But meeting the necessary demands of daily life is *not* the same thing as chronically and reflexively satisfying everyone else's needs to the neglect of yourself Any genuinely necessary occasions of giving will be a lot easier to fulfill if you have been gratifying your needs along the way.

Most of us worry that this necessary stage of self-absorption will cut us off from other people and undermine our most important relationships. The usual fear is that following our dreams will result in throwing caution to the wind while we drop our responsibilities and wreck our families. But this is not necessary! Following your dream and honoring your responsibilities are not mutually exclusive. We want the best of *both* worlds, our old world and our new world. It is the mistaken belief that there must be such desperate, impossible choices that makes people give up their dreams in the first place.

I want you to find a way to honor your responsibilities and commitments *while you put your self first.* Putting your self first is a mental attitude, an orderly efficient starting point, not a callous rejection of all the relationships you hold dear.

Just Don't Put Yourself Last

You may have made it all the way through this chapter and still feel too guilty to put your self first. When you have spent many years repressing your true self, that's normal. Trying on the idea of putting your own self first is extremely uncomfortable for many people and continues to smack of selfishness even when they know better. Believe me, I can relate, and so can almost every one of the magnificent people with whom I have worked. To you, I simply ask: *at least do not put yourself last.* Even if following the suggestions in this chapter do nothing more than move you up a notch or two on your own to-do list, it will be well worth it. You can go a long way toward reversing symptoms and emotional distress simply by giving your self even just a little bit of extra attention, a few extra minutes of taking your dreams seriously, even if you cannot yet put your self first.

Just remember that there is a difference between *selfishness* – which has momentary indulgence as its only goal – and putting your self first, which is the necessity of loving your self enough to fulfill your larger purpose.

CHAPTER 9

Mindreading:
The Still Small Voice

As long as the voice within appears to be telling us something that we don't want to hear, it may be an indication of how far we have separated ourselves from knowing what we truly want.

As the Growth Group was getting ready to leave one evening, I announced to everyone that our topic next time would be "mind reading." One woman shot me a quizzical glance as she slung an oversized handbag over her shoulder and gathered up her papers. "Oh? Are we having a séance?" she asked.

"'No, no," I laughed, "We're not going to read each other's minds; we're going to read our own. That's *much* harder."

And it is. When I think about my job as a psychotherapist, it basically boils down to teaching people how to read their own minds. The problem is that we spend too much time reading the minds of those people around us, reacting and plotting on the basis of our guesses about what is circulating in the thought stream of someone else. There is much less curiosity about what's going on in our own minds. Our mental strength is pulled outward and stretched thin with worry about what others are thinking. We forget to pull our focus back in and just *listen* to what is happening inside ourselves. The subtle art of reading your own mind is a skill crucial to the development of your individuality. It also prepares you for handling the inevitable arrival of *dilemmas*, which are nothing more than failures of imagination and a lack of faith in our ability to have what we truly want.

When we are faced with questions that have no answers except those found within ourselves, ironically we often do not know where to turn for advice. Accustomed to weighing the opinions of others or judging the appropriateness of our desires by the values of those around us, it does not occur to us just to listen to our inner voice. It certainly does not occur to us to just listen to that still, small voice without judgment!

Yet, in its quiet persistent way, the underlying mind keeps delivering the mail. Message after message piles up, whether we are opening them or not. How do we usually react when the underlying mind is trying to get our attention? We regard it as an inconsequential bulk mailer. When people bemoan feeling that they don't know what to do with their lives or where to go, I wonder if they have been paying attention to their inner messages. The underlying mind can only deliver; it cannot force us to open the envelope. We can never get the message if we don't want to. Perhaps we should practice opening and reading our internal signals, even if we decide not to do what they suggest.

Usually the reason we don't want to read our own minds is that our deeper mind is shockingly unconcerned with how our behavior and attitudes look to other people. It just goes on telling the truth like a child, oblivious to the flabbergasted stares. Often it moves us against the wishes of others, although that is not its purpose. The mind is not a rebel; it just seeks to live.

The Still, Small Voice

The subconscious, or underlying mind, approaches us through daydreams, intuitions and night dreams. It constantly sends signals toward creative solutions to our problems or dilemmas. Whenever we "zone out" or let our minds idle in neutral gear, a gap in our noisy conscious brain chatter is created. It is then that we can hear the still, small voice. In those moments, we can create and solve as effectively as any artist or scientist.

When we first begin to hear the still, small voice speaking inside us, it usually doesn't make perfect sense. It appears as a snippet, a data bit that is unconnected to the rest of our lives. It feels foreign, like an aberrant occurrence. But if the voice keeps coming back and whispering the same thing in our ear, it's a good idea to assume that it does fit in somewhere – it may just be misplaced in time. For instance, the voice might be very readily understood in the future, perhaps even just a few months from now. However, presently, it can seem unrelated to our wishes at hand. In spite of that, your job is to trust that you are being given the message for a good reason. It is to lead you toward the activities and interests that you love and which give you energy. That is the eternal push at the center of us.

The problem with the little voice, the little nudges from the underlying mind, is that it often speaks in symbolism as dreams do. It can be a challenge to decipher the message's meaning. The mind often will give you the impulse, or the image, but may not tell you *how* to get there or *what* to do next. The still, small voice is not trying to confuse you. It's just that you have a backlog of old messages built up and it may take awhile to discern their meaning when you finally start paying attention to them. Therefore, in the beginning stages of listening to the voice within, it should be regarded as the wise voice of suggestion, not the voice of command or of supernatural authority. As you may have noticed, even the gentlest suggestions, repeated enough, begin to have a major cumulative impact on the way we think about things.

The little voice is hardy and can take a lot of rejection. It never goes away, even when it is lying low for a period. It has no sense of time. It can wait forever but the voice wants to express its interests and desires. It doesn't care when and it doesn't care how. *You* are expected to handle the logistics.

What the Voice Sounds Like

Most of us have thought of our "still, small voice" as being our conscience, that little inner nudge guiding us between right and wrong. It is a little known fact that the still, small voice has *two* jobs: one as the conscience and one as the voice of deepest self-knowledge. Both jobs guide, but the voice of self-knowledge is far easier to ignore than the pricks of conscience. When we override our conscience, we feel guilt later and usually know why. If we ignore our deepest self-knowledge often enough, we will eventually feel anxious or depressed – but we often do not see that causal connection as easily as we can identify the roots of a guilty conscience.

The still, small voice is like an astute observer at each crossroads in our life, making its wisdom available whenever it is listened to. The voice never threatens or makes demands. It whispers in our ear, but has no need to take over as the ego does. The voice offers its truth then steps back, allowing us complete freedom to choose. Sometimes we then choose the kind of ego-orchestrated trap that I have heard described many times in psychotherapy sessions: people tell me they clearly recall *knowing* at the time of choice that they should *not* have chosen that mate or that job.

One such person, Daniel, remembered clearly – after thirty years of unhappy marriage – standing at the altar, watching his bride coming down the aisle and thinking *This'll never work*. He went through with the ceremony anyway and stayed with the marriage for decades until he finally faced the truth that this miserable union was something his true self had never wanted.

Professionally, I think the still, small voice often seems so weak simply because we block it out so thoroughly. We turn away from our inner voice because it so often tells us to take directions that might cause rifts and risk criticism. We are afraid that if we listen to this voice too long, we will end up doing something that might threaten our most important relationships. However, any relationship that has no room in it for each person to grow is a prison of stagnation and fear, where someone is being used as an object instead of being appreciated as a person.

Many times people feel alienated from and resistant toward what their little voices have to say. As long as the voice within appears to be telling us something that we don't want to hear, it may be an indication of how far we have separated ourselves from knowing what we truly want. When we are more fully conscious of what we need to be happy and truly alive, we will work willingly with the little voice inside, consulting it for all important decisions.

Unfortunately, many people find that they cannot tell the difference between the still, small voice and the nagging of the uptight, fear-filled ego. They don't know who is telling them what. Here are the rules for recognizing genuine guidance from your true self:

1. **The still, small voice uses short declarative statements. The ego uses lots of words and "yes, buts" to argue its position.** The still, small voice says things simply, like "She's the one" or "Don't do it." The ego loads you down with reasons and repercussions and lots of rationalizations.

2. **The still, small voice is not emotional; it has the quality of a statement or simple command. The ego can be recognized by the high degree of emotionality that always saturates its advice.** The still, small voice can be strong or weak in its signal, but it is not full of emotion. It has a simple, factual quality. The ego's edicts, on the other hand, contain anxiety, fear, euphoria, embarrassment or countless other emotions to sweep you away.

3. **The still, small voice is a quiet realization of one essential fact at a time. The ego is countless opinions based on a thousand different fears.** When listened to, the still, small voice simplifies and clarifies, while the ego confuses. Your inner voice will give you knowledge of one little step, the one thing to do next. In this way, it calmly guides us on a kind of mental scavenger hunt, in which the clues are given out one at a time. The ego, on the other hand, demands that we do a hundred things at once, increasing our agitation and clouding our vision.

4. **The still, small voice leads you to commit to one way or the other. The ego promotes the illusion that you can satisfy two contradictory goals at once without fully committing to either one.** The still, small voice tells you what to choose in order to be your true self and therefore true to other people. The ego tells you to pretend you want something you really do not, making genuine commitment impossible.

5. **The still, small voice supports originality and individuality.** The ego fosters childish fears of being left out, not fitting in, and being rejected.

6. **The still, small voice tells it like it is.** The ego tells it like it ought to be.

7. **The still, small voice points to action that will make you feel vastly relieved and peaceful inside once you have made the decision.** The ego leads to stressful action that you continue to regret later.

8. **The still, small voice changes direction easily as circumstances change; it can turn on a dime. The ego resists change and prides itself on consistency and predictability.** The ego gets nervous when things are not as they always have been, and it makes us feel guilty for changing our minds or suddenly not feeling a certain way anymore.

In summary, when you are hashing out a problem and having trouble figuring out whether the answer you get is from the real self or the ego, use the following checklist to decide if a thought or intuition is coming from the still, small voice of personal wisdom or from the ego, the voice of fear and uproar. Put a check next to the descriptions that best capture the tone of your voice within:

Still, Small Voice

☐ Uses short, firm statements
☐ Unemotional, factual
☐ One fact or message at a time
☐ Leads to commitment
☐ Promotes original solutions
☐ Tells it like it is.
☐ Actions relieve stress.
☐ Changes direction as needed.

Ego Voice

☐ Wordy, pros and cons, reasons why
☐ Anxious, emotional, conflicted
☐ Many insistent opinions all at once
☐ Sets up contradictory goals
☐ Fears rejection and ridicule
☐ Tells it like it should be.
☐ Actions increase stress
☐ Is rigidly consistent, resists change.

How to Contact the Still, Small Voice

To get in touch with the still, small voice is quite easy. Go someplace that is on nobody's turf, not even your own. This might be as lofty as a walk in the woods or an uplifting stroll on a beach. Or it might be as ordinary as eating a hamburger at a place you've never been to before. It might be lying on the ground looking up at the stars after the kids are in bed. It might be skipping work or classes in the afternoon and going to a movie you've been dying to see. *The key is to put yourself out of the ordinary* – whether this is a new physical space or the use of a familiar place in a new and original way. Of course vacations are the most pleasant way of doing this, but who can take a vacation every time he or she needs to consult the real self? The point is that you simply need to step outside of *what* has always been done and *where* it has always been done. Most importantly, it must be an activity and a place in which there is *absolutely no demand that you interact with anyone else.* In other words, you make yourself a temporary stranger. Movie theaters, unfamiliar restaurants, walks on the beach or in the woods, reading the paper in a coffee shop, solitary bike rides, or sitting in a nice public library are just some of the places where we are accepted as strangers and no one expects anything from us.

After you have put yourself in new surroundings – as a stranger with no ties to anyone around you – the next step is to ask yourself, "What is it I really want in my life?" (It is not a good idea to ask this question as you are fulfilling your responsibilities in a familiar routine because your ego will immediately take over.) Next, you pay attention to what pops into your mind. What's the answer that makes everything clear? It makes absolutely no difference if what you think changes completely in the next day or two. It is not some Ultimate Truth of the Universe you are seeking, unchangeable and timeless. You are hunting down *your* truth, and that might change back and forth quite a lot when you first start consulting your true self. You ask the still, small voice the "what-do-I-want" question not to take *immediate* action, but to discover the true self's desires over time and thereby ultimately take the *right* actions for your unique life.

Even if your still, small voice seems very contradictory at first, the more you listen to it, the more consistency it will begin to have. That's why you do not automatically do whatever it tells you at first. It is quite likely the next day it might tell you something different! But this is just your thoughts coming out in their own mysterious order; after awhile, one message will become clearer and clearer, with less switching back and forth. And then you will really know.

─♏

Your Two Brains

Medical science would have us believe that we have only one brain, reigning in gray-topped splendor over all that we do. But practically speaking, we have two brains: our head brain and our body brain. Wisdom comes from using both. We know this already because we intuitively know that the person with the highest IQ is not necessarily the wisest. We all know about the differences between "book smart'" and "street smart," about the difference between intellectual knowledge and gut feelings. So when you start reading your own mind, make sure you are reading both of them!

Your body brain resides in the trunk of your body, sometimes as high as the throat area and sometimes as low as the pelvis. A more descriptive way of saying it is that your body brain is your "like-dislike" center, where you feel dread in the pit of your stomach or joyful expansion in the chest area. It's where we feel alarm or safety when exposed to a new situation, and it is what guides us toward what we need in order to feel happy and fulfilled. As you well know, children operate mostly out of their body brain, refusing to eat what they don't like and pointedly avoiding people that make them uncomfortable. Unfortunately, as children we all are trained to override these body signals, as we are told that broccoli is good for us and that creepy old man is our Uncle Roy. We are trained to distrust the body brain and to worry instead about how our true instincts might hurt someone's feelings. We learn to ignore our body brain, to rationalize and explain away many things we might feel as viscerally true. We are taught to use only our head-brain, and in this way we close out our capacity for real wisdom.

Remember that the body brain gives you the most personally authentic feedback. Your head brain tells you how the rest of the world expects you to respond, but your body brain is concerned only with *your* survival and well-being. It speaks with the silent voice of your true desires – and your unreformable dislikes. When you finally start doing your own mind reading, pay close attention to that primeval counselor that talks to you in stomach churns and shortness of breath, in heart pain, tight throats, and waves of adrenaline. It doesn't use words, but it speaks volumes about likes and dislikes, fear and excitement. With a little practice, you will even begin to be able to tell when you are lying to yourself.

Remember that we often override this inner guide because of loyalty and guilt to our families. It is easy to pretend that we like what we really cannot stand if it means we will be accepted by others. We often have a horror of hurting our loved ones, so we will lie to ourselves just so no one feels rejected. Fortunately, however, our body brain continues to work just fine underneath the surface: it has to, having been assigned our survival instincts. Unlike the rest of your mind, your body brain's first loyalty is to yourself, and its purpose is to keep you physically and psychologically alive. All we have to do is begin to take it seriously once again, to let it guide us back to the reality we knew before we started pretending to be something we are not.

Let's take a look at Jerry, a person who had done a lot of pretending in his life, overruling his own instincts to the point where he felt he could not survive emotionally on his own.

The High Cost of Not Knowing Your Own Mind

When Jerry first called my office, he was a wreck. His wife had just told him she was unhappy in their marriage and was not sure they should stay together. This shocking revelation completely rocked Jerry's world, which until that point had been an orderly, completely predictable existence with financial security, three smart children, and a high level management job in a computer manufacturing firm. The troubles in Jerry's marriage actually had a long history that had been completely lost on him in his complacency. The responsible, only son of a minister, Jerry had unquestioningly assumed that he would be married for the rest of his life, and so his wife's pronouncement immediately threw him outside the reality he knew. Jerry panicked. Having played by head brain rules all his life, he had never before had to rely exclusively on his own gut feelings in a crisis.

His wife's news hit Jerry like a ton of bricks because it had never crossed his mind that his life could take such a completely unexpected turn for the worse. He had grown up in a sheltered, secure family in which everything revolved around serving his father's congregation. His devout parents taught him a very tidy view of the world, based firmly on conservative Christian principles of doing (and thinking) the right things. He was loved and guided and disciplined and taught to ask himself "What would Jesus do in this situation?" But there was a dark underside to Jerry's secure life. In effect, his upbringing prepared him perfectly to be his parent's obedient son and his wife's hardworking husband, but it did not prepare him to know his own mind, nor to be honest about his feelings.

Jerry had stayed on the straight and narrow, marrying, succeeding in his job, looking forward to playing golf, until this emotional catastrophe swept away his underpinnings. Jerry had nothing to fall back on internally when his wife brought up divorce. He thought he had done everything right, and now it wasn't working. What was he supposed to do now?

All Jerry could think about at first was how to get his wife to stay. In other words, how he could change her mind by making the right kinds of promises to her? If he lost his marriage, Jerry felt he could not continue to be who he thought he was – a man successful in all his roles, who could count on being rewarded for living a good life. When his wife confronted him, Jerry was so terrified of being abandoned that he never thought to ask himself if *he wanted* to stay married. Consulting his own feelings had never been a need before. Instead of reading his own mind and heart, Jerry only thought about how his actions would appear to others and what he had to do to save his status as a "good" and "successful" person. However, Jerry's wife longed for a real relationship with a man who could be emotionally intimate and honest, the one thing that Jerry had never learned to do.

In his therapy sessions, Jerry realized he had never had any practice in sorting through his true feelings in order to really know himself. He also did not have a clear sense of his real strengths and abilities for dealing with a crisis.

As Jerry thought about his life, he was able to begin to read his own mind honestly for the first time in his adult life. And what he found was a writhing nest of contradictions. Many of the feelings he was admitting turned out to be the opposite of his ideals, bringing him shame and confusion. In Jerry's words:

> I'm trying to be honest with myself. For most of my life I've acted like I was ashamed of having these contradictory feelings, like I should've disciplined them out of me. I was holding myself to a higher standard than anyone else in the world. But I find that when I bring my feelings out into the open, the shame starts to go away. It no longer feels shameful, only human, I guess.

When Jerry committed himself to marriage, he believed that he was not only committing himself to another person, he was committing himself to the "right" way of feeling and thinking. In his adult life, Jerry relied on his roles and commitments to tell him how to feel. When the marriage commitment was shaken, the only cure for Jerry's terrible abandonment panic was to teach him how to turn inside and begin the fine art of reading his own mind. Jerry began to understand the need to know how he felt inside, apart from what he thought he *should* do. It was a completely new way of thinking for him to ask: "How do I feel about myself? What do I want for myself for the next forty years on earth?" Up until now, he had simply used his head-brain to decide what he should do, and then he did the backfill work of making his feelings and thoughts fit the now-fixed decision he had made. As Jerry wryly remarked one day after a particularly honest review of his life, "It has *not* been a very fulfilling way to live."

When Jerry first tried to read his own mind and ask himself what he *really* thought and what he *really* wanted, he felt like he was consulting a vacuum. It seemed that he had walked back into himself and the place was empty. This is a very common experience for anyone who begins to try to live from the inside. When one has denied and suppressed one's true feelings for so many years, it feels as if one *has* no true feelings – and hence no internal guidance. I told Jerry it was as if he had entered the huge, empty foyer of himself, while all the interior doors seemed locked shut. But maybe someone was home after all. And sure enough, by being honest with himself and accepting whatever he discovered, one after another of his real thoughts and feelings began to open their doors and come out. He and his wife began a genuine dialogue about what each of them really wanted and what had gone wrong in their relationship.

In touch with his own mind about things, Jerry no longer felt himself to be on a roller coaster of reactivity to his wife's moods. He no longer panicked when she expressed herself honestly about her unhappiness. He was sad about the breakdown of their marriage, but he was no longer willing to manipulate his wife into staying married at any cost. Jerry had begun to believe that he could operate from the center of himself and survive no matter what his wife decided to do.

Now able to read his own mind, Jerry was no longer so dependent on his social roles and family relationships to tell him what to do and how to think. Later when rumors started circulating in his job about a possible takeover and restructuring, Jerry was amazed that he did not feel his customary panic in response to such news. He was well aware that he would have felt *terrified* in the past. Now he felt butterflies in his stomach and realistic worry – the normal range of feelings in such a situation – but he did not feel like his whole world was caving in on him.

Jerry's case reminds us that in our current society, nobody has the guarantees that more or less were taken for granted years ago. Our world is increasingly forcing new kinds of situations on us all: spouses who don't want to stay married, jobs that evaporate, companies that fold, corporations that merge. Those of us who define ourselves solely by social role and family relationships are increasingly at high risk for just the sort of devastating wake-up call that Jerry received. Knowing yourself and what you want becomes your anchor in times like these. Everything can change in an instant, and if you are not in touch with your inner core you can feel like you have nothing "but panic," as Jerry said.

There is a high price in the adult world for not knowing your own mind. This search for yourself, the quest to read your own mind, is not a luxury item. It is the greatest coping mechanism there ever was. If you know how you feel (contradictory or not) and pay attention to your own thoughts, you are inoculated against the kind of helpless panic that many people feel when their world takes an unexpected turn.

Revelation vs. Inspiration

When we feel as desperate as Jerry did, we often start hoping for the *Big Revelation* to tell us what to do. The still, small voice may seem pretty unsubstantial and ghostly when we need a fast answer. We hold scant faith in such wispy little hints. We hope instead for a burning bush, something so dramatic and commanding that we would *have* to pay attention and realize what we should do. Understandably enough, we want something outside ourselves to take that responsibility and to hit us over the head with it. We don't want mere inspiration; we demand *revelation.* We put responsibility on the outside world, on Fate, or on God, to not only supply us with a vision but to make it irresistibly compelling.

When our minds are attended to and listened to, we usually get very *mild* suggestions and hints that vaguely float through and quickly evaporate. Rarely are we knocked on the head at first. That tends to come later, when you have already been listening to your still, small voice for awhile. Then all your inner attentiveness pays off in a spurt of certainty that can be very exciting. But that only comes when you have legs to stand it up on. Our inspirations at first may seem very ordinary, like an art class or signing up for tennis, or maybe trying square dancing or volunteering at the animal shelter. These do not seem like grand steps toward big successes; they are just little activities that seem like a good idea at the time. However, these little leads are crucial. It is not your job to guess in advance what is being prepared for with these experiences. Your job is only to read your mind, and follow up by showing up. As we honor our instincts and let ourselves follow our noses, the inspirations will get stronger, and we will be guided back toward who we were really meant to be in this life.

Marbles Out of the Tube

When you are determined to listen to your own still, small voice, there is a simple way to go about it. In the Growth Group, we call this technique "taking the next marble out of the tube." In our group meetings, I used a little, hollow plastic tube, capped at both ends, which is stacked full of marbles, and I told them, "This is a model of how your mind works." Uncapping the tube at one end represents your willingness to receive your own inner guidance. Wanting to do something about it is tilting that end of the tube slightly downward from horizontal. The movement of the marbles out of the end of the tube is the flow of inspiration, instigated by the parts of ourselves that know *exactly* what we have to do to become fully ourselves. Each marble, or idea, is the perfect next step for our growth.

If we take each marble (or idea) seriously and let it come out to be considered, we have just opened the way for the next one. However, if we feel that a marble is silly or unacceptable and we refuse to even take it out to look at it, then the next marble never comes out. There is a stoppage, a block in the flow that backs up all the other ideas that are just dying to come out and help us. The fifth or two-hundred-fifth marble might be the perfect idea you need, but you would never be able to get to it if you had refused a less likely marble earlier.

Many fairy tales, like the *Frog Prince* or *Beauty and the Beast,* have this theme of not being fooled away from great blessings later by rejecting ugly first appearances. The ideas, the marbles – ugly or beautiful – will come to you in fantasy, daydreaming, idle wishes, and memories.

Your job is to pay attention and consider them seriously. Not necessarily to act on them, but to realize that they are another piece of the puzzle. Often the marble comes out in the form of a very simple urge to find out more about something, to visit a place, or to check up on an old acquaintance. Each time these urges are taken seriously, you are signaling your true self, your underlying mind, that you will welcome the messages and use them. There is no better way to ensure they will keep coming. Your true self has feelings just like everybody else, you know! How many times would you keep calling someone who did nothing but hang up on you?

When we are trying to discover who we were meant to be, for maximum personal satisfaction and benefit to others, *it is important not to let our conscious minds be the boss.* Our conscious minds take the limited options they know and immediately start flinging them into boxes labeled "Possible" and "Impossible." Remember, your conscious mind prefers the familiar, the predictable, and the logical. Real creativity is not its thing. And to move out into a new way of being, a new life, requires creativity and being open to inspiration. You may get stuck on the rigid options your conscious mind has selected, but your underlying mind will keep trying to get you to take that next marble out of the tube. So occupy your conscious mind with what it does best, by making lists of costs and benefits, reasons and objections. And as it sits huddled in obsessive worry over its account books, you can start leisurely opening the mail from your underlying mind. You don't have to do what it says right away; you just owe it a look. One marble at a time.

How Far to Trust the Little Voice?

But what if the little voice, the next marble, tells you to do something dramatic, something that would have a huge impact on the rest of your life? Suppose it declares you should sell your house, for instance, or leave your partner? Should you do it? Well, let's look at it this way. If someone you respect immensely came up to you and made the same recommendations, would you automatically follow them? Of course not. You would want to know why they thought that, or you might dismiss them out of hand immediately as preposterous. But you'd probably keep thinking about what they said.

It should be the same with the little voice. Treat it as a respected but rather inscrutable advisor, who gives pearls of wisdom that initially may seem implausible or ridiculous. Soon you will learn that this sage has an uncanny way of pointing toward the deeper truth. After awhile you might learn to listen even when you don't understand and file it away for future use. Any idea still has to be evaluated by your conscious, rational mind, of course. You always need your *whole* brain for important decisions, even when you are trying to be more intuitive and receptive to your inner voice. The best policy is to treat the messages from within as little pieces of truth that have not been fully understood yet.

For instance, the thought of wanting to leave your spouse may not have been intended as a command to leave your family unsupported while you find yourself. Instead it may be a symbolic call for more individuality on your part, in which you "leave" them psychologically at times in order to pursue your dream. Similarly, the persistent thought that you need to sell your house may be indicating not supernatural market savvy, but an awareness that too much of your creative energy is being siphoned off by the demands of keeping up a household that may be bigger than your needs. The little voice likes to give us ideas of how to lighten our load, so that we can know our deeper purposes more clearly.

Some people in their enthusiasm try acting directly on whatever hunches and intuitions they get at first, and in this way become too uncritical in the process of reading their own minds. In fact, they can get downright fascinated by their own psyches, as though the only source of wisdom for these individuals is the voice within. However, there are many sources of knowledge and we need to consult all of them, the ones outside as well as the ones inside. We don't want to become an unthinking slave of our unconscious inner influence, otherwise we have merely replaced the tyranny of public opinion with the tyranny of our next impulse.

Enter the Dilemma

Once we start reading our own minds and we get the idea of what it is that we want to do, the very next thing we will do is make it into a problem. We practically never say, "Oh, right! I see now! To be perfectly fulfilled, I must do this and that. I'll get right on it!" Remember that we are cut off from our real selves for very good reasons that have a long history. Those reasons are not about to evaporate instantly; we are all very attached to our problems. After all, if we were to realize all at once that we have been cowering before an illusion for twenty years, it could be downright discouraging. Nobody needs to know that they wasted *that* much time. So when we finally get the right idea for ourselves, our first instinct is to fight it. We immediately think up its opposite – i.e., the reason it cannot be done.

What do you gain psychologically from hamstringing yourself in this way? You get time. Time to get used to the idea, time to think it over, and to weave the new thought into the rest of your life. As we feel pulled between two apparently conflicting desires (for instance, our family responsibilities and following our dreams), we set up a *dilemma*. This state of tension between two opposites is something that we human beings seem to have a real affinity for. It's also known as the "Yes, but" position. It serves to keep us from making mistakes, but it also serves to hold us back for no good reason. As we said before, a dilemma is a failure of imagination and a negative faith in the belief that we can't have what we truly want. Our lack of imagination and trust guarantees that the tension between the two poles will not be easily resolved. You feel that you're damned if you do and damned if you don't.

The good news is that this is not a cosmic reality undermining your life, even though it may feel that way at times. No, it is simply an old way of thinking that dies hard. It is the belief that you cannot have what you want without pain and isolation and giving up all that you hold near and dear. So you dither between your two alternatives and drive yourself crazy with equal doses of excitement and hopelessness. But as you will discover, a dilemma by definition can never be resolved on its own terms. Inside its own mutually exclusive system, it must perpetuate itself as long as it is perceived as a forced choice. The expression, "being on the horns of a dilemma," captures the intense discomfort and lack of control such a predicament brings.

Often at this point in our search for who were meant to be, we feel stuck and discouraged. Dilemmas are made up of black-and-white, all-or-nothing thinking and often represent conflict between the way we think we are *supposed* to be and what we *wish* we could be. We cannot see how to resolve the dilemma without being "selfish" (doing what we want) or "trapped" (doing what others want). When faced with such dreadful alternatives, we often resort to the kind of avoidant compromises we have used over the years. We do for others, play the role, make the money, and indulge ourselves in little ways through eating, shopping, drinking, or hobbies. We buy time and try to escape. We stop reading our own minds, at least until we become symptomatic, depressed, anxious, addicted, or physically sick.

It is hard to believe there could be a creative answer that does not involve sacrificing one thing for another, but this is the solution that Robert Fritz comes up with in his book, *The Path of Least Resistance*[34]. Instead of being pulled back and forth from one option to the other, we simply assume that our future solution will incorporate *both* sides of the dilemma, even though we have no idea what it could be. We trust that if we keep taking marbles out of the tube and reading our own minds, the answer will come. All we have to do is keep desiring it and tolerate the tension that is necessary for creative solutions to emerge.

If we become impatient and act too quickly, we will break the tension by choosing one horn of the dilemma and renouncing the other. Clearly a one-sided choice is not a good solution or there wouldn't have been a dilemma in the first place! No, we must insist that *both* sides of the dilemma have to be included; we just need to find the creative solution that addresses them both. Instead of pinging back and forth between two polarities, we can draw a third point to make it a triangle, as Fritz suggests in this diagram:

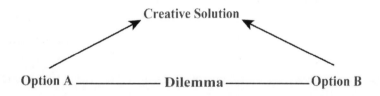

In this way, we treat the two incompatible options as the squabbling siblings they are, refusing to get involved in their fight and seeking a solution that will be better for all. The key, as Fritz points out, is that the creative solution must dissolve the dilemma by lifting up both points of view into a perspective that is larger than either of them. It doesn't have to be so hopeless and one-sided. Your dilemma is a perceptual illusion of narrow thinking, not an actual fact. If you don't want to give up one thing for the other because both are important to you, then that feeling is telling you that you need to figure out a way that you can do both.

An apparent dilemma should never be accepted on its own terms. The dilemma will always tell you, "Choose!" and by so doing, you will always be giving up one essential thing for another essential thing. It's a no-win situation. Reject that way of looking at it, and insist quietly to yourself that there is an answer if you are honest enough with yourself and give yourself time. The dilemma is simply a preliminary step in the process. But it is a tripping step that causes many people to give up because they don't know how to think their way past it.

The dilemma stage is an important period of examination to give yourself time to help clarify what is really important to you and *why*. By refusing to make a premature decision and by tolerating the strain of being caught between the old way and the new dream, new solutions have a chance to percolate.

In psychotherapy, I often suggest to people that they resist making a decision as long as they feel caught up in a dilemma. I start with the assumption that there is something they need to understand about the meaning of the choices facing them in this dilemma, and that to rush a decision would be to throw away a tremendous chance for growth.

Dilemmas are hard – and inevitable. Having some idea of what a dilemma is like and what its underlying purpose is can help keep you from getting demoralized. Now, when a dilemma hits, you can actually smile to yourself because you know it means you are on your way. Nobody ever had a dilemma if they weren't being tempted to grow.

CHAPTER 10

PICKING YOUR PROBLEMS

Our problems have messages for us, if we take the time to enter into a relationship with them and listen to what they are trying to tell us.

Sitting in a circle together in the late afternoon, Growth Group members were sharing ideas about living out their dreams. Molly, ordinarily a very capable, middle-aged woman, shook her head and talked in a dispirited voice about how much money and time it would take to open her own restaurant. As Molly listed one obstacle after another, her face began to sag and her dispirited mood was contagious. It seemed as though a wall of discouragement were rising up before us, forbidding us to climb it. Molly had been in an unhappy early marriage, suffered through a financially devastating divorce, got a good job with a high level of responsibility, raised her children alone, and recently had mastered the art of motorcycle riding.

Clearly Molly had what it took to take hold of life and prosper. Nevertheless, she was now hampered by her belief that while she could handle problems that were dumped on her, she would not be able to handle problems she had instigated in the pursuit of her dream. "Molly, you're always going to have problems," I reminded her. "Wouldn't you rather choose them yourself for a change?"

In this chapter, we will look at the illusion that held Molly and holds many of the rest of us captive: if we avoid actively creating problems in our lives by trying something new, we will have fewer problems. Nothing could be further from the truth. There are no fewer problems. The problem variable in life is a constant, whether small or large, but there are pleasant problems and there are unpleasant problems. In many cases, we can pick where *we* want our problems to be. We just cannot choose to have no problems. Becoming who you were meant to be means happily trading in old problems for new ones, the kind of problems better known as challenge and accomplishment.

Wishing Can Bring Problems

When we finally become aware of what we want and begin to make the move toward getting it, we will bump into problems. As a direct result of our wishing, we will have more to deal with than we did before. There will be obstacles and discomfort, lack of support, and discouragement. There will be times we'll wish we never started wishing! This is because we have been trained to think of problems as bad things to be avoided as much as possible. Most of us have that little ego voice inside us telling us not to make it harder on ourselves, to take it easy, and not rock the boat. Play it safe and keep the problems to a minimum. This is the destructive strategy of *avoidance* that keeps us running from our problems rather than entering the ring with them. This mind-set tells us there is only so much energy to go around and that we must conserve this energy by avoiding problems as often as possible. But think about it: how much energy does it take to keep avoiding something? Quite a bit, and there is absolutely no return on your investment for this kind of energy expenditure. The more you avoid, the less you get.

Perhaps there was or is someone in your family or life who lived like this, avoiding problems, seeming drained and stressed by them and generally accepting a lower level of living in exchange for apparently fewer problems. If you grew up around or are now with someone who deals with life this way, it may have rubbed off on you. You may have become afraid of tackling problems and may now believe that the safest route is to keep things simple. Therefore, when you begin to think about going after your dream, you are reminded of this deep, unconscious belief that it's smart to avoid anything that makes life harder.

But life is hard anyway! And what could be harder than adjusting at a level that is ungratifying, unsatisfying and below your abilities? Life gets *really* tough when you try to simplify your life to the point where it is problem-free, because that means you are going backwards to a childish helplessness. People who chronically seek to avoid all problems ultimately end up leading marginal lives, without much money, very little security, struggling with addictions, and surrounded by people who are not going anywhere either.

Wishing makes problems, but the alternative of not wishing makes your life a dead end. You may think it is easier to give up your dreams and ambitions than to take on a bunch of new problems. Yet do you know how hard it is to...

...watch yourself get older and not see anything ever changing?

...know you gave up your whole life because you were afraid of what others might say?

...turn the big fifty, sixty, or seventy and realize you did not do what you wanted with your life?

...be stuck in a job you hate until retirement?

...see your children grow up and leave you behind with no new purpose in your life?

...die unfulfilled?

Now those are what I call problems.

Why You Can Do It

The fact that you have made it as far as you have already proves you have something going for you. You have already made countless tough decisions by this point, have you not? Life has already put plenty in front of you that you have not chosen, right? And you have reacted and dealt with it and survived. You have found your way around the jungle so far, by reacting and wanting to live. You are experienced!

Why then would you think you are unprepared or unable to change your life path and become more of who you were meant to be? Perhaps it is because *reacting* to problems that are thrown at us seems easier than actively *selecting* the problems that are going to come to us.

When you start out to make your dreams come true, you are signing on for a whole set of new problems, and subconsciously you know this very well. You can see that your dreams may put you in some debt, cause strained family relations, or maybe make you lose sleep and get anxious. It may be very plain that these things might happen if you choose this new path. So you back up, and tell yourself that you do not want to take on a whole set of new problems. Things in your life are complicated and hard enough already and you have no desire to add to them. You begin to regard your latent ambition as something that will deplete your energy, which is already considerably tied up with just getting through everyday life. The dream and its pursuit can seem like just one more chore and you are already tired.

However, your dream is about adding to you, not taking anything away. It is about reconnecting to your energy, your power source. Not draining you, but irrigating your dried up life with hope and excitement. Everybody's life is full of problems. And that's the way it's going to be. Why not actively choose problems you would enjoy solving, the ones that can give you some rewards for tackling them?

The Bed of Nails

Maintaining the status quo instead of pursuing your dreams is like lying on a bed of nails. After awhile, if it's the only bed you have and you learn not to move around too much, you begin to adjust. You say to yourself, this is how my life is. It feels like your familiar fate, as if it were simply your destiny to cope with whatever has been dumped on you. We get used to dealing with the addicted spouse, the backstabbing boss, the ungrateful child. They don't seem like problems in the same way that doing something new and different looks like a problem. We slip into our old problems like a pair of well-worn slippers.

Here's another way of looking at it: whether deliberately or not, you actually may have chosen many of the very problems you have now. You may have chosen *passively,* by letting things evolve and allowing other people's desires to dominate your own – but you may be the one who let it happen. Now you have all the problems that went along with that original passive choice. You may be in the mental habit of seeing your life as something that has been happening to you. Maybe you are not as helpless as that. Maybe you are less a victim than an unwitting collaborator.

Our Childish Hope

Many of us hold onto the childish belief that perhaps we can find a way to escape from *all* problems. We think that maybe if we do not step forward and choose our problems, we will not have any. We tell ourselves the ones that we have are accidental and could go away. If we start out on a new path and actively select our problems, then we know for sure we will have problems. We have the childish hope in our heart of hearts that our problems may go away on their own if only we are good enough and wait long enough.

Unfortunately, this is not true. Life is wonderfully complex, but it is not easy. Once you are grown, things do not get easier, because the further you go, the more there is to handle. Ask any explorer; problems go with new territory. Problems will either show up at your door, passively allowed, or you can go after them and pick the ones you prefer. We cannot always choose what *kind* of problems we are going to have. But we can narrow the field. Are you going to choose the unfulfilled-life problem or the unsatisfying-marriage problem? Perhaps you'd rather choose the longhours-studying-to-get-that-degree problem? Or the effort of the making-a-dream-come-true problem?

One thing is true, as far as I can see. When you *choose* to solve problems actively, you take yourself out of the passive victim mentality and get a sense of control and forward movement back in your life. Following your dream and becoming who you were meant to be brings its own set of problems, no question. Its selling point is not the absence of problems. But that's not what should make up your mind to find the future you were meant to have. Instead it should be the satisfying sense of control, the feeling of integrity, and the boost in energy that comes when the problems you solve are in the service of your greater goal.

Sometimes we are drawn to whatever we see as offering the easy way out, whatever we think would cause us to expend the least amount of energy to get what we want. The fact is that when we are expending energy in the direction of something we love and enjoy doing, even though this activity has its demands, we feel joy and satisfaction. Exciting goals bring us pleasure along with the problems inherent in achieving them. At times there will still be hard work, problems still have to be solved, but we feel good about ourselves as we solve them.

Problems that are *actively chosen* are what we call a *challenge*. We refer to our problems as challenges when we are working toward a chosen goal. Some people resent it when optimists try to reframe the problems they endure as "challenges" because this label does not reflect those people's experiences. They did not freely choose this problem, so it is not a "challenge" to them, it is a colossal *problem!* However, when you turn from passivity to active acceptance of freely chosen problems, you literally are turning problems into challenges. A challenge is just something that stands between you and your goal. It should call up your fighting instinct and your stick-to-it-ness.

Don't Let Your Feelings Drive

Remember that the negative ego voice is highly emotional and uses emotion to steer you away from anything that might take you off the old path. It will make the new problems you choose seem to be much worse than any of the old ones you had. So remember to listen to the unemotional, still, small voice – the one that knows. It is your compass when things get difficult due to emotional frustrations. A bad day does not mean you are not supposed to be doing something. It may mean that it's hard and is causing problems, but it does not necessarily mean you should not be doing it. Your emotions will always distort your judgment and handling new problems means handling plenty of emotions, too. Your job is to experience the emotions, slog through them, and keep handling the kind of problems you believe are worthwhile.

Emotions of discouragement and resentment often travel with problems, but they do not have to become your advisors. These emotional opinions are notoriously skewed in the direction of ego agendas, so take them with a grain of salt.

Once, while working on a section of this book, I was feeling that the morning was being totally wasted because of my frustrated frame of mind. I made myself keep writing to turn out the number of pages I wanted, but it felt like I was just going through the motions. I saw myself in that scene in the movie, *The Shining*,[35] where the insane hotel caretaker spends all day typing out a single meaningless sentence over and over. My *feelings* were telling me I had accomplished exactly nothing and writing this book seemed like a problem well worth dropping. Yet when I read my notes a week later – now back in a hopeful frame of mind – I was amazed at how much sense I made despite my state of mind at the time. My writing was about as good as it ever was, and the ideas were coherent and on subject. I learned that my emotional state was not a reliable compass for determining whether I should go on or not.

How Do You Handle Complications?

Life seems to get harder whenever you try to achieve something, but it really just gets more complicated. *Problems are nothing more than complications.* There's more information to process, more emotions to feel, more decisions to be made. In other words, more of you is required to grapple with whatever is going on around you. Your brain must weigh facts, make judgments, and figure out consequences. To deal with a problem successfully, we not only have to think about right now, we also have to think about the future. Therefore we must mentally live in two places at once, in the now and in the yet-to-be. Not least of all, we have to both feel and think at the same time – we have to solve problems wisely even though we are feeling scared and upset. Think of all the neuronal activity that goes on inside our poor brains under these circumstances!

Many people experience these cognitive demands as noxious, because they dislike dealing with complexity and complications. When things get complicated, they run. Bear in mind I am not talking about people who mentally *cannot* deal with complexity; I am talking about people who have gotten into the habit of *avoiding* complexity. For instance, Molly, whom I referred to at the beginning of this chapter, took one look at the complexity of opening her own little restaurant and gave up. She did this in spite of the fact she had been very capably handling plenty of problems for a long time. If Molly could find no way out of a complication, she faced it and dealt with it like a champ. She was a passive hero, not an active one. She did not seek out challenges, even though she would roll up her sleeves and beat them into submission if they showed up at her door.

How do you deal with complications? Is your first instinct to run away from them? Do you avoid the extra brain effort?

Many normal developmental steps in our society require people to make their lives more complicated, and we accept this as the price of admission. These are familiar, socially-sanctioned complications, and so we just forge ahead and tackle them because we see everyone else around us doing it. Getting married, going to college, getting a job, having children, buying a home – all these are huge developmental steps in adult life that by definition make your life more complicated. Why then do we accept these without a whimper and yet turn pale with fear over pursuing our own dreams?

The answer is simple: complications like marriage and childrearing are socially supported activities, even though they look like individual choices. But when we pursue our own dreams and thereby pick a whole new set of problems for ourselves, we might feel the lack of society's back-up. We feel the existential aloneness of being an adult making difficult choices.

One Piece at a Time

Complications make you work harder. They require more from you. When several problems arrive at once they demand your attention. If you are unfamiliar with complicated situations, you may believe that you are being asked to deal with everything simultaneously. As you know, that is the recipe for feeling overwhelmed and unable to cope. Anyone can get demoralized trying to handle too much at once. This is the reason why most people tend to avoid complications. It feels like they are being asked to do the impossible, like learning to juggle on a moment's notice.

Masters of complications never see themselves as doing everything at once. Therefore, they do not feel overwhelmed and like running away. Instead of focusing on the complexity as a huge, monolithic thing, they "chunk" it. They break the complexity down into single chunks that they tackle piece by piece. They think in terms of steps and what to pick first. Items are prioritized and they look for the best starting point. What is the first thing they need to do? What should come next? This is exactly what anyone has to do when they have a problem. After you are done running around, you still have to quiet down from the panic and make the choice of what to do next. Master problem-solvers just save themselves the trouble of panicking first. They don't resist complications, because they know that "overwhelming" complications are just a whole string of sequential decision points.

For master problem-solvers, problems are not emotional events; they are mental events. They know that a complication only becomes an "issue" when you add fear to it. They completely mentally accept the presence of the problem (they don't waste energy bemoaning their fate). They stop themselves from emotional reactivity; instead of asking "Why me?" they think, "What needs to be done next?" If they don't know what to do next, they consider who might give them the best advice.

Decisions, Decisions

This is as good a time as any to ask you how you feel about having to make decisions. Many of us do not like to make decisions and see decisions as problems to be avoided. When you pick new problems to handle in order to follow your new path, you will also be handling a lot of decisions. Remember, problems are nothing more than complexity, and complexity just means lots of little decisions bunched together. You must learn to tolerate the risk of making a bad decision, a mistake.

Maybe there's something about that word "decision" that sounds too final to us. A decision sounds like the end of the story, doesn't it? How about "choices" as a better word? When you think about making a choice, you are focusing on getting what you *want*. Too often, when we think about making a decision, we focus on what we are giving up. Think about your decisions simply as choices. You made the wrong choice? Whoops, just make another choice and keep on until you get it right. Don't wait until you are trapped in a corner and feel forced to make a choice reactively. Make your choices early and actively to get where you want to end up.

The Two Biggest Problems

Whenever you are trying to move ahead with your plans for a more fulfilling future, there are usually two problems that stand above all the rest: time and money.

Time: The way we see the amount of time we have left in life is a function of which stage of life we are in. In our early twenties, time is in abundance. But in our forties, we are likely to see ourselves as not having enough time left to start anything new. Gail Sheehy writes about this abbreviated view of the future in her book, *New Passages*[36], and points out that in middle age, people often have an unrealistically shrunken estimate of how much time they have left in their lives.

Let's say that you are forty years old and are thinking about a career move. If you are like most people, you will think about yourself as already being forty years along the road you are currently on. Forty years is a long time; how can you think about switching now? Actually, that time frame is a fallacy. You're probably less than twenty years old in *work* years. You probably started seriously working for a living around the age of twenty, give or take a few years, and this means you are only at about the halfway point of your work life. *At age forty, you probably have more work years left in your life than you have already worked.* You have worked for twenty years and still have twenty-five years or more to go until retirement. Think back on how long it seems to you that you have been working. Think about how long it takes for your children to grow up. We humans are blessed with really long lives if everything goes well. We have much longer than we act like we have. You have time. The next five or ten years are going to pass anyway. Go ahead and pick yourself some good problems to handle in order to make these years interesting and productive!

For instance, a person might be thinking of going back to school and starting a different career, but then tell herself that at age forty-five she only has a few years left until retirement. It will take five years or longer to get the degree she wants. What would be the sense of making the investment of time and money if she will have so little time to enjoy it? By then she thinks she would have practically no time left to make a living from her achievement.

The reality is that at age forty-five this woman has at least twenty work years left. Even if it took her ten years to get her degree, she would still have *ten years* to devote to her new occupation. Ten years can be a long time. In material terms, do you know how much money you can make in ten years?

Money: Let's say your education for your new career takes four years and costs you a hefty $40,000 in loans. To make it an even worse case scenario, let's say you are fifty-five by the time you get finished. If your career change or higher degree results in an increase of only $10,000 a year in income over what you were making before, you will increase your earning power by $100,000 in present day dollars over the next ten years until retirement at sixty-five. Even taking out the $40,000 plus, say, 8% interest for loans over the next ten years, you are still left with more than an approximately $40,000 increase on your investment. Now re-compute the potential gain if you are only thirty-five, or forty-five, and you will see what I am getting at. There's more time left and more money to be made than you probably feel there is.

What about the problem of getting the money to pursue your dream in the first place? It's not that there's no money available anywhere. There's quite a lot available for good causes and new projects. The catch is that most people or places that loan money expect you to pay it back. They are placing you under contract to be a responsible adult who will succeed and repay your debts. If you are not quite sure that you want to sign up and be accountable, then yes, money may continue to be a problem. The key here is your attitude. If you are willing to go after your goal by tackling the complications and problems that arise in its pursuit, then you will probably be willing to pursue the funding for it as well.

Borrowing money and having a debt to pay back are not such bad things. Every time you go into debt for your dream, you are committing to succeed. You are saying that you see yourself in the future as able to pay the money back. It can be motivating to put yourself on the hook a little with some official debt. Going into debt for something that is going to increase your earning power later on is a good investment.

Lack of Sympathy

If you decide to complicate your life in order to become who you were meant to be, will your family and friends give you empathy and encouragement? Or will they think you have gotten yourself into that mess in the first place and therefore are undeserving of sympathetic help? You may have found that if you are a helpless victim, others will rush in to assist. But if you have chosen to complicate your life for the purpose of personal growth, you may fear they won't see your need for help as legitimate.

This is a good time to sort out who your real friends are. Anyone who is not willing to encourage you to grow and achieve those things you need to be fulfilled is not on your side, no matter how willing they are to help out when you are in trouble. When you are perceived as helplessly victimized by external troubles, these false helpers offer you sympathy to bring you closer together to them and the group. However, when you are picking problems to solve in the service of creating a more fulfilling life for yourself, they might not offer help, because they may resent your springing free of the group in order to achieve on your own. The people who are truly on your side will help you succeed even if it means you may take off and not come back.

Many families pride themselves on always "being there" for each other, which basically means that when someone is having problems, the family will do whatever they can to help out. It seems that often this guarantee of "being there" is very contingent on the problems being beyond the person's control, something that the person has been saddled with through no choice of her own. But when a family member chooses new complications in her life in order to become more truly who she is, her family may get quite judgmental about this and actually withhold support. That's when you get to see the real terms of the family contract, the fine print enforcing mutual dependency. There are other people willing to really be there for your self-initiated growth struggles: sign on with them instead.

Sharon Picks Some New Problems

Sharon already had her hands full. With three school-age children and a husband frequently out of town, she was used to holding down the fort on her own. Her work as a high school guidance counselor was busy but routine, and she was beginning to feel stifled by the same old problems day in and day out. There seemed no time for anything creative or exciting and the next twenty years were looking like more of the same. Maybe it was turning forty, maybe it was seeing her youngest step on the bus for junior high. But Sharon felt something changing inside her, something beyond her conscious intention and certainly beyond her busy schedule. Sharon began to feel she would curl up and die if she had to spend the rest of her life being the same person she was right now. When her fear of change was outweighed by her restlessness, she was ready to tackle new problems.

For years Sharon had observed the high levels of frustration and burnout among her professional peers. She became inspired to provide burnout prevention training to guidance counselors statewide. It became her mission. Sharon was convinced that she knew why the counselors were so demoralized and she came up with a program to reconnect them with their enthusiasm for helping and teach them how to support and help one another. Writing out her ideas in the evenings and weekends, Sharon soon had a workshop proposal that she submitted to the state guidance counselor association. They were impressed with her idea and gave her the endorsement necessary for offering continuing education credits. Sharon was on her way toward a new consulting and training career.

Sharon had carved out a load of new problems for her life. Planning the workshop was one thing, but designing a catchy brochure and getting it out to a statewide system of schools was time consuming. But perhaps the hardest step came when she had to reserve the hotel conference room for the workshop three months in advance with a non-refundable deposit. Sharon had to put her own money down, not knowing if anyone would show up. This was unlike anything that she had ever done before, but she knew that without some experience in giving a real training workshop, her new career as consultant would never get off the ground. She also had to plan the workshop's group activities not knowing if there would be ten or two hundred attendees, plan a luncheon at the hotel, and generate publicity. Sharon now had a full crop of new problems.

What was it like for her? She was scared, full of self-doubt, and regularly woke up at three o'clock in the morning to worry. Did she want to stop? No, because she knew this was the only way to get going in the right direction and she was willing to put up with short-term anxiety in favor of a long-term goal.

It turned out that despite the two thousand brochures that Sharon mailed out, only nineteen people attended the two-day workshop. Then, incredibly, the hotel where the workshop was being held caught fire the first evening and workshop participants staying at the hotel were evacuated until twelve o'clock that night. Nevertheless, the workshop went on the next day and Sharon still got what she had needed: experience in writing, organizing, advertising, and giving a bona fide two-day workshop. She had taken the necessary first step in her new consultant's career.

Did Sharon have to do any of this? No. She deliberately picked a bunch of new problems to solve for herself and got plenty of unexpected ones as well. However, she was moving in the direction of her dream and all those problems added up to another notch on her resume. Shortly after the workshop, with her new experience, Sharon successfully pursued an opportunity to give a speech at the national conference of professional guidance counselors. The prestige and exposure this gave her soon resulted in invitations to run other workshops – for pay.

Sharon had picked the problems to solve that were going to help her realize her mission: to become a consultant and to help burned-out counselors who so badly needed her encouragement. Sharon looked at her old problems of being demoralized and tired of her job and then she looked at her new problems. She now had proof that when she tackled the new problems, she ended up stronger. Sharon is now dealing with solving problems she *wants* to solve, and that makes all the difference in how she feels about herself.

Your Relationship with Your Problems

As soon as a problem shows up at your front door, you have a relationship with it. Like any relationship, it is full of feelings and bias. The kind of relationship you decide to forge with your problem will determine the outcome, just as it would with another person. The one option you do not have is wishing the problem away. A problem – whether it shows up uninvited or is actively picked by you – demands a response. It will react back to you, just as a real person might. Being stuck with a problem we don't want can bring out the worst in any of us. But just like with people, forgetting our manners creates more problems than it is worth. Problems have feelings too, don't forget. You must give your problems the courtesy of listening to their message instead of slamming the door in their faces. Believe me, you don't want to make your problems mad. They're likely to show back up with some of their friends.

If a problem you did not invite shows up on your doorstep, don't pretend you are not home. It probably has the right address. Ask what it wants. Our problems have information for us, if we take the time to enter into relationships with them and listen to what they're trying to tell us. These are usually messages about what we have ignored, what we have been hiding from, or simply what we need to do next. Your problem is about some area of incompleteness in your life, something that has not been attended to. In fact, if you think about it, this is probably not the first time this problem has tried to ring your bell. It is very likely that you waited until the problem was about to break your door down before you were willing to listen.

Problems have a habit of hanging around people who like them the least. The more they upset you, the more they are attracted to you. All you have to do to be convinced of this great truth is to look at times in your life when you were especially vulnerable and upset by the problems you were facing. Haven't you noticed how being in that state of fear and emotion attracted yet more problems to you? There is the old expression "When it rains, it pours," meaning that the more that problems upset you, the more others soon show up.

If you look back over your life with calm detachment, you will probably observe that your problems have not been randomly and evenly dispersed over time, like molecules in a solution. Instead, they tend to cluster, to glop around little mental fear states in your mind, forming high density pockets of antimatter that suck any problems in the vicinity right into your life. This is also known as the phenomenon of if-it's-not-one-thing-it's-another. Don't ask me why a fight with your spouse should create flat tires or broken water heaters, but such small complications seem to follow. Problems thrive on being rejected. Problems are absolutely besotted by intensely negative human emotion, and wild elephants could not pull them away from you as long as you are oozing fear and avoidance. Face up to them and they lose steam. It is your fearfulness that gives them their impressive size.

Dealing with People, Dealing with Problems

Your problems are like the people who complicate your life and you will probably relate to them in the same way that you deal with difficult people. Do you take them on early and set the ground rules from the beginning or do you let them get into the habit of treating you badly? Give some thought to how you deal with difficult people and how they make you feel.

There are two common reaction styles:

"They Hurt My Feelings": If difficult people get under your skin and make you feel badly about yourself, then your problems probably will too. In this case, picking some new problems to solve for yourself may feel to you as though you are signing up for low self-esteem. With this mind-set, you are understandably highly reluctant to take on any new problems. Just as critical people do, your problems make you doubt yourself and your projects. Subconsciously, thanks to the negative impact of your ego, you believe that your problems are a sign that you really are not cut out to be whatever it is you are trying to be. You have a secret and irrational conviction that if you were really doing the right thing, then these kinds of problems would not be showing up. You secretly believe that problems are a sign of your inadequacy, just like you secretly concur when some mean, critical person devalues you. You handle difficult people *and* problems by backing down and acting as though you believed that you are not competent or equipped to go on.

"They Can't Do This to Me": Anger is another way of saying that both problems and difficult people scare you. Anger is a fear reaction, designed to pump up your adrenaline so you can fight or flee. It is also primarily emotional, involving little thinking. You become indignant or even furious when difficult people treat you badly, and react by spending all your energy fantasizing rebuttals or plots for revenge. When you encounter problems, you feel persecuted. It is not just a few difficult people, but the world itself that is out to get you. You do not feel bad about yourself nor are you in a state of low self-esteem. Instead, you are angry about being treated this way and do not feel that you deserve all the strain and frustration that your new problems are bringing you. With this way of looking at things, you are burning up a lot of emotional fuel just to stay offended by the difficult people and problems in your life.

Now what do these two styles have in common? They both are about getting lost in your reactions. So lost that you forget what it was you were going after in the first place and why. This is what happens when your *emotional reactions* to a problem become the focus, rather than figuring out what to do about the *problem.* They are also about seeing the source of power as being outside yourself. Whether you get depressed or angry, the mechanism is the same: you are reacting to feelings of fear and helplessness.

We often say that a person or problem is "making" us upset, which is a very accurate way of stating it. There are plenty of times when we can be made to feel all sorts of things, whether we want to or not. It is a fact that difficult people and problems can have a big impact on us, *but only as long as we have a secret desire to avoid our problems.* These negative situations have power over us and make us upset only as long as we hold onto the secret wish to not have to deal with any problems in our life. This desperate avoidance is what gives problems power over us.

When you cherish the secret fantasy that maybe your life can be problem-free if you just avoid problems as much as possible, then it makes sense that you will get *very* upset when somebody or something reminds you that problems are still there. It is natural to want to avoid problems, but it is a bad habit to get into. Remember, problems that need to be solved are a constant. Either you choose to handle them or they will handle you. When you get scared or indignant about problems, you are just delaying the inevitable task of dealing with them.

You Are Not Alone With Your Problems

This is where mentors, friends, educators, therapists, support groups, coaches, and self-improvement books come in. The reason you shy away from new challenges is not that there is something fundamentally, terribly wrong with you as a human being – it is because you have had an information and training deficit in the proper attitude toward problem-solving. In the next chapter, we will be looking at the importance of finding a community of people with similar ideas and interests who are capable of helping you to grow emotionally and personally.

As you pick new problems to handle, pick some new friends too. They are easy to spot, because they are the ones who make you feel like your dreams might just be possible. They also have useful ideas for how to make the future better and want to help you get where you want to go.

CHAPTER 11

Fitting In:
Finding Your Lifestyle
and Community

The purpose of our closest relationships is to build energy. Using this energy barometer is a foolproof method for recognizing people you need to be with.

Sooner or later most of us will feel the need to be with people who make us feel alive and full of possibilities. Fitting in and belonging are basic human needs. We all have the powerful drive to become a part of something outside ourselves. We feel the urge to find a place and a group of people that make us feel comfortable, telling us we are in the right spot. Under these conditions we can relax and be ourselves. Unfortunately, not all of us feel this way in their relationships, and if you are one of these people, this chapter is written for you. To live in a group or community where we feel fundamentally different is a special kind of psychological suffering. It means that we must always be playing a role in order simply to communicate.

If a person's deepest needs are chronically unmet by his main group, he or she will naturally begin looking for a new person or community with which to bond or else risk feeling isolated. Those who are beginning to wake up to their true selves will recognize their need for a new group and will seek out people who energize them and help them fulfill their potential.

Yet sometimes there can be a very uncomfortable transition period between our old lifestyle and our new interests. If we want to move toward our true purpose it is extremely important to *tolerate* this discomfort for as long as it takes to find our new niche. We need to know about this transition stage in advance so that we do not retreat just when we are on the verge of making some marvelous changes in our lives. Most people do not have a ready-made new life just waiting for them to choose it. Instead, we have to begin taking some chances on new situations in order to create opportunities for lives more compatible with our true needs and interests. We begin to make small forays into uncharted territory, trying on bits of new lifestyle here and there. We may start tentatively responding to the attraction we feel toward new groups of people with similar interests. Predictably, it can be an insecure time of transition, as we deal with our own fears and the reactions of those people closest to us.

The Alienation Stage

When you move out beyond your old role and your old group, at times you may experience the feeling that you have no real friends, there is no back-up, you are all alone, you don't belong, there is nothing but emptiness, you are stuck in the darkness, and so on. *These are the sensations of change for the good.* These feelings are just a bit of rocky road that is often encountered when you start to reverse old repressions. When you begin to live more out of your true self, you are going to pass over that old piece of ground again and feel the fears of your first alienation experiences. Fortunately that fear now is only an illusion because *you are no longer helpless.*

When you hit the alienation stage, which can feel like existential abandonment for a little while, the first thing you do is congratulate yourself. Just as if you had succeeded in finally finding a trail you had lost while wandering in the woods, you now know that you are on your way back out. Unfortunately, not many people know to congratulate themselves or others at these moments. They are too busy being afraid and thinking discouraging things about themselves. Even therapists sometimes mistake these moments for going backwards instead of going forward, because the client's anxiety is so convincing. However, if you have been working on finding your own true self and the life you were meant to live, the alienation sensation means you are on the right track. Give yourself credit. Things are really happening.

When your feelings are finally validated as legitimate, real, and reasonable, you may feel emotional pain. This is the pain of re-assimilating a part of yourself that has been forced off into the shadows for years. Reintegration of a lost piece of your soul can really hurt at first. Seek out the help you need during these difficult times. Such moments are what the mystics used to call the dark night of the soul, but they really are encounters with the truth. The painful truth is that until now, those around you have not been able to understand you or give you what you needed at the soul level. When this truth is finally realized, whether painfully or with relief, you become free to form new relationships or to reinvent old ones based on who you really were meant to be.

Getting Along With Everybody

Perhaps you have sought intimate relationships with people you do not even like. Instead of using your natural ability to know whom you like and do not like – every child's innate ability – you have learned to get along with everybody even when they hurt you.

Lila, a lovely, softhearted lady I worked with for several years, used to come into my office and metaphorically wring her hands while saying, "Why are they so mean to me?" or some similar variation, such as "Why are they treating me like this?" or, incredulous and full of hurt, "I wouldn't do that to them." Lila was highly sensitive, a person who thought of other people's needs as naturally as breathing. In fact, she *felt* other people's needs sometimes even before they did. She watched what she said, did not impose, tried to think of others, and yet found herself routinely flattened by the full-bore insensitivities of her husband and her bossy siblings. After each of these squashings, this sweet lady would wonder how they could act this way, since she placed such high value on getting along with everybody.

Finally, though, Lila began to ask the right question, which was not *Why do they keep doing this,* but *Why did their actions keep catching her by surprise?*

Slowly her denial of her loved ones' egocentrism and lack of empathy began to lose its power over her, until one day she was able to admit: "I guess I've never gotten it through my head that people can be like that." This was because she had been taught—brainwashed perhaps – from the earliest stages of her interpersonal consciousness that *they* weren't selfish and insensitive, *she* was. Given this upbringing, how was Lila supposed to see the truth of their egocentrism? Because her family denied the essential fact of their own self-centeredness, Lila was always missing the piece of data that would make sense of the story: her family really did not care how she felt, and worse, they did not regard her as a substantial person worthy of being considered. Because it was her very nature to consider the feelings of others, their emotional neglect was a foreign concept to her and thereby fueled her denial.

Each of us can create such traps in adulthood. Like Lila, we can try too hard to get along with people, tolerating such things as an inhibiting, joyless marriage or negative, critical friends. There is no need for this once we wake up from denial about the very human, but often very self-involved motives of our loved ones. We do not have to fault them for being human, but neither do we have to go on pretending they know better than we do about what we need.

Shooting You Down

When people first start out on new paths of their very own, following ambitions that arise from their cores, their families and friends can perceive this as implicit rejection. Resentment and envy can be the instant reaction rather than support and encouragement. Yet these are the people who're supposed to be on your side!

Some of the stories I have heard are so staggering as to be unbelievable, but they happen all the time. Just at the moment of take-off, the closest relationships in our lives can start pulling us backwards. It is incredible, but there is something about seeing someone proudly realize a dream that stirs up the urge in some people to find the weak spot, the disappointment, the little piece of it that is not so great. Cathy, a woman who had been determinedly working on her writing skills, finally had a short story published in an amateur writer's competition. When Cathy told her husband, the first words out of his mouth were "Are you getting paid?"

Another person, a man in his thirties, had struggled for over ten years trying to get on with an airline as a pilot, and finally landed a plum job on a cargo carrier airline. His brother's first words were, "Oh... I was hoping you'd get on with a passenger airline so I could get those reduced fares." An artist who had her work accepted for the first time to a juried art show proudly sent her best friend the catalog with her work listed. Her friend never mentioned it.

If you have gotten similar reactions from those closest to you, what is this telling you? It's telling you to shake the dust off your feet and go find a new group – one where the people like you and want to see you do well. There's no need to hate the old crowd, but don't put your hopes for support in their hands either. By this point, you have probably proved to your satisfaction whether or not your current relationships or family of origin are capable of helping you fly. If they cannot, it is essential to find those people and communities who can.

Nobody Does It Alone

Before we go any further, there is a basic human fact that must be accepted. If you are an especially independent type you may not like to hear this, but we all need other people to fulfill our highest potential. You cannot have relationships by yourself, and you cannot have career successes by yourself. In his book on creative geniuses, Howard Gardner[37] researched the development of each of these stellar individuals and found that every one of them had emotional and/or financial support, encouragement, and cross-pollination of their ideas with like minds. Not one of them had sprung into genius out of nothing. They all stood on the shoulders of people who had come before them, and they bent others' ideas into their own new framework, incorporating them as they went.

In Freud's lonely work at the beginning of psychoanalysis, his correspondence with his friend, Fleiss, was crucial to Freud for inspiration, feedback, and respect for his radical new ideas. Einstein borrowed heavily from the scientific theories that preceded him and actively engaged with the scientific community as a fellow seeker.

Gardner called this necessary pattern of supportive, invigorating relationships – found in the life history of every genius – the "Triangle of Creativity." Gardner's research confirmed that each of these exceptional people had not only a commitment to their creative work, but also had at least one important supportive person in their life who believed strongly in their worth and work. In Gardner's view, the necessary elements of creativity must include:1) the creative person, 2) the work, and 3) at least one other supportive person. You can do no less for yourself.

Am I Being Dependent?

Unfortunately some people really do not like the idea that they need other people to get where they want to go. We may not like the laws of physics when we stub our toe either, but that does not change the field of physics. If you are fiercely independent, the drawback is that you will never be as big a success on your own as you could be with the right kind of people involved. The sad thing is that many stubbornly independent types got to be that way because they saw their earliest relationships holding them back rather than encouraging them forward. The good thing is that as adults we aren't trapped in that past any longer. We are now free to adjust our thinking.

People who value their independence often worry that by asking for help, they are being "dependent." If they are dedicated to an stereotyped masculine view of strength, they may even equate getting help with being "feminine" or "weak." However, remember that the true genius mentality comfortably relies upon other people's help and support. For a genius, support for their creative work is crucial and not a reflection of anything else.

Ralph, a very wise client of mine, once put it this way, after thinking long and hard about the difference between *dependency* and *support*: "*Dependency* is static, by definition it is going nowhere. It means staying in one place for good. *Support* is a synergistic relationship which helps you move forward, and in which when one person changes and grows, the other one does too."

Finding these special soul-supporting relationships starts first with the realization of our need for them.

"Get Yourself to the Border of a Friendly Nation"[38]

Vicky was thirty-two years old and had been divorced for several years when her ex-husband who had initiated the break-up died suddenly in a work-related accident. With two children under the age of ten, she sought out psychotherapy to help her cope with the overwhelming demands of being the single parent in a grief-stricken family. Vicky made excellent progress in therapy and was able to discontinue after several months. I did not see her again for over a year. When she returned, Vicky was coming back for a different purpose. She had done well enough coping with her sense of loss and her children's grief, but now she was reevaluating her whole life.

Coming out of a long period of readjustment that followed her divorce and then her ex-husband's death, Vicky was finding that she had changed so much that her old lifestyle and community no longer fit her. In Vicky's words, "I need a new kind of interaction. I've become disassociated from my old crowd and friends." Her ex-husband's death had stirred up powerful questions in Vicky about how she wanted to live her life, and what kind of people she really enjoyed being around. Prior to this major event in her life, except for the divorce she hadn't wanted, Vicky had tended to go with the flow of already established relationships, even when they were frustrating and inhibiting to her emerging sense of individuality. Now she felt a strong urge to find a more compatible group of people to which she could belong. Vicky used the vivid metaphor of imagining such people living happily in another land, separated from her by a wide body of water. "I just need to get from here to where they are," Vicky said simply.

Vicky was describing the instinct to find her right community, the one that would fit and encourage her true self. However, Vicky needed more than her good instincts to pin down what she was blindly moving toward. She needed to understand what were the characteristics of a really good community. Although individuals will differ in what types of friends or community groups they like best, there are certain characteristics that are found in *all* "friendly nations" of the soul.

The Kind Of People We Want To Be With

In a nutshell, your right community is made up of other people who: 1) like you and 2) let you be who you feel you were meant to be. This can just be a general feeling of acceptance or it can actually be spelled out as the principle and purpose of a formally organized community, such as a church or self-development group. As one person told me, "When I'm around these people it allows me to feel a certain way; it allows me to *become* myself." When pressed to describe how she recognized her new community of friends as being ideal for her, she noted how "relaxed" and "comfortable" she felt around them. She also reported the feeling with her group that "it is okay to try out new parts of myself."

The purpose of our closest relationships is to build energy. Using this energy barometer is a foolproof method for recognizing people you need to be with. If you come away from a contact with someone feeling drained and less interested in doing things, you have been in the wrong place for your true self. It means that you felt stuck in playing some kind of role, and also that the other person was relating to you through a rather rigid persona of his or her own. It is hard to generate much good energy between two personas. It's like rubbing two pieces of cardboard together; there's never a spark.

When we are with the right kind of people, we feel lifted up, more alive, and more alert than usual. After contact with these kinds of people, we feel like we can do things and do them well. It is as though our interaction with them takes us to another level of optimism and possibilities. Whether our goals are large or small, it makes no difference. The right kind of friends gives life a sense of enjoyable adventure.

As noted above, another characteristic of a desirable community of friends is a palpable feeling of freedom to be your true self. You do not have to feel guilty if there are disagreements or you have to say no. In other words, you're free to have free will. In good relationships and supportive communities, the roles people play are flexible conveniences, not moral mandates. These roles can be modified to fit individual needs and real friends will accept the changes and adjust accordingly. This freedom and flexibility are not about being impulsively selfish or abusing the rights of others according to your whims. It just means that your relationships with important others are not threatened when you need to change your mind about something. Differences and changes can be negotiated without threatening the underlying bond of the relationship.

This idea of freedom and flexibility in friendships was a hard one for another client of mine, Celeste, to grasp. She had been trying to define for herself the kinds of friendships she wanted to keep. With some guilt, Celeste realized that one of her oldest friendships actually left her tired and exasperated whenever she and this friend spent much time together. Celeste felt badly about saying no to this friend because she had always prided herself on "being there" for her friends. It was like a code of honor for Celeste: to be consistent, reliable, and trustworthy. It meant that once Celeste made you her friend, you could count on her to be committed. However, Celeste was surprised to learn as we worked together that her noble goals were not necessarily appropriate for close friendships in the same way they might be for other types of relationships, such as a marriage or childrearing. Remember, we need to choose our friendships in order to *increase our energy* and to create *mutually uplifting energy* with other special people. Once we begin to put strict rules of consistency onto something as alive and spontaneous as a truly good friendship, it becomes an obligation instead of a joy.

I discussed with Celeste how her ideals of consistency, reliability and trustworthiness (i.e. absolute predictability) fit well into *goal-directed relationships of responsibility* like raising children, doing your job, keeping good credit, or fulfilling an agreed-upon commitment. However, friendships are not "goal-directed positions of responsibility" and if they go too far in this direction, we all want out. Instead a good friendship is based more on affectionate communion, play, creativity, caring, and support for the purpose of keeping each other's energy high and sustaining a positive outlook on life. We may help each other out at times, but our connection has to be based on enjoying each other's company. No one has to stay with friends or in a community that does not offer these essential gifts of the spirit.

Good friends respect your boundaries, what you can do and what you cannot do. They do not make you feel guilty when you cannot do what they ask. Nor are they miffed if you don't take their advice. True friends see your real self and believe in your potential, and so their guidance is always offered with your growth in mind. They are willing to encourage, praise, and appreciate you, while showing their support for your hopes and ideas. You can be yourself and know that they will not exploit you or run you down behind your back. They urge you forward rather than holding you back from new things you might want to try[39].

The best kind of friends and community are also able to provide helpful guidance and wisdom when you need it. They know the real you and therefore can be realistic problem-solving partners. Objective enough to point out where you might be sabotaging your higher goals, they keep you from getting in your own way.

Supportive communities and good friends are also optimistic. They see the universe as a friendly place and trust that their efforts will pay off. They are not naive Pollyannas, but do believe they can have an effect on making good things come their way. In other words, they do not feel fated or helpless. They see our potential because they believe in their own. They enjoy their successes and don't take hard times personally. They take setbacks in stride without getting too bitter or paranoid, and they believe that their improvement or recovery is within their control. These kinds of people are safe to be around because they don't need to feed off your energy in order to stay afloat.

Interestingly, most of my clients, no matter how difficult their childhood circumstances, all remember these special kinds of people in their past. For one woman it was an adored teacher who encouraged her to pursue her dreams of college, an unheard of goal in her family. For another client it was the family of his best friend in childhood, a family that provided an unforgettable model for what a supportive and fun-loving group can do for its members. The memories of these special types of relationships never leave us, because they resonate so deeply with the truest feelings we have.

The most important points to remember about desirable friendships and communities are:

1. The purpose of good friendships is to build energy.

2. We can exercise our own free will and say no without jeopardizing our friendships.

3. Friendship roles are not set in stone; we can be flexible and negotiate changes in expectations as needed.

4. Good friends respect our boundaries, our likes and dislikes.

5. Friends admire our potential and want to see us grow and succeed.

6. Praise, encouragement, and appreciation are given easily.

7. They are able to give realistic guidance when you ask for it because they know you and have sensible ideas.

8. A person capable of being a good friend is essentially optimistic.

To sum up, Ann, one of my clients, used the following question to evaluate potential new friends or groups she was considering joining. After spending some time with these individuals, she would mentally ask herself: *Does this feel right to me? Is this where I am supposed to be?* She always got her answer by the way she felt.

Fake It Until You Make It

If you are to become who you were meant to be, finding the right community is essential for another reason as well. The people we are around tend to rub off on us. You may have noticed this if you have had to spend a great deal of time around someone who is negative and complains a lot. Most of us do not have invincible armor that protects us from such negativity and hopelessness in the attitudes of others. It is nice to think that we could "choose" not to be affected by this kind of draining influence, but misery loves company and will keep on wearing you down until you provide it! Being the social beings we are, we form an emotional network with the people we spend the most time with and those bonds either lift us up or pull us down.

By being with other people who want the same things you do or who can model what you want to become, you are giving yourself a head start toward getting there. Jennie, a group member, expressed her hopelessness about ever being able to be assertive in a committee meeting, something that was very necessary for her line of work. She had always been shy, and had no idea how to hold her own with more extroverted colleagues in her new job. I asked her a simple question: "Have you ever known someone who seemed to find it easy to speak up in committee meetings?" Jennie did, of course, and I told her to secretly pretend she was that person next time she went into a meeting. My suggestion surprised Jennie because she viewed it as a kind of dishonesty or cheating.

We had a very productive group session that evening talking about how we learn any new skill: usually it is in the form of copying someone else. The way we laugh, cut our meat, or make up our beds were all patterned after what we saw someone else do. There is no reason that we should stop copying who and what we admire just because we grew up. Mimic, borrow, pretend to be someone else, and add to your identity. This does not mean that you are being false or untrue to yourself. It only means that you are increasing your range of behaviors and adding to your effectiveness in dealing with the world and other people.

Your core self, who you were meant to be, cannot be changed, but the accessories can. Adding necessary skills and bits of identity from others you admire adds to your basic self, giving it more polish and richness, and broadens your genius. When you find a community that speaks your language, laughs at your jokes, and leaves you feeling better each time you see them, don't be afraid to make a nourishing psychological soup out of all the good things you find there. The groups we belong to are meant to enrich us, and we are meant to grasp whatever we need to bring us closer to our soul's fulfillment. Nobody does it alone.

Lifestyle Changes

Community is *where* we feel comfortable; lifestyle is about *how* we feel comfortable. Lifestyle always changes to some extent as you start living your life from inner prompts instead of outer demands. When the still, small voice finally has your ear and you start reading your own mind, you begin to wonder why it has taken you so long to make things easier on yourself. Instead of living from externally imposed roles in which you are *told* what to value, you start to *experience* the value of making self-directed choices and changes in the way you live your life. A satisfying lifestyle flows from going after what truly gives you energy as you uncover your real self and its interests.

Your own lifestyle changes may be on a small scale and yet far-reaching in terms of the change in your energy level and enjoyment of life. You don't have to change your name, quit your job, or join a commune to have a completely new experience of life. Radical changes are not necessary, only *real* changes. Sometimes the small ones are the best ones.

There seem to be two ways that people go about changing their lifestyles for the better. One is to add to their lives by creating new opportunities and another is to do old things in new ways. Either way we make important shifts in how we live so that there is less stress and discrepancy between who we really are and who we appear to be. A person with a well-matched lifestyle is not wasting energy on irrelevant activities that were originally designed to please a false self or impress others.

Michelle, who had come to me because of a deep depression, found that the discovery of her true self led her into a passionate interest in writing. She had always been interested in it but didn't know how to get started. Plus she was too busy pouring her energy into being a full-time wife and mother. Michelle had always prided herself on being home with her children and not using day care, especially with the last child who had arrived unexpectedly when Michelle was in her forties. However, after taking her first writing workshop, Michelle was filled with excitement and enthusiasm for her new creative outlet. Then she had to face the fact that her goals now as an older mother were quite different than those she had enjoyed when her other children were little.

It was hard for Michelle, but she made several changes in her lifestyle in order to give herself time to pursue her writing. Initially feeling very guilty and worried about this new step, Michelle nevertheless pushed past her concerns to find a good baby-sitter several days a week so that she would have blocks of time to work on the book she was authoring. She also started a writers' group and thereby added a new opportunity for affiliation with other creative people. Incidentally, the depression for which Michelle had sought therapy began to alleviate as she made these changes.

By doing the same old things in different ways, some people find a freshness and joy that reinvigorates their lifestyle. This might include little moves as simple as altering work schedules to allow time for pursuing other interests, making a plan to meet with like-minded friends on a regular basis, taking out a special magazine subscription, or corresponding with people who share your passion about certain topics. They do not have to be big changes or additions to give a definite energy boost; they just have to match your interests and emerging sense of true self. Stacy, one woman with whom I worked, had one of her best holidays ever when she changed her goals for her trademark annual New Year's Eve party from an expensively lavish affair to a much smaller, more casual and intimate get-together. She had discovered her need for this change when she began to feel depressed and overwhelmed at the prospect of yet another huge celebration with a crush of people she really did not care much about. Rather than canceling the party altogether, Stacy took the opportunity to change the party to reflect her new interpersonal style, moving from impressing others to nourishing and relating to others. When your lifestyle is geared around *creating opportunities for happiness,* whatever that means to you, you will be living from the real self that you were always meant to be.

Plugging Energy Drains

One of the most important lifestyle changes a person can make involves finding and plugging up the places where energy is leaking out of his or her life. Once we start looking for these spots, we will see plenty of them. Some of these empty spots may be obvious, like social or volunteering activities in which we have little interest. However, there is another kind of energy drain that is much more subtle and hard to catch – and sometimes can be extremely hard to stop. These are our own unthinking emotional reactions to certain kinds of events in our lives.

Are there predictable and repetitive experiences in your life that leave you feeling completely drained of energy when they happen? Most of us have experienced these energy-drainers, whether at work or in our closest relationships. It seems to us as if another person or the situation is deliberately trying to frustrate us or drive us crazy. It's predictable that we react with paranoid self-righteousness to our perceived persecution. At such moments, we take all our energy and pour it into anger, mental accusations and judgments about the other person's character. Often this is not even shared with the other person as we silently boil with resentment over our mistreatment.

Why? Why should a part of our preferred lifestyle – our way of living our lives –include drumming up scorn and rage toward people and circumstances over which we have no control? Believe me, if we could have controlled the situation, we would have done so by now, right? Changing your lifestyle for the better means recognizing what you can change and what you cannot. To feel chronically persecuted or emotionally upset suggests an avoidance of real problem-solving, as well as an unhealthy fascination with the false excitement of exaggerated emotions. In other words, if you keep finding yourself reacting with overwhelming emotions of whatever type, you could be sinking your energy into overdone drama and the vindication of self-righteousness at the expense of more rewarding pleasures in life. When we do this we are choosing a dramatic, superficial lifestyle over a truly enlivening one.

Joan was a client who regularly experienced emotional meltdowns whenever her husband or teenage son pressured her at the wrong times to do things she did not want to do. Since this seemed to happen fairly often, Joan could easily have filled our sessions with one example after another of how stupid, insensitive, thoughtless and demanding these two were being that week. Even though Joan had made major progress in listening to her true self and living out a more authentic and rewarding life in many respects, she still had a weakness for these self-righteous eruptions about being exploited or let down by her husband and son. She was hooked on mini-drama.

Joan's feelings of persecution and being taken advantage of may have started back in her difficult childhood, but now *she* was the one keeping these souped-up emotional reactions going in her adult life. In Joan's mind, she was right, they were stupidly thoughtless, and that was that. Unfortunately, Joan was emotionally blind to the high cost of this reactivity to her own life and happiness. It took many good-natured confrontations in therapy before Joan began to see that she had the power within herself to respond differently to other people's "stupid" behavior.

Joan was full of excitement on the day when she finally came into my office with the report that she had averted a self-induced crisis by realizing that she had the freedom to respond differently when her husband made one of his insistent requests just as Joan was coming in the door from a grocery shopping trip. Instead of blowing up at him ("Can't you see I just walked in the door?!"), Joan paused and thought a second, then told him that she would be happy to help him once she had gotten something to eat and had a little rest. It turned out that Joan had been causing much of her upset by never questioning that she had to do something as soon as someone else asked her to do it. This self-imposed pressure was added to the demands of her family members, magnifying the situation out of all proportion. Joan had finally realized how important it was to protect her energy by giving up the starring role as her family's beck-and-call martyr. Joan's story gives us a good example of how we can have much more control over the quality of our lifestyle when we set limits on how much energy we are willing to spend on being emotionally reactive.

Drama or Happiness: What's it Going to Be?

It may be hard to believe, but happiness can take some getting used to. True happiness comes from knowing your own mind, reading your true needs accurately, and meeting them. If you are not accustomed to doing this, you can create a great deal of dissatisfaction and unhappiness in your life as you pursue one wrong thing after another. Yes, the original sources of unhappiness may have lain in our pasts, but reading our own mind *now* is the key to happiness and is available to each one of us every second. It is available, that is, if we are willing to trade the false excitement of emotional drama for real happiness.

Drama is what happens when we substitute imaginary persecution and emotional reactivity for knowing what we really want. In his writings on the human condition, Vernon Howard[40] stresses that we can become addicted to emotional excitement – and even pain – because we fear going through the process of discovering what we really desire for a peaceful, fulfilling life. When people have lost touch with their inner voice, they often have the secret (irrational) fear that maybe they have no real self, no actual inner guide. This intolerable sense of emptiness leads them to re-embroil themselves in superficial, repetitive dramas that give them a fleeting but false sense of being fully alive.

In order to be happy we have to be willing to step off the stage of our own habitual roles and – are you ready for this? – give up our pet miseries once and for all. Major lifestyle changes from an unhappy life to a happy life are possible, but can be very uncomfortable. For far too many of us, our sufferings turn into our main source of identity, and we don't even realize we are clinging to such negativity.

Terri, one woman whom I counseled, called her newly happy feelings "strange" and "weird." For the first time in her life she found herself not constantly preoccupied with one self-imposed crisis after another. Thinking about her experiences growing up, Terri had the staggering realization that "We only knew how to function with conflict in our lives. If it was not there we had to create it because it made us so uneasy to be without it. That's the weird thing, having to learn how to be happy." Terri is not the only one. There are many of us who have to learn to get used to peace and happiness after a lifetime of repetitive melodrama.

How do you know if you are putting more energy into drama than seeking out opportunities for real happiness? People who have become hooked on the false excitement of suffering and drama have a very distinctive pattern. There is always a lot happening in their lives, but it is rather like the activity of an animal chasing its tail: the animal goes round and round without actually going anywhere. Drama-hooked lifestyles are similarly repetitive: it may be lurid stuff, but it's basically the same old emergency dressed up in different clothes. In contrast, a lifestyle devoted to discovering and meeting the needs of the real self shows gratifying evolution and change as we go along.

New opportunities are seen, goals are accomplished, and our energy is used creatively instead of reflexively. By reading our own minds and listening to the voice of the true self within, we come up with new responses that improve our way of living rather than trapping us in the same problems over and over.

Perfectionism or Happiness: What's It Going to Be?

Fran had come to see me for tension, anxiety, and outbursts of anger in which she became viciously critical of her husband over the slightest transgression. She knew she was out of control and finally sought out therapy to get a handle on why she was being so mean. Fran and I did not have to spend a lot of time revisiting and uncovering her childhood wounds, because Fran knew exactly where they were and who had inflicted them.

Fran prided herself on never being considered a lazy person. Consumed with busyness, Fran drove herself into the ground, making lists and being so organized that even small events became full-scale operations. Fran tormented herself (and her husband) with the exaggerated pride she felt in having everything neat as a pin. In Fran's lifestyle, happiness was a moot point as long as she could feel satisfied that she had done everything just right. With that kind of self-imposed pressure, no wonder she was always ready to bite someone's head off!

The pressure did not come from outside. *Fran was doing this to herself* with her insistence on a lifestyle of perfectionism and over-control of everything around her, including her husband. As we worked on discovering more about what Fran really enjoyed, what genuinely gave her energy and enthusiasm, she began to be less focused on duty and more aware of what gave her pleasure. As she accepted the idea that enjoying life is not the same thing as being shiftless and lazy, Fran began to relax some of the extreme demands she placed on herself and others. Now she could stop and ask herself what she really felt like doing in any given moment instead of heedlessly driving herself to be fully occupied every second. It was a big day for her when she talked about her newfound ability to stop and watch some baby ducks at a nearby pond, or to not fly into self-reproach if she did not get a birthday card off on time. Fran's new lifestyle was more relaxed and fit her, rather than being so rigid that *she* was supposed to fit *it*.

A Good Lifestyle Requires Setting Limits

Todd was a single parent who was remorseful about his frequent yelling at his ten-year-old son. It turned out these episodes usually happened in the evenings after supper, when this man had done a full day's work, fixed dinner, and checked his son's homework. The pattern was that before the evening was over he would blow-up over some small thing – "the last straw" – and then would feel guilty about it. He would resolve to be an even better father the next night, but invariably the pattern repeated itself.

It turned out that Todd was allowing himself no time to relax and had set no limits on his son's access to him, even though the boy was clearly old enough to amuse himself on his own for awhile. Sensitive to being his son's only parent, Todd had set up a dutiful lifestyle devoted to his son, determined to make up for the lack of a mother figure in the home. It had never occurred to him that he could consciously change his lifestyle in a small, but crucial way by simply telling his son that he needed some time each night to unwind and spend by himself. Now if his son forgot and interrupted his quiet time, Todd reminded him of their talk and the boy went off to find something else to do. As long as Todd honored his essential need to have a little bit of time for himself, there was no more yelling and no more guilt.

Setting these limits on our energy is mandatory for a lifestyle that can support and nourish our true self. This includes listening to our bodies, our muscular tension and our physical needs for rest and sleep. When these body-based cues begin begging for attention in the form of excessive fatigue, irritability, or illness, it is important to ask ourselves how we might be allowing our lifestyle to run us instead of the other way around.

Tricia, one particularly alert and psychologically insightful client, used to ask herself when she began to feel bad physically, "Why did this happen? What did I do to bring this on?" Since Tricia was in a high-demand medical profession, it was easy to fall prey to accepting more assignments than she really wanted because the pay was so good. Nevertheless, through her work on discovering the fulfillment of making choices from her real self, Tricia became very firm in her ability to set limits for the kind of lifestyle she found acceptable. She found better things to do than exhaust herself for a little more money.

A Good Lifestyle Involves Staying Aware

Anita had made huge strides in changing her way of reacting to life. When she first came to see me she was in danger of losing her job as a laboratory technician because of her irritability and barely concealed resentment of her co-workers. After a number of sessions, Anita was able to see how she was letting herself become impatient and overwhelmed because of her difficulty with clearly communicating her needs for certain limits and structure. The rather loose and freewheeling tone of her workplace aggravated her to no end until she realized that the only thing she had control over was how she chose to conduct *her* own work. Anita started keeping her focus on her own work, directly asking for what she needed to do a good job, and letting others get theirs done in their own style. She was getting great results from paying attention to herself and meeting her own needs quickly in order to avoid accumulating unnecessary fatigue and resentment. In her words, "I feel much calmer internally, I'm more focused on me."

Being only human, however, Anita soon began to complain about the amount of effort this all took. She wanted me to tell her how long she would have to remain so aware of all her feelings, needs, and reactions. When would she be able to not think about all those things so consciously and effortfully? Anita remembered how automatic and easy it used to be, just to give into her reactions and let the chips fall where they might. A part of her wanted to go back to the illusory ease of this old reflexive, unconscious style of living.

I remember sitting and staring at her for a few moments before the answer came to me. "You know, Anita," I said, "There isn't one of us who would get in our car, drive somewhere and then complain about how we had to spend all this effort keeping our eyes open and our hands on the wheel in order to get there. In driving, we just accept that we have to do certain things to avoid our car's going into a ditch or hitting another car."

Now Anita was the one who sat and stared at me. "I'm going to have to give that some real thought," she said slowly. Anita now was keeping her car out of the ditch, so to speak, but she had to realize that her new efforts at conscious awareness were going to have to become part of her new way of living life.

In order to build a new lifestyle that keeps us out of self-constructed negative consequences, our goal always must be to *maintain* conscious awareness. It is this *habit of awareness* that ultimately gets to be second nature and protects our true selves from being depleted by incompatible situations and people. When your awareness has been practiced to the point of becoming automatic, that's when it starts seeming easier and more natural. We can't go back to closing our eyes, popping off any old response, and still expect to get where we want to go.

Take Your Time

There is probably no task suggested in this book that will take you as much time and work as making changes in your lifestyle and community. While the internal work of connecting with your real self takes some effort, time and opportunities are required to make new friends and change. But the first step is to just practice being aware of how you feel around various people and in different situations. Gradually you will find yourself being drawn to what you need. Subsequently, you will find it ever easier to avoid things that are not right for you in your journey toward becoming all you were meant to be.

It takes time to practice this kind of awareness. If you push yourself into big new changes too soon, you may find yourself with the same old problems in a different setting. Take your time, and enjoy the process of finally being able to listen to where that still, small voice within is guiding you.

CHAPTER 12

WHO YOU WERE MEANT TO BE: PLANNING FOR THE REST OF YOUR LIFE

Don't hold back from falling in love with the dreams of your deeper self. Deep within you is a field of energy craving outlet, craving completion through action.

You are the axis on which your world turns. There is no one else but you who knows the answer to the question of who you were meant to be. That question has been answered for years. It was answered the day you were born. If you have come this far, you won't feel settled until you remember it. Every day you will begin to answer this question with each authentic thing you do, every pleasure that you enjoy, and all the dreams that pull you forward. Once you know how it *feels* to be moving toward who you were meant to be, you will have your touchstone of identity. Your energy will rise, your eyes will shine, and your mind will feel clearly directed.

Hopefully, our work together in this book has helped you to sweep aside the cobwebs of guilt and self-doubt so that you can see clearly what you want to do. If you now realize how you've been held back, you can work toward regaining yourself. You have begun to wake up, to snap out of the childhood trance that has kept you feeling like a powerless, guilty child even into your own adulthood. You have explored the profound act of becoming yourself, and why so often people lose their nerve when they try it. Now you can find your truth and know the inner wholeness that cannot be in conflict against itself. You no longer have to let your compassion for the limitations of others stand in your way of living. You now know that finding your own destiny is a requirement for full living. By doing something *for* yourself in this way, you know that you are not doing anything *against* your loved ones.

It's Not Selfish

A central point in this book is that egocentric people try to make us believe that when we follow our dreams, we are being selfish. Unless we become who *they* think we should be, we fear we will be seen as inconsiderate and self-centered. But this is misplaced guilt and unnecessary self-doubt. It is not selfish to want to have your best life, even though the most immature and egocentric people in your life might make you feel that way. Once you see through their guilt-trips, however, you will be freeing yourself from the confusing self-reproach that ties you up in helplessness. You are not self-centered for wanting a more personally rewarding life. It's other people who are excessively self-focused if they try to hold you back out of their own insecurities.

The purpose here is not to blame anyone else, but to stop blaming yourself. Often people worry that if they examine the influence of their families or parents, they would be evading responsibility and "blaming" others. They're concerned that finger-pointing might be needlessly harping on the past in a non-productive way. However, the reason for researching your family's part in your unhappiness (witting or unwitting) is not to blame them so much as it is to get the story straight.

Once we are clear about what we want and are moving toward our own personal goals, we naturally begin to lose interest in how others have failed us in the past. (It gets to be boring!) However, first we have to understand what *did* happen to us and how it trained us to think badly of ourselves and to judge ourselves as selfish. Otherwise we are stuck in a constant tug-of-war between anger and guilt, never stopping long enough to figure out the real reasons for our resentment and exhaustion. True, there is no need to spend

WHO YOU WERE MEANT TO BE

the rest of your life blaming others – just as long as you don't spend the rest of your life erroneously blaming yourself either.

Once we finally see that our loved ones may not be the best ones to rely on for good advice about our future, we are free to turn to our own inner guide.

Your Inner Guide

The truth is that we have an inner guide who inspires and speaks with simplicity and certainty when we listen. You can call this inner guide your intuition, your instincts, your subconscious mind, Spirit, God, or Higher Power. It does not matter what you call this guide, because it works just the same. It doesn't matter what you name it because you can still make use of its principles and effects. Call your inner guide anything you like, but appreciate how it works so you can use it.

You have this guide backing you up all the time. It never stops whispering in your ear. It is totally internal, totally self-contained. It does not come sweeping at you from the outside, like a pushy salesman. It does not boom out advice in an authoritarian way. You may not see a burning bush or have a life-transforming mystical experience. You may not even feel very enlightened. But it remains there, in its quietly insistent way, no matter how many times you try to turn it off.

Honor your still, small voice. Not the critical ego voice, but the still, small voice that shows you the next steps, one at a time. Your inner voice is not interested in being an authority and standing over you as if you were a child. It wants to be your equal partner. It speaks at your level. It has been within you all the time even if, like Brenda below, you haven't always heard it or been aware of its presence.

Brenda's Story

The more Brenda felt dissatisfied with her life, the more she felt the itch to escape her homemaker role. However, she allowed herself no time to explore her true interests. Instead she impulsively latched onto the idea of becoming a real estate salesperson, something others had told her she should try because of the flexible work hours and her friendly personality. Brenda jumped into taking all the required courses, yet wondered all the while if she was doing the right thing. When it came time for her final exam, she had a massive panic attack and could not complete her test sheet. It was as though her true self had finally had enough of this nonsense and told her in no uncertain terms, *"I'm no real estate agent!!"*

Brenda's heart was in the right place, but she made the mistake of listening to others instead of herself. Having been a dutiful wife and daughter all her life, Brenda had learned to mistrust her instincts. Usually when someone does not know what to do with his or her life, other people will rush to fill the vacuum with suggestions. Brenda needed to look to herself and find her true interests before she could succeed in the outside world. Fortunately, that is just what Brenda did, and she is now in a field that matches her true interests.

You may be terribly out of practice in hearing your inner voice or, like Brenda, you may have spent most of your life ignoring it completely and instead looking outward for guidance. The key is to use the outside information to help you *recognize* what you already know deep down about yourself, not to try to become something that you are not. You may recognize inner truth when it appears on the outside, but you *know* it from the inside. Think back to your own *recognition moments,* those times when you knew that something was definitely *you.*

Recognition moments can also occur when you suddenly become unusually aware of what another person just said, as if a light bulb lit up. Perhaps you are in a class, listening to a conversation, or simply talking with a friend over lunch. Suddenly something they say stands out to you as if it were a neon sign. It may be a phrase or a word, but suddenly your consciousness is on full alert and you know that something has just spoken to you. You may not understand it or know what it is about, but you have an instant moment of recognition: This feels like a message! This is what I needed to hear!

Look forward to the day when this inspired feeling will emerge reliably from within yourself. Soon it will be your own thoughts that are catching your attention, and your self-recognition will become more internal. You will get to the point where you have your own inclinations and no longer need to be plugged into the receptacle of others' opinions. At that point you will have "Aha!" experiences and these insights will carry a kind of knowing that lets you know they come from your true self. You will have reached the point of trusting yourself and respecting your own opinion. At this stage, you will not be totally immune to others' input, but it will be filtered through *your* knowledge of who you really are.

When you allow yourself to be more and more willing to receiving guidance from inside yourself, opportunities will begin to cross your path. Articles in the paper will begin to appear on a subject of interest to you, a class will be advertised, a friend will call to introduce you to someone who knows someone in a certain field. In her book, *The Artist's Way*, Julia Cameron[41] talks about how reliably these things happen once you start channeling energy into your dream. This certainly has been my repeated experience with psychotherapy clients. As they get more in touch with their real self, other elements in their life began to fall into place in totally unplanned-for ways. It was as though as soon as they resolved their inner conflicts and got their energy all flowing in the same direction, the outside world shaped up too. The next steps appeared, and as they took those steps, the next ones appeared. Listening to our inner guide and faithfully taking the next marble out of the tube keeps us aligned with the natural psychological forces in our lives. In this state you realize that it is only your fear and conditioning that holds you back, not reality. Once we get straight in our minds and hearts what we *know* we want and are determined to do it, circumstances begin to arrange themselves for the fulfillment of our goal.

Listening to your inner guide enables you to think straight. You develop a sense of conviction that there must be a way, and you have the confidence to find it. Finally you fully accept that if you have to do it on your own, so be it. Once you turn that corner of willingness, your natural creativity and instinct

LINDSAY C. GIBSON, PSY.D.

for growth applies itself to the task. You settled for limited options before only because you secretly were too scared to act on anything. You now are capable of flexibility and creativity in your planning.

When you shift to listening to your inner voice, it feels natural and right, like you're in the groove. You may not even pause to remember how long you have stood in your own way with fearful obeisance to others' opinions, as well as your heartfelt efforts to save them from themselves. The change just seems easy and right. You no longer have to ask for permission because you are no longer ambivalent. You do not feel guilty anymore.

Where Will the Confidence Come From?

Where do you get the confidence to move ahead? Confidence comes from within, but it is also encouraged from the outside. You need some people in your life who will hold the dream for you, remind you of it, and push as needed when you get scared and discouraged. Find someone you instinctively know will tell you, "You can do it!" Ask that fortifying person if he or she would be willing to meet with you regularly and occasionally be available for phone calls to help you stay on track. Do not underestimate the need for support, encouragement, and community with like-minded people. We know that even geniuses need support, so don't deprive yourself of that kind of help.

You are like a little child when you start out on the path of your dream – very vulnerable, very suggestible, and very open to negativity. Pick your companions *extra* carefully at this stage. Raise your awareness of who gives you energy and who brings you down. Follow your fascination. Resist the rut. You owe nothing to people who want to use you or feed off you. Believe me, they will find someone to take your place, someone who is still willing to be controlled by guilt and intimidation.

Many times the confidence comes from simply not putting yourself in situations that tear your confidence down.

Confidence Is Not a One-time Decision

Think of yourself as a person who has been bewitched by a wicked spell. You have been told that life is a certain way, with rules and prohibitions against your becoming who you were meant to be. Now, you sleeping giant, you are beginning to wake up. It may even begin to seem incredible that you ever believed those old things. Like one of those gestalt pictures, the shapes shift totally and you suddenly feel completely confident in your outlook. It happens all at once. It feels great. A new day has dawned. The old way no longer has any hold on you. You know you can do it. Whatever it was that you had lost or never found, you now have it. Like a jewel, it is precious to you and you hold on to it tightly. It is yours alone.

Remember, though, that the jewel that you were never going to let go of may slip out of your palm in a thoughtless moment. You lose it. You flip back into the gestalt of unhealthy pessimism and hopelessness and guilt[42]. You feel burdened again and put others' needs ahead of your own to the point where you feel deadened and exhausted once more. You commit a soul murder on yourself, if the truth be known. Be aware that when you get too far out of balance, you can count on yourself to develop symptoms guaranteed to remind you of your true self's needs.

It is important to know that this back-and-forth is how the growth process works so that you don't get discouraged. It is a predictable pattern of growth to find the jewel and lose it and once having lost it, to feel the need to find it again. As you move further along in the process, you will keep that jewel in your grasp for longer and longer. And it will be *much* easier to find the next time you drop it.

The important thing for your morale is that you *accept* the psychological nuisance of your own ambivalence: it's human nature to move ahead, then scare ourselves and jump back.

It is natural to want to feel confident all at once. Do you feel you can't wait? This is your inexperience speaking. I hate to say that, but it's true. You are a human being, not a superhero. You set yourself up for failure and discouragement when you declare that you are suddenly, completely on your own, going to do this thing all at once, and there is no holding you back. If you have not prepared your way and have not worked up to it, you are riding for a fall. It is understandable that passionate types will be frustrated by this idea of tiny, back and-forth steps toward a goal. Maybe – just maybe – this all-or-nothing outlook could be the reason you have gotten so discouraged in the past.

Remember that the newly emerging part of your self is extremely vulnerable to setbacks. You wouldn't let your five-year-old drive the car because *he* thinks he's ready. You would step in before he had a catastrophic encounter with his physical weakness and lack of experience. Do the same for yourself. There is nothing wrong with confidence and ambition. You just don't want to let these excellent feelings be traumatically deflated by putting yourself in circumstances that are beyond your ability to cope right now. Accept that there will be moments in which confidence disappears, and then returns slowly. Before long, you'll be moving forward again.

The Gods of Timing

Give yourself room for the timing factor. In the excitement of personal growth, sometimes we forget we are a part of a bigger picture. Our lives follow a confluence of forces that makes certain times better than others in terms of opportunities. Here's an unforgettable dream I once had on this subject:

> *I'm driving my car fast on a winding road, in a big hurry to get somewhere. Suddenly I see a car stopped in front of me, just before a blind curve.*

> *I lean on my horn, exasperated by this upcoming obstacle. Swerving past the stopped car, I swoosh around the bend, only to screech to a stop in front of a lifted drawbridge. I suddenly understand why the other car had stopped*

> *Sheepishly, I look in my rearview mirror at the car behind me. The other driver has a compassionate, amused smile on his face, as if he'd been watching to see what would happen when I saw that drawbridge. I was deeply embarrassed. But that didn't hold*

*me back. I was still driven by my internal hurry! In the next mo-
ment, I am hooking together these straw mats, making a flimsy
raft to get across the river anyway. The mats are light and un-
stable and keep flipping me over into the water.*

The moral of the dream was that I was in such a hurry to achieve my goal
that I was denying certain realities. Looking back on the dream, I realized
that if I had simply waited a little bit, the drawbridge would have come back
down, getting me where I was going with speed and ease. The dream was
reeling out a metaphorical movie about human impatience and the high cost
of the "Gotta have it now!" mentality. It's not a virtue to go ahead at all costs.
That may feel heroic and exciting, but it will often leave you a tragic figure
who jousted with the gods of timing and lost.

If you are on your true path, having to wait a little will not take you off
the track. It is when we get frantic and believe we have to drive ourselves
against all odds that we wear ourselves out and then give up. The highway
remains there, even if we get interrupted briefly when unforeseen delays cross
our path. At such moments the proper response is to wait expectantly and not
give up. Rushing our goals always signals an underlying lack of faith and the
bullheaded belief that we have to do everything alone. I whizzed right by a
wise helper on that curving dream road, convinced that I had to figure everything out for myself.

Everything has a rhythm, with melodies and rests. Your life – and the creation of your dream – follow this natural law. Push when you can, but don't
think you can get around the gods of timing!

Your goals may shift and even take you places you didn't know you were
going. That is normal and even ideal for your optimal development and
growth. Shifting and twisting on the road of self-discovery is part of the ride.
Setbacks and interruptions pop up when least expected. But these are just
necessary road tests for your growing maturity, just old obstacles coming up
again in another form. Your job is not to take these obstacles too seriously, but
to expect and accept them. When the drawbridge is up, there's nothing to do
but show up and wait. That's not hopelessness; that's timing.

You will feel confident even when you have to wait because you now understand the process of growth described in this book. You are like the wise investor who knows better than to sell as soon as the market drops. Don't give up on your dream. Soon you will have enough experience in which to plant your faith.

You cannot do it all at once, but you can work on bits and pieces and get there very effectively. Your job is to take divine dictation[43], open your mail from the true self within, and let the still, small voice make its suggestions. You came into this life fully equipped, with batteries included. As one of my clients looked back on the road she had taken, she recalled the hard times but she also talked about what it's like on the other side: "I'm a little amazed at all the changes. Before, I felt like I was struggling all the time. Now it doesn't feel like that. It's more natural. I'm trying not to let anything overwhelm me. I know it will all get done and I am on my way."

Why You Will Succeed

The unfortunate truth is that many people do not live their dreams and do not allow themselves to find out who they were meant to be.

Why will you succeed where others fail? You will succeed because you are becoming a *realist-idealist*. That is what we have worked on in this book, not only to support your dreams and idealism, but to help you become realistic about the forces in your way and how to move ahead daily in a practical way. You now allow your dreams to inspire you, to give you energy and hope. By reading this book, and thinking things through, you have also looked at many hard and painful emotional and family realities. You have come to realize that you can have compassion for the suffering and limitations of others, yet not allow that compassionate loyalty to stand in your way of living.

Hopefully, you have come to understand the nature of the growth process, and the map of growth has taken away some of the uncertainty and helplessness. You now know about excitement and collapse, ups and downs, exhilaration and despair, confidence and hopelessness, and this unavoidable pattern of growth no longer alarms you nor makes you give up. *You recognize the roller coaster of inner conflict that accompanies freeing yourself from the fears of the past.* Everybody loses their nerve once in awhile, but it is the people who expect setbacks and then go on anyway that make it.

Just because you fall down and *feel* lost, this is not a statement of reality. It is only a mood commenting on a bad day. Einstein had bad days. Picasso had bad days. Nevertheless, they kept on being themselves. They just kept showing up. They kept working at it. Sports stars know this very well. They have a whole language for the psychology of competition and doing their best in spite of fears, doubts, and setbacks. They expect it, accept it, brush it off, and go on. Remember the stock market graph; there will be little variations on any course of action through time, but it is the overall upward trend on which you want to focus.

Raising Expectations

Care enough to expect good things from yourself. When things get rough, be kind and comforting like a concerned mother. However, when you are tempted to give up, be a stern father. Be the implacable coach. Be the kind of mentor to yourself that will not stand by and watch you waste your potential. You are not mediocre. Your discontent is telling you that where you belong is not where you are.

Why Take Fear, Shame, and Hopelessness Seriously?

I hope at this point you have come to some perspective on your feelings of fear and shame, those henchmen of the failure mentality that have scared you into submission. Surely you can see now that these feelings have never been about you, but about other people's reactions to you.

Shame makes you hate your real self and feed your false self. It makes you invest your energy in what is worthless, while it bankrupts that which is most precious about you. Shame is always about distorted loyalty that has gotten so out of hand you think the oppressor's needs are in *your* best interests. Turning against yourself, shame makes you disown your real self, discounting it as deserving of whatever ridicule and humiliation it has suffered. That's the societal mallet of shame coming down on your head. *Shame is when you blame yourself for doing something that another person dislikes.* It makes you apologize for being in the way when someone pushes you down.

Shame is your glory turned inside out. It is the dark lining of that radiant coat that is your birthright. Instead of shining your light outward and displaying your gifts to the world, you turn it in toward yourself, so no one can see. What a waste of life. That shining glory is what we experience when we are doing what we love to do and are good at. When we can shine in a community of loved ones and mentors who back our potential, not our conformity, we close the original wounds of our shaming.

Feelings Aren't Facts

Hopelessness and disappointment are just passing *feelings.* Taking them seriously – or mistaking them for *facts* about you or your life – creates additional problems that do not need to be there. Treat them like viruses. Do not identify with them. Endure and work past them instead, and get over them as soon as possible. Decide in advance what you are going to say to hopelessness when it shows up, because it will come. Figure out the right slogans to deflate it. Look at encouraging online sites or through magazines and books for inspirational quotes. Then write or paste these reminder slogans on a few index cards, and put them safely in a drawer for when you need to get yourself going again. Your ego will not want you to do this, so prepare for that voice of resistance. Think of the cards as a rapid antidote to the mind poison of hopelessness. The cards will rebuild the bridge between the healthy you and the temporarily despondent you. You then can dispel the doom-and-gloom mirages of others' pessimism with a dose of your healthy side. Using these cards will remind you that there is much more to you than these temporary moods. Hopelessness is nobody's natural state.

And fear? What is fear but excitement turned sour by the cold finger of your discourager, the ego. Your fears will tempt you back into the family trance-state that has defined you for many years. In the ego chapter, I asked you to write down some of the withering statements that the ego makes to you. You did this necessary work of getting down on paper what had previously been scrawled on your heart. The stains left by the ego may require repeated washings.

When fear and hopelessness tempt you, review that awful list of old ego criticisms and look at it with an objective eye. You will see that these beliefs that speak so authoritatively inside your head are really only the envious, snippy remarks of people from the past who had given up on their dreams, and unconsciously wanted to drag you down with them. One man I worked with summed up his successful struggle with ego fears in these words: "Instead of being *really afraid,* now I'm just a little scared." He had kept just enough anxiety to motivate himself, but not so much fear it would make him stop.

The Courtship of the Self

There is a courtship that needs to go on between you and your true self. In many ways, finding out who you were meant to be is more like falling in love than pursuing a goal. In fact, if you do not develop this infatuation with your true self at the outset of an endeavor, your heart will not be grounded in a deep enough place. It will be like a seed that never put down much of a taproot and can be pulled up or blown over by the first bit of challenge.

Deep within you is a field of energy craving outlet, craving completion through action. Your dream will try hard to push up into reality, and the inner pressure can be enormous. To resist it, to deny it the object of its desire – which is felt as a part of its very soul – is to give it the experience of withering and dying inside. But in this interior realm of dreams and goals, this is a quiet death because people around you cannot know how important these dreams are to you. The death of a dream is a profound loss. And you can feel just as weakened and demoralized by such a loss as someone would feel in the aftermath of a broken love affair.

Don't hold back from falling in love with the dreams of your deeper self. Giving yourself over to this experience is essential for your success. Accomplished, successful people intuitively have given in to this process naturally and without shame. It's up to you to allow a falling in love with your deeper self as a necessary part of the plan. It is a return to health, a reconnection with who you really are, and a deepening of your true integrity as an individual. All the great and admired people in the history of civilization were people who were in love with *the deepest part of themselves.*

Wait! Before your ego jumps up with its hysterical objections to that last statement, take the time to think about this objectively. Where *did* their great energy and certainty come from? Consider this truth: if you are not in love with your truest self, you cannot love your work. It is a logical impossibility. Neither will you be able to fully love another person, because your inner insecurities will limit you to either *competing* with them or *shaming* them.

A committed relationship with yourself is essential. This is not New Age malarkey. It is pure practicality and the foundation of success and fulfillment in the real world. Falling in love with yourself is accepting who you were meant to be and becoming that person.

A Final Meditation

In our final session of the Growth Group, we used the following meditation as a way to remember what we had come to the group for and what we needed to take with us. You can use this group meditation for yourself by recording it in your own voice and then listening to the meditation as you relax in a quiet place, especially at one of those times when you need extra support.

> *Close your eyes. Get comfortable where you are. Outside noises will not distract you; they are not a concern for you. Just allow yourself to relax and feel the safety of the room around you. Imagine that you are sitting in a group of like-minded people. Their feeling toward you is positive, excited and helpful. Relax comfortably and feel what it is like to bask in this climate of encouragement and enthusiasm. Everyone wants only the highest good for you. We want you to have what you want. We support you in becoming who you were meant to be. We are your comrades, supporting, encouraging, and renouncing any forces of negativity that block you.*

Pause and let yourself feel this support for a few moments of silence.

God and all the powers of the universe want you to be who you were meant to be. Allow yourself to gently relax knowing this. You belong in this world, with your interests and gifts. Fears may come, you may feel deflated, hopeless, or collapsed, but resolve to follow your dream. It is the way out of fear, out of depression. Make up your mind to persevere. Be determined. Say to yourself:

Even when all the forces in my life are opposed to my desires, even when negativity saps my courage, I will keep moving toward my goal. Even if I only have strength just to think about it, I will be proud of myself that I have not let my dream go.

Each day a choice is put before me: life or stagnation. Therefore, I am choosing life. And as I keep choosing life, opportunities will come – opportunities full of risks and effort because that is the way – but also full of life and interest and energy.

As you practice this pure state of relaxation, you will peacefully and comfortably absorb into your subconscious mind all that we have learned together. As you emerge from this meditation, you'll remember the certainty of your growth and learning. Bring all that you have learned so well into your daily life, living the life that your true self urges you toward, the one that lifts our energy and gives you ideas. This is who you were meant to be. It was just waiting for your support.

ACKNOWLEDGEMENTS

We need each other's help to make our dreams come true. Never was this truer than on this project. Every principle about needing a community of like-minded souls to provide support and stimulation has been thoroughly tested and proven through the writing of this book. First and foremost, my deepest appreciation goes to my husband, Skip, who kept believing in me and in the possibility of this book. Real love is encouraging your loved one's success, even when it means picking up the slack to give her the room to follow her dream.

Much love to Mary Babcock, my sister, who has encouraged my creativity from the beginning, and to Esther Freeman, who was unfailingly there to help me figure out the next step. They held the enthusiasm and vision for me even when I had misplaced it, and never expressed one pessimistic thought no matter how much I tempted them to do so. Special affection to Barbara Forbes, for holding the vision of being at the booksigning, and sincerest thanks to my other official mentors for this project: Ted Stevens, Judi Meyer, Scott Carter, Judi Carter, and Tom Bird, whose writing class showed me how to get from there to here. Judy Snider has also been an extraordinary friend through this whole process, and her contagious excitement has been glorious. Thanks also to Kathy Brehony, who had already blazed the trail between psychologist and author, and then generously gave me the benefit of her advice and experience. I am thankful too for the wholehearted encouragement and interest shown by Morna Owens, Debbie Stevens, and Karen Neymark, and for my Uncle

Louie, who believed in my potential as a writer from the very beginning. I am also grateful for my contact with Unity Renaissance church, which celebrates individual creativity as a divine partnership.

This book could not have come into being without the tireless efforts of my wonderful agent, Susan Crawford. She never gave up in her insistence that this book had to get out there, that its message was too important to lose, and her determination was a marvel to behold.

Finally, my love and high hopes to Carter, Lindsay, Catherine, Randy, Landon, John, McKenzie, Adam, Chris, Josh, and Asher. May your best dreams come true.

About the Author

Lindsay C. Gibson holds both Master's and Doctoral Degrees in clinical psychology. She has been a psychodiagnostician and psychotherapist for over thirty years, working in both public and private practice. In the past, Dr. Gibson has served as an Adjunct Assistant Professor for the Virginia Consortium Program for Clinical Psychology, teaching doctoral students clinical theory and psychotherapeutic techniques. Dr. Gibson is the author of two other books, *Adult Children of Emotionally Immature Parents* and *Recovering from Emotionally Immature Parents*. She has also written a monthly column on *Well-Being* for *Tidewater Women* magazine (www.tidewaterwomen.com) for nearly twenty years. Dr. Gibson lives and works in Virginia Beach, Virginia.

APPENDIX A:
IS THIS THE RIGHT
DIRECTION FOR ME?

Have you thought about, dreamed, or imagined an idea for your true life's purpose? Are you sure it's your dream and not the desire of those around you? To know if you are choosing a direction from your true self, rather than one derived from the opinions or beliefs of others, answer the following questions as honestly as you can:

1. **Every time you think about this area of interest, you feel a definite increase in energy.**   T   F

2. **When you have tried to make yourself give up this dream, you have felt let down, resentful, and depressed.**   T   F

3. **Anything related to the topic of your idea catches your attention instantly.**   T   F

4. **You find yourself automatically thinking "I could do that!" when you encounter a person doing something related to your idea.**   T   F

5. You feel envious when you see or read about people
   doing activities related to your idea.   T   F

6. You are impatient with people who are less proficient
   than you think you would be in this particular area.   T   F

7. An irresistible attraction keeps bringing you back to
   this idea.   T   F

8. The thought of spending as much time as possible in
   your area of interest energizes you.   T   F

9. You have a sense of physical lightness when you think
   about your idea, as though a burden were lifted.   T   F

10. There is a sense of pleasant well-being and ease of effort
    as you imagine yourself doing this activity.   T   F

11. When you consider doing this, you feel optimistic
    and hopeful.   T   F

12. Your fantasies about this ideal purpose are stimulating
    and enlivening; your mind keeps returning to it.   T   F

Now add up the number of true statements you circled and compare your responses to the following scoring guidelines.

If you scored...

10 - 12 True Responses: ...Your idea is very well suited to your true interests. Excellent choice!

7 - 9 True Responses: ...There are many things about this purpose that are right for you, but you need to define exactly which parts of the idea you like best.

4 - 6 True Responses: ...Rethink your idea. There are some important needs being met by this purpose, but not enough. You may be in the ball park, but there is something important you are missing. Zero in on it.

1 - 3 True Responses: ...Whose idea was this? It doesn't sound like yours! Following this idea may be draining and frustrating. Are you choosing for yourself, or because other people have sold this to you as a great idea?

APPENDIX B:
TEST YOUR SELF-DISCOVERY
KNOWLEDGE

Now that you have read the book and actively begun your search for who you were meant to be, let's see how well you remember some key points from the chapters. Answer each of the following true or false questions. Then look at the scoring section at the end to check your responses and to understand the meaning of your score.

1. There is always a path to take that fulfills you and your potential without harming others.   T   F

2. We are obliged to clean up our own dissatisfactions before they contaminate our relationships with others.   T   F

3. Our naturally occurring human feelings are tools to tell us when we are on or off the track toward fulfillment. T   F

4. A moment of success is still a success even if it is followed by a disappointment.   T   F

5. It is selfish to want to find your true purpose when other people need you to help them.   T   F

6. You cannot mentally decide what will interest you or what will energize you.   T   F

7. Our fears of the future are only our pasts projected forward.   T   F

8. The first stage of growth is dissatisfaction.   T   F

9. Turbulence always precedes a breakthrough in growth.   T   F

10. A strong feeling of panic indicates you should quit.   T   F

11. Overexcitement is a natural reaction to the return of hope and energy.   T   F

12. Challenge junkies are people who are hooked on their own competence in handling negative situations.   T   F

13. You should follow encouraging signs and serendipities.   T   F

14. Your energy level tell you if you are on the right path for your true self's needs.   T   F

15. Getting the permission of family members and loved ones is an important part of testing out your new ideas.   T   F

16. Asking for someone's blessing means that you would like their support, but still plan to do it anyway.   T   F

17. The ego is made up of ancient prohibitions against individual self-fulfillment.   T   F

18. Self-doubt is the ego's way of distracting you when you are about to reconnect with an important part of yourself. T   F

19. The ego uses grandiose dreaming to sabotage real accomplishment.   T   F

20. The ego is the same thing as the voice of your conscience. T   F

21. The ego's statements are always borrowed from other people and the past.   T   F

22. The primary goal of the ego is to destroy your motivation toward fulfilling your hopes and dreams.   T   F

23. When you're motivated, you may collide more frequently with other people's wishes.   T   F

24. We often take on characteristics of family members whose dominance and power impress us.   T   F

25. Helplessness and hopelessness are naturally occurring moods in small children.   T   F

26. Depressive backslides are nothing more than reenacted memories of childhood feelings of despair.   T   F

27. Inexperience can give us unrealistically hopeless views of the future.   T   F

28. It is normal for the course of growth to have plenty of ups and downs.   T   F

29. Sensitive, empathic people are often extremely strong psychologically.   T   F

30. Motivation and enthusiasm as more reliable than
persistence and endurance. T F

31. Survivor guilt in sensitive people is often instilled by
family members who project blame rather than take
responsibility for their own problems. T F

32. The *gap* is that highly insecure but necessary
transition space between who you were and who you
are becoming. T F

33. Putting the self first is the practical first step toward
a more rewarding and more loving way of living. T F

34. When you have neglected and forgotten about your
real self long enough, it will create symptoms or
problems to get your attention. T F

35. The best way to read your own mind is to ask other
people what they have observed about you. T F

36. The still, small voice speaks succinctly, quietly, and
often uses images and symbolism. T F

37. Never accept the forced choice of a dilemma as
the only possible solution to your problem. T F

38. When we reject and criticize our normal wishes, they
can show up in the form of scary, obsessive thoughts. T F

39. Family members may be very supportive when you are in
the victim role, but may lack sympathy if your problems
are the result of trying a new direction for your life. T F

40. If you don't try anything new, you will have fewer
    problems in your life.   T   F

41. Feelings of alienation are normal when you move out
    beyond your old role and old group.   T   F

42. Even geniuses need like-minded supporters; nobody
    does it alone.   T   F

43. When we are with the right kind of people, we feel
    lifted up, more alive, and more alert than usual.   T   F

44. The purpose of good friendships is to build energy.   T   F

45. Being consistent and reliable are the most important
    considerations in being a good friend.   T   F

46. Drama is false excitement, not happiness.   T   F

47. A rewarding lifestyle always requires setting limits.   T   F

48. Awareness helps protect our true selves from being
    depleted by incompatible people and situations.   T   F

49. If you are not in love with your deepest self, you cannot
    love your work nor can you fully love another person.   T   F

50. It is necessary for you to spend the rest of your life doing
    a highly skilled impersonation of someone you're not.   T   F

Scoring Key:

All statements are true except for every fifth one: numbers five, ten, fifteen, twenty, twenty-five, thirty, thirty-five, forty, forty-five, and fifty are false. For each statement you correctly marked true, give yourself one point. For each statement you correctly marked false, give yourself one point.

If you scored:

40 – 50 points ...   Congratulations on your careful reading! You have an excellent understanding of the main points in the book. You are well on your way to self-discovery.

30 - 39 points ...   Very good understanding of many points. Were there some ideas you found uncomfortable to accept? Check the ones you got wrong and consider reviewing the subject matter.

20 - 29 points ...   Keep this book around. You may have read selectively for your needs right now, but other parts of the book may have more meaning for you later.

10-19 points ...   Did you find yourself disagreeing with many key points? That's a good sign! Keep thinking and arguing this out with yourself. Go back and read sections you find puzzling. Talk it over with trusted friends.

1 -9 points ...   There is still plenty for you to get from this book. Savor it a little bit at a time until the pieces start fitting together. It is a whole new way of looking at life. Take your time.

NOTES

1   James Hillman, *The Soul's Code,* 1996.

2   This use of the term "ego" differs from Freud's meaning of the same word ("Dissection of Personality." 1933,1965.) In Freud's terminology, the ego was that part of the personality responsible for negotiating between the id and superego within the personality – and between the individual and the outside world – in order to get essential needs met through the higher-order functions of realistic perceptions, judgment, self-control, etc. In this book the term "ego" is more akin to the meaning in *A Course in Miracles* (1992), in which "ego" pertains to the destructive, delusional part of an individual that promotes misery, fear, and the belief in separation from God. Also, Edinger's (1973) conceptualization of the ego, based on Carl Jung's (1959) theories, as a small area of restricted consciousness sitting atop the enormous creative power of the Self, is also compatible with my use of the term, as it addresses the deceptive inflation of the ego's position when it tries to claim autonomy and pretend that there is no underlying, more powerful source called the Self.

3   Clarissa Pincola Estes *(The Creative Fire,* 1991) richly describes this kind of ego destructiveness and its unavoidable archetypal force in the personality as the counterpoint to the constructive creative energies. Her audiotape, *The Creative Fire,* is an excellent resource for deeper understanding of this innate destructive force and how it undermines our faith in our creative potential.

4   Freud. "Anxiety and Instinctual Life." 1965.

5   Richard Schwartz. *Internal Family Systems.* 1997.

6   Robert Firestone. *Compassionate Child-rearing.* 1990.

7   Matthew 4:1-11.

8   Richard Schwartz. *Ibid.*

9   Carl Jung. *The Essential Jung.* 1983.

10   Joseph Campbell. *The Hero with a Thousand Faces.* 1949,1968.

11   Robert Firestone. *Ibid.*

12   Hal and Sidra Stone. *Embracing Our Selves.* 1989.

13   Robert Firestone. *Ibid.*

14   Richard Schwartz. *Ibid.*

15   Martin Seligman (Overmeir & Seligman, "Effects of Inescapable Shock Upon Subsequent Escape and Avoidance Learning, 1967) is the psychologist who has been most associated with the research into learned helplessness in animals as a model to understand the origins of depression in humans. He found it was possible to make animals learn to "give up" seeking escape after numerous trials of inescapable shocks. In this classic research, they found that when the animals in their experiments had learned repeatedly by painful experience that no escape was available, the animals would no longer attempt escape even when provided a way out.

16   Hillman, 1996.

17   James Gleick. *Chaos: Making a New Science,* 1987. Gleick's chaos theory is a fascinating look at the science of unanticipated patterns in the uncertainties of nature.

18   Renee Fredrickson *(Dealing with Deniers,* 1992) presents a very clear description of this link between sensitivity in the personalities of abuse survivors and their strength to take on family problems. Her audiotapes on childhood abuse and the family dynamics of abusive families are exceptionally informative and very comforting to anyone who has been in the role of the sensitive child. They can be ordered from: Fredrickson and Associates, 821 Raymond Avenue, St. Paul, MN 55114, (612) 646-8373.

19   Elaine Aron. *The Highly Sensitive Person,* 1996.

20   Co-Dependents Anonymous (CODA) groups are widely available to help with these issues in a supportive atmosphere of peer counseling (*Co-Dependents Anonymous,* 1995).

21   W.R Bion *(Second Thoughts,* 1967, 1984) originated this concept of one person serving as the psychological "container'" for another person's disowned and projected feelings.

22   I am indebted to my friend and teacher, Robert Lovinger, Ph.D., for his deep empathy and clarity of thought on religious issues in therapy. Fortunately, other therapists can benefit from his experience and scholarship in his books on religion and psychotherapy *(Working with Religious Issues in Therapy,* 1984, *Religion and Counseling,* 1990).
23   Erik Erikson. *Childhood and Society.* 1950, 1963
24   In his studies on intellectual development, Piaget *(The Development of Thought,* 1977) describes the necessity of periods of cognitive "nonbalance" during times of intense learning and growth. In his words: "Actually it is clear that one of the sources of progress in the development of knowledge is to be found in nonbalance as such which alone can force a subject to go beyond his present state and to seek new equilibriums." (p. 12).
25   William Bridges. *Transitions.* 2004.
26   Stanley Greenspan, *Developmentally Based Psychotherapy,* 1997.
27   Freud, *The Interpretation of Dreams,* 1965.
28   This example was given by Tom Bird at his seminar for writers. If you think that writing may be a part of your real self, his workshops are extremely helpful and encouraging. For more information on Mr. Bird's seminars, please look him up at tombird.com.
29   Barbara Sher. *Wishcraft.*1979.
30   John Sanford writes reassuringly about the phenomenon of death imagery during the personal growth process in his book, *The Kingdom Within* (1970).
31   In Lenore Terr's book, *Too Scared to Cry* (1990), she describes beautifully how the foreshortened future effect influences the lives of trauma victims, based on her research into the lives of the Chowchilla bus kidnapping survivors.
32   The movie, *The Right Stuff* (1983), is an inspiring and invigorating account of men in the NASA space program who were very much following their true purpose in life.
33   Gordon Allport's concept of functional autonomy *(Personality: A Psychological Interpretation,* 1937) described the way learned behaviors can take on an autonomy of their own, independent of the original reasons for being learned. For instance, a behavior originally learned for the purpose of

self-defense or the rechanneling of unacceptable impulses may come to hold its own rewards apart from the original motive for learning it.

34   Robert Fritz. *The Path of Least Resistance.* 1984, 1989.

35   *The Shining,* 1980.

36   Gail Sheehy, *New Passages,* 1995.

37   Gardner, Howard. *Creating Minds,* 1993.

38   Howard, Vernon. *Esoteric Encyclopedia of Eternal Knowledge.* 1974, 1996. (p.181.)

39   Two books by Henry Cloud and John Townsend, *Boundaries,* 1992, and *Safe People,* 1995, are very helpful on the subject of interpersonal boundaries and the art of finding safe friends. They are written from a Christian perspective and this may not be compatible with all readers. However, it is the excellent, practical psychological insights in the books that are being recommended here.

40   Vernon Howard. *The Laws of Spiritual Development* (audiotapes). All of Howard's books and tapes stress the importance of seeing through illusion and drama to find the real truth within.

41   Julia Cameron's book, *The Artist's Way* (1992), is an excellent source of inspiration and helpful exercises for discovering your creativity and true self.

42   Andras Angyal (*Neurosis and Treatment: A Holistic Theory,* 1965) describes this phenomenon of abruptly switching back and forth between a healthy personality and a neurotic personality as a kind of total gestalt shift. This theory certainly accounts for many of the puzzling contradictions that can occur in people during the change process, as they shift from optimism to hopelessness and back to optimism in an amazing and complete flip-flop.

43   Tom Bird (*52 Weeks or Less to the Completion of Your Book,* 1995) describes writers as being "overpaid, over-glamorized transcriptionists" who are essentially taking dictation from their divine sources.

BIBLIOGRAPHY

A Course in Miracles (1975, 1992). Mill Valley, CA: Foundation for Inner Peace.

Allport, G.W. (1937). *Personality: A Psychological Interpretation.* New York: Henry Holt.

Angyal, Andras. (1965). *Neurosis and Treatment: A Holistic Theory.* (E. Hanfman and R.M. Jones, Eds.). New York: John Wiley & Sons.

Aron, Elaine N. (1996). *The Highly Sensitive Person.* New York: Carol Publishing Group.

Bion, W.R. (1967,1984). *Second Thoughts.* New York: Jason Aronson.

Bird, Thomas. (1995). *52 Weeks or Less to the Completion of Your Book.* Virginia Beach, VA: Tom Bird Seminars.

Bridges, William. (2004). *Transitions.* Cambridge, MA: Da Capo Press.

Cameron, Julia. (1992). *The Artist's Way.* New York: Putnam.

Campbell, Joseph. (1949,1968) *The Hero with a Thousand Faces* (2nd edition). Princeton, NJ: Princeton University Press.

Cloud, Henry and Townsend, John. (1992). *Boundaries.* Grand Rapids, MI: Zondervan.

_____.(1995). *Safe People.* Grand Rapids, MI: Zondervan.

Co-Dependents Anonymous. (1995). Phoenix, AZ: Co-Dependents Anonymous, Inc.

Edinger, Edward. (1973). *Ego and Archetype.* Baltimore, MD: Penguin Books.

Erikson, Erik. (1950, 1963). *Childhood and Society.* Second edition. New York: W.W. Norton.

Estes, Clarissa Pinkola. (1991). *The Creative Fire.* (audiotape). Boulder, CO: Sounds True Recordings.

Firestone, Robert. (1990). *Compassionate Child-rearing.* New York: Plenum Press.

Frederickson, Renee. (1992). *Dealing with Deniers.* (audiotape). St. Paul, MN: Frederickson and Associates.

Freud, Sigmund. (1933, 1965). "Anxiety and Instinctual Life." *New Introductory Lectures on Psychoanalysis.* New York: W.W. Norton.

_____. "Dissection of the Personality." *Ibid.*

_____. (1965). *Interpretation of Dreams.* (trans. by James Strachey). New York: Avon Books.

Fritz, Robert. (1984, 1989). *The Path of Least Resistance.* New York: Ballentine Books.

Gardner, Howard. (1993). *Creating Minds.* New York: Basic Books.

Gleick, James. (1987). *Chaos: Making a New Science.* New York: Penguin Books.

Greenspan, Stanley. (1997). *Developmentally Based Psychotherapy.* Madison, CT: International Universities Press.

Hillman, James. (1996). *The Soul's Code.* New York: Random House.

Howard, Vernon. (1996). *Esoteric Encyclopedia of Eternal Knowledge.* Pine, AZ: New Life.

Jung, Carl Gustav. (1959). *Aion.* (trans. by RF.C. Hill). 9 C.W., Part II. Bollingen Series XX. Princeton: Princeton University Press.

_____. (1983) *The Essential Jung.* (Anthony Storr, ed.) New York: MJF Books.

Lovinger, Robert. (1984). *Working with Religious Issues in Therapy.* New York: Jason Aronson.

_____. (1990). *Religion and Counseling.* New York: Continuum Publishing, 1990.

Matthew's gospel, Chap. 4: 1-11. (1990). *The New Jerusalem Bible.* New York: Doubleday.

Overmeir, J.B. and Seligman, M.E.P. (1967). "Effects of Inescapable Shock Upon Subsequent Escape and Avoidance Learning." *Journal of Comparative and Physiological Psychology.* 63, 23-33.

Piaget, Jean. (1977). *The Development of Thought.* (trans. by Arnold Rosin). New York: The Viking Press.

Sanford, John. *The Kingdom Within.* New York: Paulist Press, 1970.

Schwartz, Richard. (1995). *Internal Family Systems Therapy.* New York: Guilford Press.

Sheehy, Gail. *New Passages.* New York: Random House, 1995.

Sher, Barbara. *Wishcraft.* New York: Ballentine Books, 1979.

Stone, Hal and Sidra. (1989) *Embracing Our Selves.* Novato, CA: New World Library.

Terr, Lenore (1990). *Too Scared to Cry.* New York: Basic Books.

The Right Stuff (film). (1983.) Robert Chartoff-Irwin Winkler Production. California: The Ladd Company through Warner Brothers.

The Shining (film). (1980). California: Warner Brothers.

Made in the USA
Columbia, SC
07 October 2024

43764850R10188